THE REVELS PLAYS

Founder Editor
Clifford Leech 1958–71

General Editors
F. David Hoeniger, E. A. J. Honigmann and J. R. Mulryne

MAGNIFICENCE

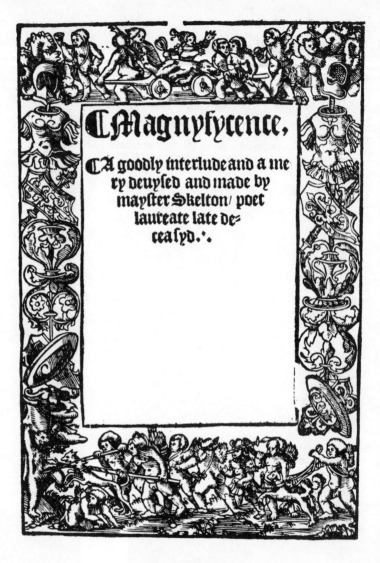

¶Magnyfycence,

¶A goodly interlude and a me
ry deuysed and made by
mayster Skelton/ poet
laureate late de=
ceasyd.·.

Title page of F,
reproduced by courtesy of the Syndics of
Cambridge University Library

THE REVELS PLAYS

MAGNIFICENCE

JOHN SKELTON

Edited by

Paula Neuss

MANCHESTER
UNIVERSITY PRESS

THE JOHNS HOPKINS
UNIVERSITY PRESS

© Paula Neuss 1980

Published by
Manchester University Press
Oxford Road, Manchester M13 9PL
ISBN 0 7190 1524 3

Published in the United States of America, 1980, by
The Johns Hopkins University Press
Baltimore, Maryland 21218
ISBN 0–8018–2337–4

Library of Congress Catalog Card Number 79–3125

British Library cataloguing in publication data

Skelton, John, *b. 1460?*
   Magnificence. – (The Revels plays).
   I. Title. II. Neuss, Paula.
   III. Series.
   822′.2   PR2347.M2
   UK ISBN 0–7190–1524–3
   US ISBN 0–8018–2337–4

Printed in Great Britain
by W & J Mackay Limited, Chatham

Contents

List of Illustrations

To the memory of
CLIFFORD LEECH

General Editors' Preface

The series known as the Revels Plays was conceived by Clifford Leech. The idea for the series emerged in his mind, as he explained in his preface to the first of the Revels Plays in 1958, from the success of the New Arden Shakespeare. The aim of the new group of texts was 'to apply to Shakespeare's predecessors, contemporaries and successors the methods that are now used in Shakespeare editing'. The plays chosen were to include well-known works from the early Tudor period to about 1700, as well as others less familiar but of literary and theatrical merit: 'the plays included,' Leech wrote, 'should be such as to deserve and indeed demand performance.' We owe it to Clifford Leech that the idea became reality. He set the high standards of the series, ensuring that editors of individual volumes produced work of lasting merit, equally useful for teachers and students, theatre directors and actors. Clifford Leech remained General Editor until 1971, supervising the first seventeen volumes to be published.

The Revels Plays are now under the direction of three General Editors, F. David Hoeniger, E. A. J. Honigmann and J. R. Mulryne. The publishers, originally Methuen, are now Manchester University Press, with Johns Hopkins University Press as co-publisher. Yet, despite these changes, the format and essential character of the series will continue, and it is hoped that its editorial standards will be maintained. Except for some work in progress, the General Editors intend, in expanding the series, to concentrate for the immediate future on plays of the period 1558–1642, and may include a small number of non-dramatic works of interest to students of drama. Some slight changes have been forced by considerations of cost. For example, in editions from 1978, notes to the introduction are placed together at the end, not at the foot of the page. Collation and commentary notes will continue, however, to appear on the relevant pages.

The text of each Revels play, in accordance with established practice in the series, is edited afresh from the original text of best authority (in a few instances, texts), but spelling and punctuation are modernised and speech headings are silently made consistent. Elisions in the original are also silently regularised, except where metre would be affected by the change; since 1968 the '-ed' form is used for non-syllabic terminations in past tenses and past participles ('-'d' earlier), and '-èd' for syllabic ('-ed' earlier). The editor emends, as distinct from modernises, his original only in instances where error is patent or at least very probable, and correction persuasive. Act divisions are given only if they appear in the original or if the structure of the play clearly points to them. Those act and scene divisions not found in the original are provided unobtrusively in small type and in square brackets. Square brackets are also used for any other additions to or changes in the stage directions of the original.

Revels Plays do not provide a variorum collation, but only those variants which require the critical attention of serious textual students. All departures of substance from 'copy-text' are listed, including any relineation and those changes in punctuation which involve to any degree a decision between alternative interpretations; but not such accidentals as turned letters, nor necessarily additions to stage directions whose editorial nature is already made clear by the use of brackets. Press corrections in the 'copy-texts' are likewise included. Of later emendations of the text, only those are given which as alternative readings still deserve serious attention.

One of the hallmarks of the Revels Plays is the thoroughness of their annotations. Besides explaining the meaning of difficult words and passages, the editor provides comments on customs or usage, text or stage business—indeed, on anything he judges pertinent and helpful. Each volume contains a Glossarial Index to the Commentary, in which particular attention is drawn to meanings for words not listed in *O.E.D.*

The Introduction to a Revels play assesses the authority of the 'copy-text' on which it is based, and discusses the editorial methods employed in dealing with it; the editor also considers his play's date and (where relevant) sources, together with its place in the work of the author and in the theatre of its time. Stage history is offered, and in the case of a play by an author not previously represented in the series a brief biography is given.

It is our hope that plays edited in this fashion will promote further scholarly and theatrical investigation of one of the richest periods in theatrical history.

F. DAVID HOENIGER

E. A. J. HONIGMANN

J. R. MULRYNE

Preface

This volume is dedicated to the memory of Clifford Leech, who first encouraged me to work on a new edition of *Magnificence*. I am very grateful for his help and that of the General Editors who have followed him. David Hoeniger has corresponded with me energetically about numerous problems, especially those posed by modernised spelling. Ernst Honigmann, upon whose desk my typescript finally landed, has scrutinised my work with immense thoroughness, correcting many errors, and making many suggestions I have been happy to adopt.

I should also like to thank the following people for helping me in various ways with my work: Neil Berry, Edward Costigan, Mike Fynes-Clinton, Tom Kelly, Richard Proudfoot, Victoria Rothschild, and colleagues at Birkbeck. Barbara Brunswick has been a most efficient and patient typist. Diane Susans kindly helped me prepare the index. Angela Conyers was good enough to check my Latin translation. My father, R. F. Neuss, has meticulously checked the proofs. Those people who have helped me with information about modern productions are mentioned in section 4e of the Introduction—I am grateful to John Leyerle and the Medieval Centre of the University of Toronto for providing me with the plate that appears on p. 134. I thank, too, Dorothy Bednarowska, who introduced me to Skelton's poetry.

PAULA NEUSS

London, 1978

Abbreviations

(A) TEXTS

(i) Skelton's poems, cited from Dyce's edition (see below, Dyce), are abbreviated as follows:

Albany	*Howe the douty Duke of Albany, etc.*
Bowge	*The Bowge of Courte.*
Calliope	*Why were ye Calliope embrawdred with letters of golde?*
Cloute	*Colyn Cloute.*
Coystrowne	*Agaynste a comely coystrowne.*
Darlyng dere	*My darlyng dere, my daysy floure.*
Dundas	*Vilitissimus Scotus Dundas etc.*
Garlande	*The Garlande of Laurell.*
Garnesche	*Poems against Garnesche.*
Hauke	*Ware the Hauke.*
Knolege	*Knolege, aquayntance, resort etc.*
Margery	*Manerly Margery Mylk and Ale.*
Northumberlande	*Vpon the doulourus dethe . . . of the . . . Erle of Northumberlande.*
Parrot	*Speke, Parrot.*
Replycacion	*A replycacion agaynst certayne yong scolers.*
Rummyng	*The tunnyng of Elinor Rummyng.*
Scottes	*Against the Scottes.*
Sparowe	*Phyllyp Sparowe.*
Tongues	*Against venemous tongues.*
Trentale	*A Deuoute Trentale.*
Why come	*Why come ye nat to Courte.*

(ii) Dramatic texts:

All for Money	T. Lupton, *All for Money*, in *English Morality Plays and Moral Interludes*, ed. T. Schell and J. D. Schuchter (1969).
Dodsley	*Dodsley's Old English Plays*, ed. W. C. Hazlitt (1874).
Enough	W. Wager, *Enough Is as Good as a Feast*, in edition cited under *All for Money*.
Farmer, *Heywood*	*The Dramatic Writings of John Heywood*, ed. J. S. Farmer (1905).
Farmer, *Tudor Plays*	'*Lost*' *Tudor Plays*, ed J. S. Farmer (1907).
Fulgens	H. Medwall, *Fulgens and Lucrece*, in *Five Pre-Shakespearean Comedies*, ed. F. S. Boas (1934).
Gentleness	*Gentleness and Nobility*, ed. A. C. Partridge, Malone Society (1950).
Ludus Coventriae	*Ludus Coventriae*, ed. K. S. Block, E.E.T.S. (1922).
Macro	*The Macro Plays*, ed. Mark Eccles, E.E.T.S. (1969). (*The Castle of Perseverance*, *Mankind*, and *Wisdom* are cited from this edition.)
Mary Magdalene	*Mary Magdalene*, in *The Digby Plays*, ed. F. J. Furnivall, E.E.T.S. (1896).
Ramsay	*Magnyfycence*, ed. R. L. Ramsay, E.E.T.S. (1908).
Respublica	N. Udall (?), *Respublica*, in edition cited under *All for Money*.
The Longer	W. Wager, *The Longer thou Livest the moore Fool thou art*, in *Tudor Facsimile Texts*, ed. J. S. Farmer (1910).
Tide Tarrieth	G. Wapull, *The Tide Tarrieth No Man*, in edition cited under *All for Money*.

Wit and Science   John Redford, *Wit and Science*, in edi-
                             tion cited under *All for Money*.

Dates given for Tudor interludes are taken from the list in
Craik, pp. 140–1. The titles of Shakespeare's plays are abbreviated as in Onions, *Shakespeare Glossary*, p. x; their line-
numbering is that of Peter Alexander's edition (1951). Jonson's
Bartholomew Fair, Marlowe's *Massacre at Paris* and *Dido, Queen
of Carthage* and Middleton's *A Chaste Maid in Cheapside* are
cited from the Revels editions.

(iii) Other texts:

Diodorus   *The Bibliotheca Historica of Diodorus
                             Siculus translated by John Skelton*, ed.
                             F. M. Salter and H. L. R. Edwards, 2
                             vols. E.E.T.S. (1956).
Dyce   *The Poetical Works of John Skelton*, ed.
                             Alexander Dyce, 2 vols. (1843).
Lydgate, *Fall of*   *Lydgate's Fall of Princes*, ed. H.
    Princes   Bergen, 4 vols. (1923–7).
Lydgate, 'Mesure'   'Mesure is Tresour' in *Minor Poems*,
                             pp. 776–80.
Lydgate, *Minor Poems*   *The Minor Poems of John Lydgate*, ed.
                             H. N. MacCracken, Part II, E.E.T.S.
                             (1934).
Lydgate, 'Song'   'A Song of Just Mesure', in *Minor
                             Poems*, pp. 772–5.
Rede me   William Roy and Jerome Barlowe,
                             Rede me and be nott wrothe, Arber Eng-
                             lish Reprints (1895).
Ship   *The Ship of Fools*, trans. Alexander
                             Barclay, ed. T. H. Jamieson (1874).
Utopia   *More's Utopia*, ed. John Warrington
                             (1965).

Chaucer's works are cited from the edition of F. N. Robinson

(1961); *Piers Plowman* from the edition of the B text by Skeat
(E.E.T.S., 1869); Dunbar's works from that of W. Mackay
Mackenzie (1932).

(B) WORKS OF REFERENCE, ETC.

Ballads	*Ballads from Manuscripts*, ed. F. J. Furnivall (1868).
Cavendish	G. Cavendish, *The Life and Death of Cardinal Wolsey*, ed. R. S. Sylvester, E.E.T.S. (1959).
Craik	T. W. Craik, *The Tudor Interlude* (1962).
Dobson	E. J. Dobson, *Elizabethan Pronunciation, 1500–1700*, 2 vols. (1957).
Du Cange	D. Du Cange, *Glossarium Mediae et Infimae Latinitatis* (1883).
Glassco	W. G. Glassco, 'Against Wolsey: a critical edition of John Skelton's Why come ye nat to Courte? and Colyn Cloute', unpublished dissertation, Toronto (1966).
Hall	*Hall's Chronicle*, ed. H. Ellis (1809).
Harris	W. C. Harris, *Skelton's Magnyfycence and the Cardinal Virtue Tradition* (1965).
Heiserman	A. R. Heiserman, *Skelton and Satire* (1961).
Kinsman, 'Old Sayde Sawe'	R. S. Kinsman, 'Skelton's *Magnyfycence*: the Strategy of the "Olde Sayde Sawe"', *Studies in Philology*, LXIII (1966).
Kinsman, *Poems*	*John Skelton Poems*, ed. R. S. Kinsman (1969).
L.P.	J. S. Brewer, *Letters and Papers, Foreign and Domestic, of the reign of Henry VIII*, Vols. I–III (1864–7).

M.L.N.   *Modern Language Notes.*

Nelson   W. Nelson, *John Skelton Laureate* (1964).

O.E.D.   *Oxford English Dictionary.*

Partridge   Eric Partridge, *Shakespeare's Bawdy* (1947).

Pollard   A. F. Pollard, *Wolsey* (1965).

Pollet   M. Pollet, *John Skelton: Poet of Tudor England* (1971).

R.E.S.   *Review of English Studies.*

Southern   Richard Southern, *The Staging of Plays before Shakespeare* (1973).

Stevens   John Stevens, *Music and Poetry in the Early Tudor Court* (1961).

Tilley   M. P. Tilley, *A Dictionary of the Proverbs in England in the Sixteenth and Seventeenth Centuries* (1950).

Ven. Cal.   *Calendar of State Papers, Venetian*, ed. Rawdon Brown, Vols. II and III (1867–9).

Visser   F. Th. Visser, *A Syntax of the English Language of St. Thomas More*, 2 vols. (1946–52).

Whiting   B. J. Whiting, *Proverbs, Sentences and Proverbial Phrases from English Writings mainly before 1500* (1968).

Introduction

I. SKELTON

John Skelton's reputation is not that of a person we would expect to have written *Magnificence*. He is Pope's 'beastly Skelton',[1] Puttenham's 'rude rayling rimer',[2] an inventor of Skeltonics; probably his best-known poems have always been *Phyllyp Sparowe* and *The tunnyng of Elinor Rummyng*. Most people would not think of him as a playwright, and indeed *Magnificence* is his only surviving play. He almost certainly wrote others; in the lengthy list of works included in the self-adulatory poem *The Garlande of Laurell* he mentions 'Of Vertu . . . the souerayne enterlude', and 'His commedy, Achademios callyd by name'. There are other items listed there that may have been interludes, such as 'Royall Demenaunce worshyp to wynne', and 'Good Aduysement, that brainles doth blame'; and 'paiauntis that were played in Ioyows Garde' (Arthurian tournaments) were perhaps intended for dramatic presentation. Possibly some of the items in this list were invented by Skelton: if he *did* write 'The Balade . . . of the Mustarde Tarte' or 'The Gruntyng and the groynninge of the gronnyng swyne; / Also the Murnyng of the mapely rote' these pieces, regrettably, have not survived. Nor has a play attributed to him by Warton: *The NIGRAMANSIR, a morall ENTERLUDE and a pithie written by Maister Skelton laureate and plaid before the king and other estatys at Woodstoke on Palme Sunday*, which was supposed to have been printed by Wynkyn de Worde in 1504.[3] Bale attributed to the poet an interlude *De bono ordine*, a fragment of which has survived, but it is probably not written by Skelton.[4]

There are fewer facts known about Skelton's life than there are conjectures based partly upon them and upon legends that began to develop soon after his death, particularly those stories in the *Merie Tales of Skelton* published in 1567. The name Skelton was common: 'systematic inquiry reveals about two hundred and fifty Skeltons during the fourteenth and fifteenth centuries, of whom one hundred or so are named John'.[5] Thus when a John Skelton is discovered in contemporary records he may not be the poet. Even the things we 'know' about Skelton's life have mainly been gathered from his own writings, and he had a notoriously vivid imagination.

The earliest certain reference to him survives in the dedication to Caxton's *Eneydos* (printed in 1490). There 'mayster Iohn Skelton, late created poete laureate in the vnyversite of oxenforde' is asked to 'ouersee' the book and correct any faults he may find in it:

> For hym, I knowe for suffycyent to expowne and englysshe euery dyffyculte that is therin/For he hath late translated the epystlys of Tulle/and the boke of dyodorus syculus, and diuerse other werkes oute of latyn in-to englysshe, not in rude and olde langage, but in polysshed and ornate termes craftely, as he that hath redde vyrgyle/ouyde, tullye, and all the other noble poetes and oratours/to me vnknowen: And also he hath redde the ix. muses, and vnderstande theyr musicalle scyences, and to whom of theym eche scyence is appropred. I suppose he hath dronken of Elycons well.[6]

It is not known exactly what requirements had to be fulfilled before the title of poet laureate was conferred, except that it involved advanced studies in grammar, rhetoric and verse composition. The honour was not, as now, restricted to one man: there were other poets laureate contemporary with Skelton, for example the grammarian Robert Whittinton. That it was considered a great honour we can infer from Skelton's frequent references to it.[7]

Skelton dated many of his works by a private calendar which began in October or November 1488, clearly an occasion of great significance in his life, and so possibly the date of his laureation by Oxford[8] (Caxton's remarks show that this occurred not long before 1490). Because of the long list of achievements Caxton mentions, and our tradition of a span of threescore years and ten, Skelton is assumed to have been born about

1460 (he died in 1529). His birthplace is not known; legend assigns it to somewhere 'up north', either in Cumberland or Yorkshire. Soon after the ceremony at Oxford, he was also laureated by the University of Louvain, and, in 1493, by Cambridge[9] (where he may have taken his B.A.[10]). About this time he may have entered the service of the king (Henry VII). That he was tutor to the young prince Henry we learn from Erasmus, who accompanied More on a visit to the king's children at Eltham in 1499. More had taken a volume of poems with him as a gift, and Erasmus (annoyed at not being briefed by More to do the same) put together a collection which he presented to prince Henry. The dedication includes the words:

> There is in your household that light and glory of English letters, Skelton, who is capable not only of stimulating your appetite for learning, but of satisfying your hunger as well.[11]

He compares Skelton to Homer and Virgil, observing in one poem that 'the boy Henry, happy in the name of his father, is introduced to the sacred fountains of the Muses by the poet Skelton'.[12] Skelton himself informs us:

> The honor of Englond I lernyd to spelle,
> In dygnyte roialle that doth excelle: . . .
> I yaue hym drynke of the sugryd welle
> Of Eliconys waters crystallyne,
> Aqueintyng hym with the Musys nyne. . . .
>
> It plesyth that noble prince roialle
> Me as hys master for to calle
> In hys lernyng primordialle.
> (*Garnesche*, IV, 95–6, 98–100, 103–6)
>
> The Duke of Yorkis creauncer . . . Skelton was,
> Now Henry the viij. Kyng of Englonde,
> (*Garlande*, 1226–7)

Henry was born in 1491, and so Skelton may have become his tutor as early as 1494.[13]

During this period Skelton wrote various occasional pieces, the earliest known being an elegy on the death of the Earl of

Northumberland (1489), and a lost poem celebrating Arthur's becoming Prince of Wales. There were satirical works like *Agaynste a comely coystrowne*, satirising an upstart court musician, and the allegory *Bowge of Courte* (printed in 1499), which shows the lively characterisation and preoccupation with court vice that are features of *Magnificence*. *Uppon a deedmans hed* (the first poem in 'Skeltonics'), was probably written at this time, as well as instructive pieces for prince Henry like the *Speculum Principis*, which contains conventional advice about the best way of ruling life and realm. His teaching seems not to have had much influence on Henry, for one of the precepts the *Speculum* includes is 'choose a wife for yourself; prize her always and uniquely',[14] and Lord Mountjoy, Erasmus' pupil, remarks in a letter to his teacher after Henry's accession that the king 'said that he regretted that he was still so ignorant'![15] However, Agnes Strickland's view that 'the corruption imparted by this ribald and ill-living wretch laid the foundation for his royal pupil's grossest crimes' is certainly exaggerated.[16] 'When ladies attempt to write history, they sometimes say odd things.'[17] Skelton *may* have left the court because he was found unsatisfactory at his job or because his behaviour was not beyond reproach, but there is no proof that he was dismissed. In 1501 a complaint was made against him by one of the king's chaplains, and in 1502 he was imprisoned as surety for a debt owed by the Prior of St Bartholomew.[18] A payment of forty shillings to the Duke of York's schoolmaster in 1502[19] may indicate the end of his service: certainly by 1504 the prince had a new tutor, and Skelton was at his rectory at Diss in Norfolk witnessing a will.[20]

He had taken holy orders in 1498[21] and seems to have lived mainly in Diss between about 1503 and 1511, as rector of the parish. The rectory was in the king's gift, so that his departure there does not necessarily imply that he was in disgrace. The living was granted to him along with the final payment for his services, perhaps both as a reward and a way of getting rid of him.

His reputation as a 'ribald wretch' seems to develop from his time at Diss. According to the *Merie Tales*, he had stormy relations with his bishop, one Richard Nikke or Nix. To 'appease' the bishop Skelton made him a present of two capons:

> Skelton sayde, My lord, my capons haue proper names; the one is named Alpha, the other is named Omega: my lorde, sayd Skelton, this capon is named Alpha, thys is the fyrst capon that I dyd euer geue to you; and this capon is named Omega, and this is the last capon that euer I wil giue you: & so fare you well, sayd Skelton.[22]

Skelton also was supposed to have had a 'wife' and child, and, when his parishioners objected to them, refused to be ashamed, bringing them into the church for all to see:

> Thou wyfe, sayde Skelton, that hast my childe, be not afraid; bring me hither my childe to me: the whyche was doone. And he, shewynge his childe naked to all the parishe, sayde, How saye you, neibours all? Is not this child as fayre as is the beste of all yours? It hathe nose, eyes, handes, and feete, as well as any of your: it is not lyke a pygge, nor a calfe, nor like no foule nor monstruous beast. If I had, sayde Skelton, broughte forthe thys chylde without armes or legges, or that it wer deformed, being a monstruous thyng, I woulde neuer haue blamed you to haue complayned to the bishop of me; but to complain without a cause, I say, as I said before in my antethem, *vos estis*, you be, and haue be, & wyll and shall be knaues, to complayne of me wythout a cause resonable.[23]

These stories may be apocryphal, but they are not entirely unlikely for a man who wrote a mock epitaph for two of his parishioners which included the words:

> The deuill kis his *culum*!
> With, hey, howe, rumbelowe,
> *Rumpopulorum*,
> *Per omnia secula seculorum*!   (*Trentale*, 60–3)

a vigorous diatribe against a neighbouring 'pekysh parson' who exercised his hawk in Skelton's church, and a mock mass for a dead sparrow whose relationship with his mistress Jane Scrope was not altogether innocent.

When Henry VIII came to the throne in 1509 Skelton attempted to get back into royal favour by writing *A lawde and prayse made for our souereigne lord the kyng*, one of many congratulations Henry received from such people as More, Erasmus, Barclay, Bernard André and Hawes. His name is included in a general pardon issued by Henry (for what cause is unknown), where he is described as 'John Skelton, of London, clerk, poet laureate, *alias* late of Disse, Norf., poet laureate and rector of Dysse'.[24] He also added a dedication to the *Speculum Principis* in which he laments his neglect and asks for royal favour.[25]

He does not seem to have returned to London permanently, for he was at Diss witnessing a will in 1511.[26] However, on 5 July 1511 he dined with the Prior of Westminster Abbey (on plaice, sole, conger eel, salt fish and butter)[27] and after this there are various references that connect him with Westminster, including definite evidence of his residence there in 1518.[28] He must have moved there some time after Henry's accession, and he remained there until he died. That he did again find favour with the king is suggested by the fact that from 1512 he began to use the title *orator regius*, and certainly at least the poems against Garnesche were written 'By the kyngys most noble commande-mennt'. He again wrote the sort of occasional pieces that would be expected from a king's poet: Latin poems on the defeat of the French at Therouanne and the Scots at Flodden, and English poems on the defeat and death of James IV (all in 1513), and a Latin elegy for Lady Margaret Beaufort (mother of Henry VII), in 1516. About this time too, though, he probably wrote *Elinor Rummyng*. He participated in the 'Grammarians War', a quarrel between writers of rival Latin grammars for schools, in which he sided with his fellow poet laureate Whittinton, holding the more conservative view that Latin should be taught by instilling a thorough grasp of the precepts of grammar, rather than through the imitation of examples.[29] In 1519 Whittinton published a long ode in praise of Skelton (the volume also included poems to the King, Wolsey and More), while William Lily, the headmas-ter of St Paul's, who belonged to the other camp, attacked him in Latin verses which end (as translated by Fuller):

> Skelton, thou art, let all men know it,
> Neither learned, nor a Poet.[30]

About 1520 he started writing virulent satires against Wolsey: *Speke, Parrot* (1521), *Colyn Cloute* (1521–2), and *Why come ye nat to Courte* (1522). The reasons for Skelton's enmity against Wolsey have been the source of much speculation. It might have been the result of a personal grudge or jealousy dating from early in their careers. There are a number of coincidences in their lives:[31] Wolsey must have obtained his B.A. at Oxford at about the time that Skelton was laureated; they were ordained in the same year; Wolsey came from Ipswich, just a short journey from Diss, and from 1505 to 1506 he was rector of Redgrave, a neighbouring parish to Diss with which Skelton was afterwards connected;[32] they must have known each other at court; Wolsey's rise at court coincided with Skelton's dismissal; he became chaplain to Sir Richard Nanfan, deputy of Calais, in 1501, Henry VII's chaplain in 1507, and Royal Almoner after Henry VIII's accession in 1509, when Skelton was trying to get back into royal favour; they even died within a year of each other (Wolsey in 1530). Or, it has been suggested, Skelton may have written his satires at the request of Wolsey's enemies the How-ards, Dukes of Norfolk.[33] Diss was in the county of Norfolk, and Skelton retired to the duke's castle at Sherriff Hutton shortly after writing *Why come*, where he wrote *The Garlande of Laurell* at the request (so he says) of the Countess of Surrey, the Duke's daughter-in-law (and mother of the poet).

However, '*difficile est / Satiram non scribere*' (*Why come*, 1213–4). When such atrocities are thought to have been com-mitted as the murder of the Duke of Buckingham (1521), and such wasteful extravagancies occur as the display at the Field of the Cloth of Gold (1520), there is no need to look for any personal or patronised motive. A number of other satires of Wolsey were written in the 1520s.[34]

After *Why come* Skelton apparently suddenly repented, for *Garlande* and *Albany* (both written in 1523) contain dedications to the Cardinal. Skelton even suggests that *Albany* was written at Wolsey's instigation. He hints that Wolsey has said some-thing about an 'amass gray' (a prebend), and this promise (which was never fulfilled), may have been the reason for his obsequiousness, or he may suddenly have become frightened for his life. Five years later, in *A replycacion agaynst certayne yong scholers* (an attack on two Cambridge students, Lutheran heretics), Wolsey is again spoken of as his patron. It is hard to reconcile these facts with Bale's statement that Skelton died in sanctuary escaping the wrath of Wolsey.[35] Perhaps the tone of their relationship can best be captured by this story from the *Merie Tales*:

> On a tyme Skelton did meete with certain frendes of hys at Charyng crosse, after that hee was in prison at my lord cardynals commaundement: & his frende sayd, I am glad you bee abrode amonge your frendes, for you haue ben long pent in. Skelton sayd, By the masse, I am glad I am out indeed, for I haue ben pent in, like a roche or fissh, at Westminster in prison. The cardinal, hearing of those words, sent for him agayne. Skelton kneling of hys knees before hym, after long communication to Skelton had, Skelton desyred the cardinall to graunte hym a boun. Thou shalt haue none, sayd the cardynall. Thassistence desirid that he might haue it graunted, for they thought it should be some merye pastime that he wyll shewe your grace. Say on, thou hore head, sayd the cardynall to Skelton. I pray your grace to let me lye doune and wallow, for I can kneele no longer.[36]

If Skelton was imprisoned by Wolsey, it might have been some years before his death, before he wrote the ingratiating words in *Garlande*. In 1523 Wolsey dissolved the convocation at St Paul's:

> wherof master Skelton a mery Poet wrote.
> *Gentle Paule laie doune thy swearde*:
> *For Peter of Westminster hath shauen thy beard.*[37]

If Skelton did write this home thrust he would hardly have escaped prison. Perhaps the visit to Sheriff Hutton was, like the poem's form, a dream vision, and Skelton wrote *Garlande* in prison, resolving to check his tongue on the doings of Wolsey thereafter.

Skelton died at Westminster on 21 June 1529. He was buried in the chancel of St Margaret's with the following inscription on his tomb:

> *Iohannes Skeltonus vates Pierius hic situs est animam egit, 21 Junij 1529.*

He had aroused startlingly different reactions in his contemporaries: fulsome praise from Caxton, Erasmus and Whittinton; invective from Lily and Alexander Barclay. Though there may have been political or personal reasons for these contrasting attitudes, they do also point to certain inconsistencies in the poet himself. A combination of learning and ribaldry is not particularly surprising; it is a fairly common characteristic of clergymen (we need only think of Sterne), and both More and Erasmus mingled jests with more serious matter in their writing. Nor should we wonder at this supposed celibate keeping a 'wife' and having a child (if he did): Wolsey himself had a mistress,[38] and at least one illegitimate son, Thomas Wynter. Yet Skelton was so extraordinarily concerned with his own importance ('the history of literature affords no second example of a poet having deliberately written sixteen hundred lines in honour of himself')[39] and he nursed grudges for so long (Barclay's criticisms of 1509 are still remembered in the *Garlande* in 1523), that for him to be able to grovel before Wolsey as he seems to have done *is* startling. But the same Protean quality is found in his writing. On the one hand he pours out formless Skeltonics, which run on until he is exhausted (often long after the reader); on the other hand he produces patterned and controlled works like *Bowge* and *Parrot*. He is conservative about the teaching of Latin, objects to the introduction of Greek[40] and to Erasmus' translation of the Bible,[41] yet he is concerned about the state of the English language,[42] makes advances in the writing of poetry, and probably coined or brought into common use many words now part of our everyday language.[43]

He uses all the resources of the language in passages of outspoken, vigorous invective, yet at other times writes so obscurely and cryptically that some of the puzzles set in his poems are still to be solved. His obvious vanity is balanced by his strong sense of humour. Of one of his earliest and dullest works he observes, in one of his latest:

> Diodorus Siculus of my translacyon
> Out of fresshe Latine into owre Englysshe playne, . . .
> Who redyth it ones wolde rede it agayne;
>
> (*Garlande*, 1498–9, 1501)

The translation runs to 395 dense pages in a modern edition!

Writing poetry, for all his laureate dignity, seems to have been a sort of game to him, in which he played whatever part seemed fitting.[44] His liking for the dramatic is suggested in the *Merie Tales*, and at Diss he 'was esteemed more fit for the stage than the pew or pulpit'.[45] Probably he was a little mad, like all the best people.

2. THE TEXT

(a) *Folio and subsequent editions*

Magnyfycence, | *A goodly interlude and a me*= | *ry deuysed and made by* | *mayster Skelton/poet* | *laureate late de*= | *ceasyd* ∴ (STC 22607), was printed *c.* 1530, probably by John Rastell, though it contains no date or imprint. The type is that of Peter Treveris, who was printing from 1522 to 1532 and was closely associated with the Rastells.[46] The edition is a folio in fours: A-G4, H2, thirty leaves numbered ii–xxx (the title-page is not numbered), misprinting iii as xxix, xxiv as xxi, xxvi as xxi. It is in black-letter (both text and stage-directions). Two copies and a fragment of this folio edition (hereafter referred to as F) survive:

1. Cambridge University Library, AB.8 46⁴. (Received in 1715 from the collection of Bishop Moore.)
2. British Library, C.34 m.1, wanting A1. (From Garrick's collection, perhaps originally owned by the Nat or Nathaniel Wilkinson whose name is written twice in the margin. A1 is replaced by a transcript made by George Steevens of the CUL copy.)[47]
3. Bodleian Library, Douce fragment d.7 (G2 and 3 only).

It appears to have been carefully printed: there are few obvious errors, more in the Latin stage directions than in the English directions and text. There are seven variants.[48] There is evidence of proof correction in two formes, B1 and B4v (BL corrected), and F2 and F3v (CUL corrected).

This edition was reprinted by the Roxburgh Club in 1821. In 1843 the play was newly edited by Dyce in *The Poetical Works of John Skelton*, and in 1908 it was re-edited by R. L. Ramsay for the E.E.T.S. (E.S. 98). An extract (966–1159) is included in R. S. Kinsman's edition of Skelton's poems (1969).

(b) *This edition*

The present text is based on F, collated with those of Dyce and Ramsay. It is the first full edition to appear in modern spelling, though Philip Henderson included an unannotated version, based on Dyce, in his *Complete Poems of John Skelton* (1959). Modernisation of spelling creates special problems for an editor of a text as early as this. Firstly *Magnificence* contains many words either obsolete, or whose meaning has altered considerably since Tudor times. Secondly a modern form inevitably distorts the sound of the original: *run* does not accurately represent the sound of Skelton's *rynne* or *renne*, nor *pretty* his *praty*. Yet to retain original spellings which apparently differ in sound from modern ones would be illogical, for even when the Tudor and contemporary spellings do not greatly differ, their pronunciation must have done. Modern spelling versions of Elizabethan texts generally considered acceptable do not accurately represent the sound of their original either. But an extra difficulty arises in *Magnificence*. In this play the metre is based on stress rather than syllable, and there can be considerable variation regarding the number of weak syllables in any line (see below, pp. 53ff.). There is therefore no *internal* evidence to help an editor decide whether, for instance, final *es/ys*, *en/yn*, *ed/yd* were syllabic. If we examine the original spelling of the first line of the play:

Al thyngys contryuyd by mannys reason

we can see that there are four strong stresses (on *thyng-*, *-try-*, *mann-*, *reas-*), but we cannot be sure how many weak syllables the line contains. It might be eleven (if the plural and genitive *-ys* and *-yd* are syllabic), or nine (if only *-yd* is syllabic), or eight (if none of these three endings is syllabic). The *external* evidence is inconclusive. Dobson feels that the weight of evidence suggests that in most cases final *es/ys*, *en/yn* were syncopated by Skelton's time, but that *-ed/-yd* was often a separate syllable.[49] I have therefore omitted the e/y in *es/ys*, *en/yn* endings, but have always printed 'ed', though never 'èd', preferring to leave the reader free to decide whether this ending is syllabic. Besides these general cases, there are a number of individual words which *might* have lost a syllable by modernisation, e.g. *commaundement*, *ellys*, *whilest*. In these cases, where the weight of evidence suggests syncopation, I have felt justified in printing the modern equivalent. With other words, e.g. *capytaynes*, *hinderaunce*, *tappyster*, where syncopation may not have occurred, I have simply regularised the spelling as described below. In some special cases, where I have used modern spelling but have felt guilty about possibly losing some of the quality of the original, the F spelling is recorded in the collation.

It is impossible to reach a completely satisfactory solution to these problems, and the rules I have arrived at after much cogitation and consultation with the General Editors will doubtless not suit everyone. At best they are a compromise between being faithful to the original and making the text available to the general reader.

Original spellings (in a regularised form) are retained, then, as follows:

(*a*) When the word is obsolete. Where more than one form of spelling of such a word occurs in the text I have adopted the one used most frequently for all occurrences. (This may not necessarily be the spelling given the main heading in *O.E.D.*) There are several cases of two different words existing in Tudor English, with approximately the same meaning, which have merged in Modern English, one form becoming obsolete (e.g. *fet* (OE *fetian*), and *fetch* (OE *feccan*); *lese* (OE *leosan*), and *lose* (OE *losian*)). In such cases I have tried to decide whether the F spelling represents the obsolete form or the ancestor of the modern one, modernising the latter cases, and treating the former as other obsolete words. In practice, of course, it is frequently difficult to distinguish between different forms and different spellings of the same form.

(b) Where a modernised form would seriously obscure the intended sense, or where a special feature of the text, such as a play on words, would be lost.

(c) Where rhymes would be *seriously* affected, or lost. Not agreeing with Folly that 'It forseth not of the reason, so it keep rhyme' (1150), I have not felt it right to retain the original spelling *merely* for the sake of exact rhyme, especially when modernisation produces near-rhyme or eye-rhyme in any case. Where I have felt doubtful, but have decided against retaining the F spelling, the original spellings are recorded in the collation.

(d) Where metre clearly requires the retention or reduction of a syllable.

In these instances, spelling is regularised so that, for example, y becomes i, u becomes v, final e is dropped and reduplicated consonants are reduced to single ones. Snatches of Latin, French and Flemish in the text which are obviously intended to be distorted are left as they are.

Certain other special cases are mentioned at relevant points in the Commentary. Anyone who is interested in studying the original language of *Magnificence* is advised to consult Ramsay's edition, and quotations from Dyce's edition of Skelton's poems in the Introduction and Commentary will also give some idea of Skelton's (or of his printers') spelling.

The present text is punctuated more lightly than that of Ramsay, which contains the heavy punctuation typical of Victorian editors. Differences in punctuation are collated only where they affect the sense of a line. Since F has only full stops and the occasional virgule[50] and question mark, and often has no punctuation where we would expect it, it is not cited in collations concerned merely with punctuation. Lineation creates few problems: it differs in this edition from that of Dyce, because he frequently prints as two lines one metrical line divided between two characters, and occasionally from that of Ramsay, who sometimes incorporates parts of stage directions into the text.

Abbreviations have been silently expanded in the text and

Collation. There are not many of these in F: ampersands; the suspension mark over a vowel indicating omission of m or n; abbreviations for 'that', 'the[e]', 'thou', 'with', for *es* or *ys* endings, and, in the Latin stage directions, those for *quam*, *qui*, *quod* and endings in *us*. Roman numerals are occasionally used instead of words. F's black-letter is changed to roman in the Collation.

A special problem occurs in this text when the same word is used for the name of a character and for the abstract quality he represents (Conveyance or conveyance), often standing for both at the same time. In F these usually appear with their initial letters in lower-case (except in the speech-headings). In Ramsay's edition upper-case is always used, even for abstract concepts that have no counterpart in the characters of the play, such as 'will' or 'reason'. It has seemed best in this edition to reserve upper-case initials for what are clearly names of characters in the play, and give abstracts the lower-case. Some special occurrences where it has been difficult to make a decision are mentioned in the Commentary.

F contains a large number of stage directions: those in Latin have been translated, with the original given in the Collation. There is no reason to assume different sources for the English and Latin directions: many early plays have stage directions in both languages, from The *Castle of Perseverance* onwards. Editorial stage directions appear in square brackets: I have inserted them where I felt certain what would be happening 'on stage', since I believe that visualising the action is an important aid to understanding the play. (These directions are collated only when they have been added by a previous editor.) Other stage business which seems likely, but not certain, to have occurred is mentioned in the Commentary.

Owing to the unfamiliarity of Tudor English, or perhaps because so many words which *appear* familiar really differ in meaning from their modern counterparts, the Commentary contains more glosses than is usual in Revels editions. Except occasionally for the sake of clarity, a word is glossed only on its first occurrence in an unfamiliar meaning. A date given in brackets after a gloss indicates the first citation in *O.E.D.* or, when a proverb is identified, the earliest in Tilley or Whiting. More notes explaining points of syntax are needed than for later plays; these have been made as brief as is consistent with clarity.

3. DATE

A reference in the play which seems to fix a *terminus a quo* was first pointed out by Ritson.[51] When Fancy is discussing the importance of Largesse, he remarks:

> Largesse is he that all princes doth advance;
> I report me herein to King Lewis of France. (279–80)

Felicity inquires: 'Why have ye him named, and all other refused?' (281) and Fancy replies: 'For sith he died, largesse was little used' (282). King Lewis is probably Louis XII, for Louis XI died in 1483, a date which precedes Skelton's earliest work. That Louis XII is meant here is not as certain as Ritson thought, however, for when Skelton refers to 'Kynge Lewes of late' in 1522 (*Why come*, 719), it is Louis XI he means.[52] Louis XII died on 1 January 1515, and so the play is likely to have been written after that date; also the reference to Wolsey's liaison with mistress Lark (discussed below, pp. 34–5), which began in 1515, shows *Magnificence* to have been written no earlier. It cannot have been written later than 1523, when *Garlande* was printed, for it is mentioned among the catalogue of Skelton's works listed there (though it could have been *re*written between then and its printing *c*. 1530).

Ramsay deduced from Fancy's statement that 'largesse was little used' that the play could not have been written after 1520, when Francis I of France and Henry VIII vied with each other in extravagant displays of munificence at the Field of the Cloth of Gold, and that Fancy was probably referring to the 'state of semi-hostility' that existed between Britain and France immediately after Louis' death, when Francis refused to return the dowry of Henry's sister Mary, who had married Louis in 1514.[53] England was 'virtually at war' with France until the treaty of

Noyon, in August 1516, and 'peace was finally arranged through the efforts of Wolsey, by the betrothal of Francis to the infant Princess Mary', in 1518. Ramsay also used Fancy's account of his difficulties in crossing from Calais with the forged letter (347 ff.) as evidence that *Magnificence* 'must have been composed while hostility was still acute', hence probably before the treaty of Noyon, and certainly before the betrothal of Francis to Mary.

It is naturally tempting to try to find a precise date for the play but unfortunately the evidence of Fancy, a notorious liar, cannot be relied upon. He is posing as 'Largesse', and trying to persuade Magnificence of the need to 'use' him. The reference to little use of largesse after Louis' death is probably ironic: Louis was 'careful' in the same way that Henry VII was, and when Francis came to the throne he started using his father's money in just the way Henry VIII had *his* father's. Or Fancy may have been referring to Louis XII's 'largesse' in bribes. The Venetian calendar reports under 1510:

> The Spanish ambassador was on his way to England but had stopped in Paris. Suspects he will be bribed by the King of France according to custom.[54]

> The Spanish ambassador still in Paris. Dread that King Lewis will bribe him, as he does the whole world.[55]

If Fancy's remark is ironic it could have been written at any date, in fact the later the better; after 1520 it might well refer pointedly to the extravagance at the Field of the Cloth of Gold. We do not know, either, whether Fancy is restricting his criticisms to France; it seems more likely that he is complaining about a general disinclination to use largesse, and that of Magnificence in particular.

Similarly his comments on the difficulties of travelling from Calais cannot really be used as evidence for 'a state of semi-hostility', for the account is given in the hope of persuading Magnificence to pay his expenses, and is no doubt a complete fabrication. Magnificence does *not* reimburse him; not even he really believed Fancy (his words 'Marry, sir, ye were affrayed' are ironic), and so there is no reason why we should be taken in.

Fancy does not say 'largesse *is* little used', but that it *was* little used. Were he referring to events in 1516, or indeed to any supposed contemporary meanness, he would be more likely to have used the present tense. The use of the verb *was* tends to suggest that the line was written some time after Louis' death.

Finally, any evidence based on the official relationship between England and France is extremely unreliable. They are traditional and respected enemies, 'perhaps Europe's oldest enemies',[56] and a treaty or a betrothal is only a political move; it does not mean that the general populace of the two countries suddenly become the best of friends. In fact in 1519, when there was supposed to be 'peace', the Venetian ambassador said his legation 'proved very irksome to him, owing to the enmity between France and England'.[57]

Reluctantly, then, Fancy's 'evidence' must be dismissed as inconclusive, and unfortunately there are no other references in the play that directly shed light on its date.[58] It must be accepted that *Magnificence* could have been written anywhere between 1515 and 1523. But because it contains similar matter to satires of Wolsey, and especially in view of the close verbal parallels to *Why come* (1522), and to some extent to *Parrot* (1521), and *Cloute* (1521–2),[59] I feel that it is closer to these poems in date, and believe it to have been written between 1520 and 1522.

4. THE PLAY

(a) 'A goodly interlude'

The description of *Magnificence* on its title-page ought to help explain what kind of work it is, but the term interlude seems to have been used with great flexibility during the Tudor period, indeed it is virtually synonymous with 'entertainment'.[60] In the epilogue, 'this interlude' (2520), 'matter . . . / Pressly purposed under pretence of play' (2548–9), is variously called 'a plain example' (2510), a 'process' (2506), i.e. 'a discourse or treatise; an argument or discussion' (*O.E.D.* sb. 4), and 'a mirror . . . / This life inconstant for to behold and see' (2520–1). These terms serve to describe the different elements or genres combined in the play. A moral play, *Magnificence* provides its audience with an 'example' which should teach it to seek virtue and avoid vice. It is also like an argument or debate in that it is concerned with demonstrating the truth of a thesis. Then like Lydgate's *Fall of Princes* or the later *Mirror for Magistrates* it shows the inconstancy of the lives of the great, and their subjection to the vicissitudes of Fortune.

A moral play dramatises a battle between Virtues and Vices over the soul of Mankind. The external struggle represents the internal conflict of every man (or Everyman): Virtues and Vices are 'the motives and impulses of man's own heart . . . taken from him, and, clothed in flesh and blood, given him again for companions'.[61] The moral play *Mankind* (*c*. 1475), though much shorter and simpler than *Magnificence*, closely resembles it in structure. Mankind enters in a state of grace, protected by the Virtue Mercy. When Mercy leaves him he is corrupted by the Vices. He falls into despair, is tempted to suicide, is rescued by Mercy, and repents, promising to lead a new life. Similarly Magnificence appears under the rule of Measure. When Measure goes away he is corrupted by the six Vices. He despairs and is tempted to suicide, is saved by Good Hope, and repents, returning to his palace to begin anew. The two plays are particularly close in their demonstration of Despair and Mischief,[62] but the shape grace–fall–repentance is common to all moral plays and moral interludes, sometimes, as in *The Castle of Perseverance* (1400–25?), or *Nature* (1495?), being run through twice. Where moral plays vary is in the choice of sin or vice they warn their audience against. *The Pride of Life* (1400–25?) deals with pride; *The Castle of Perseverance* emphasises covetousness; *Mankind* warns against sloth. There seems to have been a development from general warning ('If you sin you will be damned unless you repent') to a more specific message. *Mankind*, for instance, points out that 'the devil finds mischief for idle hands to do'.[63] This kind of proverbial statement comes to serve as a thesis for the action of the play to prove. Later moral interludes are often proverbial in title: *Enough Is as Good as a Feast* (1564?); *Like will to Like* (1568?); *The Tide Tarrieth No*

Man (1576?); *The Longer thou Livest the more Fool thou art* (1564?). In *Enough*, the Prologue, saying, 'go we to the Argument', explains:

> Our title is Enough is as Good as a Feast,
> Which rhetorically we shall amplify
> So that it shall appear both to most and least
> That our meaning is but honesty;   (79–82)

'Argument' here has the sense 'a connected series of statements . . . intended to establish a position', or 'discussion of a question; debate' (*O.E.D.* 4,5)—the sense 'theme' is not common until later. The 'argument' of the play is the establishing of the truth of the position 'Enough is as good as a feast'. The interest is as much in the argument for its own sake as in the truth it purports to 'prove', but the final aim, at least in those interludes which may be termed 'moral', is the correction of vice in the audience:

> the hearers that thereby shall be touched
> May rather amend their lives than therewith be grieved.
> *(All for Money*, Prologue, 97–8)

The argument, or thesis, of *Magnificence* is summed up in the proverb 'Measure is treasure' (125), and the play sets out to prove the truth of this statement by showing what happens when measure is lost. 'Sources' for the discussion about measure in *Magnificence* have been found in Aristotle's *Nicomachean Ethics*[64] and Horace's *Odes*,[65] but like any proverb 'Measure is treasure' is a commonplace, and we cannot prove that Skelton took it from any 'source'. He might have found it in *Mankind*, where it is cited by Mercy (237). Skelton does seem to have drawn on Lydgate's poems 'A Song of Just Mesure' and 'Mesure is Tresour'. The opening line of *Magnificence* is almost a repetition of the first line of 'Song',[66] and there are echoes of sentiments of both poems here and there throughout the play.[67] Some of the examples of immoderate tyrants Lydgate lists in 'Mesure' are cited in the tyrannical speech of Magnificence, and both Lydgate's poems and Skelton's play are concerned with the lack of measure that arises when 'he allso that is a cherll of blode'

('Song', 35) is 'Brought vp of naght vnto dominacion' ('Song', 36). Both authors cite *Wisdom* XI, 21, as an authority:

> In old auctours lyke as it is discryved, . . .
> By peyse, by nombre, tryed out by equite,   ('Song', 3, 6)

> In ponder, by number, by measure, all thing is wrought,
> As at the first original, by godly opinion; (*Magnificence*, 118–19)

In these poems Lydgate is interested in examining the qualities of measure (and showing its opposites), just as Skelton is.

Skelton's choice of this particular proverb for his thesis is connected to his use of Magnificence rather than simply 'mankind' for the hero of his moral play. Measure is essential to true magnificence, as Aristotle had pointed out and as was explained in the popular pseudo-Aristotelian treatise *Secreta Secretorum*, supposedly written for Alexander the Great:

> Ther is a maner straunge difference,
> ffor lak of Resoun twen prodigalyte
> And in a kynges Royal magnificence,
> Whan he lyst parte of liberallite
> To his sogettys as they been of degre
> So Egally I-holdyn the ballaunce,
> Ech man contente with discreet Suffysaunce.
>
> Ther is a mene peysed in ballaunce
> Atwixen hym that is a greet wastour
> To kepe a meene by attemperaunce,
> That ech thyng be peysed be mesour.
>   (*Secrees of Old Philisoffres*, 764–74)[68]

This too is a commonplace: the importance of moderation was stressed in all advice given to princes from Isocrates and Xenophon through to Skelton's own *Speculum Principis* and Erasmus' *Education of a Christian Prince* (1516).[69]

The choice of Magnificence rather than Mankind for hero gives Skelton's moral play the quality of (medieval) tragedy inherent in such works as Lydgate's *Fall of Princes*. Lydgate defines his work as showing:

> The fall of nobles, with eueri circumstaunce,
> From ther lordshippes, dreedful and vnstable,

How that thei fill to putte in remembraunce,
Therin to shewe Fortunys variaunce,
That othre myhte as in a merour see
In worldly worshepe may be no surete.

(Fall of Princes, I, 51–6)*

His stories had the same didactic purpose as a moral play:

Ther cheef labour is vicis to repreve
With a maner couert symylityde

(Fall of Princes, III, 3830–1)*

The lives of the nobles are *exempla* just as are those of the mankind figures, but there are two main differences in the type of writing. Firstly the *exempla* in the *Fall of Princes* are history. The life-story of a fallen prince is used as an example of how any man may fall. The characters at least in the earlier moral plays have no existence as 'real' people; they function allegorically, created to demonstrate a general truth, the knowledge of which precedes their existence. Secondly, in *Fall of Princes* writing the emphasis is placed less on man's inconstancy, which can be rectified, as shown in the moral plays, and more on the inconstancy of Fortune, to which all are subject, though those who are governed by Reason have more control over her:

Vertu on Fortune maketh a diffiaunce,
That Fortune hath no domynacioun
Wher noble pryncis be gouerned by resoun.

(Fall of Princes, II, 54–6)*

This concept is derived from Boethius, and Skelton uses it to open his play: Felicity (or Prosperity) explains that he can continue when everything is controlled by man's reason.

Skelton's inclusion of the characters Felicity and Adversity (aspects of Fortune, rather than qualities of mankind), in his allegory gives the play at times a tone similar to tragedies like Lydgate's. But prosperity is lost by the prince's own actions, through his submission to will rather than reason, and Adversity is seen not as an undeserved visitation of Fortune, but as a punishment for sin, coming from God: 'The stroke of God, Adversity, I hight' (1883).[70] When Adversity is seen as a punishment, it can be reversed after repentance. This is impossible when it is under the arbitrary rule of Fortune, and therefore impossible in a medieval tragedy. The repentance and renewal of Magnificence show finally that the play *is* a moral one, not a true tragedy of a prince's fall, yet the choice of a prince for hero, and the placing of that prince in a 'historical' setting with a life of his own, makes for something, if only potentially, similar to medieval tragedy.

Magnificence, then, resembles a moral play like *Mankind* in its structure, but its aims and overall effect are more complicated. Like all moral plays it aims to demonstrate a general truth by a particular example. But the thesis of *Magnificence*, 'Measure is treasure', is not merely used as the basis of a sermon intended to correct the vices of the audience, it is also examined for its own sake, and indeed defined by the concrete manifestations the play uses to demonstrate it, and the example, of a prince whose lack of measure leads to his downfall, is conveyed in a manner which convinces us of its literal reality.

Magnificence might be described as having three levels of interest, corresponding to the three 'genres' it combines: the allegorical level, in which Magnificence corresponds to the Mankind figure over whose soul, or perhaps more accurately in whose mind, the Virtues (of measure), and the Vices (measure's enemies), are warring; the philosophical level, in which Skelton is interested in considering the implications of the statement 'Measure is treasure' and the meaning of 'magnificence'; and the literal or narrative level, where we follow the story of a particular prince who ceases to be aware of the virtues of moderation, and loses his power after inviting corrupt conspirators to his court. This division into 'levels' is made merely for the sake of clarity; the different genres of moral play, debate, and tragedy naturally merge into one another; the matter cannot really be separated any more than that of any allegory. And since there is constant movement between the specific and the general, as in all allegory, the amount of attention given to one 'level' in the play changes from one moment to the next. There is more concentration on philosophical debate at the beginning of the play, when the thesis to be examined must be established; more attention given to the play's moral meaning at the end, when the message or didactic element of the play has to be firmly brought home; and inevitably more 'realism' in the part of the play which shows the gradual corruption of Magnificence by the Vices, since vice more readily assumes a human form than virtue.

The thesis to be examined in *Magnificence* is conveyed more economically than in interludes such as *Enough Is as Good as a Feast* or *All for Money*, which make use of a lengthy prologue. Personifications of concepts with which the argument is to be concerned in *Magnificence* themselves raise questions about it. Felicity and Liberty are shown discussing whether it is right for Liberty to be kept under control, and the resolution is provided by the personification who represents the proper position: Measure. In his speech at 114–25 Measure cites the authorities of Horace, and the *Book of Wisdom*, and repeats a series of maxims all aimed at the conclusion 'Measure is treasure', with which proverb he ends his speech. Liberty must be controlled by Measure: without it, it 'would prove a thing of nought'. After further discussion, the thesis is put in a different form, which defines for us what is meant by 'treasure': 'Measure continueth prosperity and wealth' (141)—moderation ensures the continued existence of good fortune. This is the same point that was being made in Felicity's opening speech.[71] He states that prosperity comes to every reasonable man some time during his life, and that a wise man will know how to make it last as long as possible. But he concludes that 'nowadays' men do not have these qualities; will has gained control over reason, and hence 'felicity is passing small' (21). The introduction of a comment on the contemporary situation particularises the general truth he is discussing. Measure is treasure, prosperity is always lost when men cease to use moderation, and it is lost nowadays since wilful rulers are in control. Felicity later states the ultimate results of wilfulness:

> For without measure, poverty and need
> Will creep upon us, and us to mischief lead;
> For mischief will master us, if measure us forsake. (152–4)

This is both a maxim and a prophecy of what will actually happen to Magnificence in the play. The sequence wilfulness–loss of prosperity–poverty–evil ('mischief' = 'evil' in Tudor English) summarises the main movement of the play, and more important, it immediately establishes the connection between unreason and evil which enables Skelton to move from examination of a thesis to a moral conclusion.

Use of personifications always entails moving between the general and the specific—Mischief is both a manifestation of evil and a character in the play who produces a knife and a halter for Magnificence to kill himself. But Skelton is often more precise and literal in his use of personifications than many allegorists. He also allows greater flexibility. In *Youth*, for example, the Virtues Charity and Humility act virtuously throughout, but they do not behave either charitably or humbly, they simply represent the charitable and humble side of Youth's personality. Measure represents the quality measure and its manifestation in the (early) behaviour of Magnificence, but is also a *character* who behaves moderately in the literal action, from his first words after greeting Felicity and Liberty: 'I perceive well how each of you doth reason' (83) which indicate his lack of bias. The Vices, as well as representing vice in general, act in accordance with their names: Folly is foolish; Crafty Conveyance conveys the letter which has been forged or counterfeited by Counterfeit Countenance. This precision gives a firm basis from which an examination of general truths can arise; a very literal meaning which pins the allegory down. Some personifications, though, represent concepts which are less easy to define, and to understand their true meaning is part of the purpose of the play. Wealthful Felicity might represent well-being or prosperity in general, or the quality of being 'well-off' financially. Measure equates 'treasure' with 'prosperity', and so does Magnificence at first, when he calls Felicity 'my singular treasure' (317). But when Magnificence starts handing out money indiscriminately, and allows the conspirators to have charge over Wealth, the financial sense is uppermost, and Felicity complains, 'Then waste must be welcome, and farewell thrift' (1445). The meaning of Liberty, 'power to do as one likes', varies depending upon what Magnificence likes to do. When Liberty is ruled by Measure Magnificence is free to act rationally, to be generous or liberal on the right occasions, but when measure is gone liberty turns into licence. Liberty himself explains for us how his meaning can shift:

> For I am a virtue if I be well used,
> And I am a vice where I am abused.   (2102–3)

Most important is the flexibility of the term magnificence. As a translation of the Aristotelian term μεγαλοπρέπεια it signifies 'liberality . . . combined with good taste' or properly measured generosity, and is frequently synonymous with 'munificence' (O.E.D. 1, 2). It can also mean 'glory', greatness in general, and qualities relating to that (O.E.D. 3, 4, 5), and here, like liberty, it can turn in either direction, becoming either proper dignity or, when abused, pride. It can also be 'a title of honour applied to . . . distinguished persons' (O.E.D. 6). When Magnificence observes:

> For doubtless I perceive my magnificence
> Without measure lightly may fade,
> Of too much liberty under the offence.   (227–9)

the first sense of the term has precedence. When he tells the audience at the end of the play

> Without our ship be sure it is likely to burst.
> Yet of magnificence oft made is the mast,
> Thus none estate living of him can be sure,
> For the wealth of this world cannot endure.   (2558–61)

'magnificence' has a neutral sense. The sense 'title of honour' is evident in the name of the hero himself, as well as on occasions as greetings.[72]

These three areas of meaning correspond to what I have called the three levels of the play. A consideration of the concept liberality forms part of the discussion concerned with proving that 'Measure is treasure'; magnificence as a neutral quality is at the centre of the struggle between the Virtues and Vices; Magnificence is the prince who is corrupted and loses his power.

But we should always be aware of all possible meanings of the term, whichever seems uppermost at any time. They are united in the figure Magnificence, and cannot really be separated any more than can the 'levels' of the play.

Once the thesis 'Measure is treasure' has been established, the play goes on to demonstrate the gradual stages of the prince's fall. Here the 'merry' part of this 'goodly interlude' appears, but it is not mere entertainment; the antics of the Vices are an integral part of the action, not just superfluous gambols.

The Vices are differentiated by their costumes and the use of different verse forms in their soliloquies,[73] and they also have distinct functions in the action of the play, both literally in their roles as conspirators aiming to oust Measure and take over the court of Magnificence, and allegorically as showing different stages in the process of the prince's downfall. They are accepted into Magnificence's service one by one, and the arrival of each shows him taking a new step on the downward path.

Fancy joins in the debate, twisting it in a new direction. He argues:

> Marry, upon truth my reason I ground:
> That without largesse nobleness cannot reign.   (264–5)

This reasoning is only 'true' to the extent that it depends on the definition of 'largesse', properly 'liberality', and, as such, a quality appropriate to magnificence, or nobleness, as Fancy calls it, but 'lavishness' is what Fancy intends. Later shown to be a fool, Fancy corresponds to the 'folargesse' or 'folee largesse' that is described as a vice in the *Secreta Secretorum*[74], which Skelton described in *Diodorus*, in an interpolation, in a manner which *Magnificence* echoes:

> yf foly by his fantasie, disguysed with his gyrded habillementis of worldly vanyte, induce noble astates to daunce the comyn trace of abusion; wherupon, sone after, ensueth extreme confusion of fallyble fortune ful of deceyte.[75]

Though neither Felicity nor Magnificence notices this, Fancy's 'reason' does not prove their talk was 'vain'; it actually supports their argument. True 'largesse' is not the opposite of Measure, though Fancy, false 'Largesse', thinks it is. It is psychologically appropriate that Fancy enters when Measure has left the stage, thereby leaving Magnificence vulnerable. Fancy ('capricious or arbitrary preference') is virtually synonymous with 'will',[76] or at least is one manifestation of it, Liberty being another.

Once Magnificence has succumbed to Fancy, a downward movement towards folly and loss of measure is inevitable. Conveyance manages by 'underhand dealing' (*O.E.D.* 11b) to get himself to court, and works at conveying the rest of the Vices there, through the 'device' (*O.E.D.* 11c) of providing them all with assumed names.[77] These names help to emphasise the differences between the Vices, as well as to show us how they each seem to Magnificence once he loses 'measure'. 'Good Demeanance' (Countenance) appropriately enters when Magnificence has accepted Fancy under *his* 'counterfeit countenance', Largesse. The appearance of Counterfeit Countenance shows allegorically that Magnificence has taken another downward step, from following his own inclinations to a loss of judgement of character. When Fancy, Conveyance and Countenance are colluding to get rid of Measure, *Collusion* symbolically arrives. That he is taken by Magnificence for 'Sober Sadness' indicates extreme lack of judgement on the part of the prince, for Collusion is like Iago: his words 'I am never glad but when I may do ill' (731) resemble that terrifying 'Pleasure and action make the hours seem short'.

As Collusion ends his soliloquy on the word *bale* ('evil'), Courtly Abusion comes in singing. He *seems* a pleasant change (and his assumed name is 'Pleasure'), from Collusion, who is 'cloaked', dark and gloomy. Abusion is 'Rich to behold/Glittering in gold' (853–4), brightly, indeed garishly, dressed. But he is worse than Collusion. 'Abusion' = 'perversion, corruption, wrong'. Collusion had expressed the idea of taking pleasure in evil, and Abusion enters to provide a concrete image of this. Magnificence is now so corrupt that he takes evil for 'Pleasure'.

The re-entrance of Fancy, now dressed as a fool,[78] shows allegorically that fancy not only *leads* to folly: it really *is* folly, when seen in its true colours. When Fancy finally reveals his true name to Magnificence he substitutes the term 'fondness' for 'largesse'.[79] Folly is taken by Magnificence for 'Conceit', synonymous with fancy in many of its senses.[80] Thus vice is shown to be self-perpetuating. As Covetise explains in *The Castle of Perseverance*:

> euery synne tyllyth in [attracts] othyr
> And makyth Mankynde to ben a foole.　　　(1032–3)

The work of one Vice naturally touches on and merges with that of the others; this is emphasised by many correspondences and cross-references in the soliloquies. All the Vices refer to the corrupt state of the contemporary world, and particular aspects of this are mentioned in several of their speeches; corruption in the Church; extravagance in fashion and language; the frequency of upstarts. They all draw on each other's terminology to describe their own activities. They argue about which of them is better and what order they come in; they quarrel among themselves. In fact, as Folly points out, they are all fools.[81] The circle is completed by the soliloquy of Conveyance, who had begun everything by conveying the letter to Fancy.

> By conveyance crafty I have brought
> Unto Magnificence a full ungracious sort,　　　(1373–4)

During the conveying of each new conspirator into Magnificence's presence the attack on Measure has been going forward off-stage, reported by one Vice as he comes back to collect the next. After the arrival of Conveyance at court, Fancy is promoted to knighthood; after Collusion reaches Magnificence a 'fray' occurs which results in Liberty's becoming a free soldier and in the weakening of Measure's power; the arrival of Abusion completes the freeing of Liberty from Measure's rule, and Conveyance prophesies that when Folly gets to the court 'All measure and good rule is gone quite' (1317).

This series of scenes, then, shows literally the destruction of the court of Magnificence by conspirators, and allegorically the disintegration of his (and any man's) personality, wilfulness leading to folly, vice leading to crime.

When Magnificence returns, significantly without Measure, though still with Felicity, the degeneration in his personality symbolised by the Vices is shown us in concrete form. His views are now exactly the opposite of those he had originally held. He had ordered Liberty to be ruled by Measure, but now this 'grieves' him (1376–7). Felicity's repetition of Measure's warning to 'beware of "had I wist"' passes unnoticed. Now the command is 'Ye shall be occupied, Wealth, at my *will*' (1381). Not only is Magnificence now shown in the company of the Vices, he has also taken on their qualities. He has adopted the 'haughty expression' of Collusion,[82] and he uses the same words that he had originally found offensive in Fancy.[83] His soliloquy shows how his 'magnificence' has shifted from proper dignity to pride. It resembles the ranting speeches of the tyrants in earlier drama, or figures like World in *The Castle of Perseverance*.[84] He thinks himself greater than heroes like Alexander, Hercules and Charlemagne, and believes, like Tamburlaine, that

> Fortune to her laws cannot abandon me,
> But I shall of Fortune rule the rein; (1460–1)

This delusion is brought out clearly by the images he goes on to use:

> I sing of two parts without a mean;
> I have wind and weather over all to sail,
> No stormy rage against me can prevail. (1464–6)

These contrast sharply with sentiments expressed by Measure and Felicity:

> All trebles and tenors be ruled by a mean (137)

> after a drought there falleth a shower of rain
> And after a heat oft cometh a stormy cold (12–13)

Felicity had shown that Fortune cannot be controlled by will, yet Magnificence now claims 'I have wealth at will'.

This part of the play is important in establishing the relationship between folly and sin, which proves Felicity's assertion that without measure a man will fall into mischief. The consequences of wilfulness are not merely *social* evils, they result in

danger to the soul. Magnificence's soliloquy shows him falling
into the sin of pride, and 'Pleasure' encourages him in lechery
and wrath.

The arrival of Adversity, 'the stroke of God', is a natural
consequence of Magnificence's behaviour:

Lo, sirs, thus I handle them all
That follow their fancies in folly to fall;   (1897–8)

For I strike lords of realms and lands
That rule not by measure that they have in their hands, (1939–40)

Hard upon Adversity, in fulfilment of Felicity's prophecy,
come Poverty and Mischief.

Had Mischief succeeded in getting Magnificence to kill himself, the play would have been a true tragedy of a prince's fall,
not merely one that 'takes a long step toward tragedy'.[85] The
advent of Good Hope here, a sort of *deus ex machina*, and the
resulting arrival of Redress, Sad Circumspection and Perseverance, are unsatisfactory on every level of the play. The thesis
'Measure is treasure' would have been proved, and Felicity's
prophecy fulfilled, had Magnificence ended here. The fact that
he is able to return to his palace 'with joy and royalty' tends
finally to disprove the thesis, for Measure does not return, nor
does 'Wealthful Felicity',[86] and so there seems no reason why
'treasure' should. Allegorically the arrival of Good Hope is
unconvincing (as that of Fancy was not). There is nothing in
Magnificence's state of mind to lead us to expect him to be
hopeful, and while Fancy came in when Measure had gone out,
Good Hope appears while Despair and Mischief are still there. It
is impossible to believe that the sudden arrival of a few good
friends (and how was Sad Circumspection summoned back
from abroad so quickly?) would enable Magnificence to regain
all the possessions taken away by conspirators who are still at
large.

This sort of unsatisfactory ending is not peculiar to
Magnificence, however: the sudden reformation of the hero
without any apparent internal motivation is common in moral
interludes. The change in the hero of *Mankind* results from the

return of Mercy, a quality at least partly coming from God. And Good Hope speaks like a churchman[87] – he can be seen as coming from 'outside', rather than from the psychology of Magnificence. Tudor audiences seem to have been optimistic about mankind's tendencies. In *Youth*, after saying that he will be guided by Riot in everything, the hero suddenly changes his mind when Charity talks of Christ's mercy. In *Mundus and Infans* Manhood repents when Conscience tricks him by twisting the meaning of covetousness. In *Nature* Man suddenly turns against his companion Worldly Affection by a thought about Reason which previously had no effect on him, then falls again, to repent when Age brings in Reason (a very optimistic view of the powers of Age!). The double depiction in *Nature* of fall and repentance emphasises man's inconstancy, his faculty 'ever to offend and ever to ask mercy', shifting like a weather-vane, as the author of *Mankind* put it. If man is changeable he must sometimes change for good as well as bad. The shape of all moral plays is based on this optimistic view, though in *Magnificence* the emphasis is finally placed on the inevitable inconstancy of life:

> A mirror encleared is this interlude,
> This life inconstant for to behold and see: (2520–1)

> A plain example of worldly vainglory:
> How in this world there is no sickerness (2510–1)

(b) *Satire of Wolsey*

Ramsay had different reasons for thinking the ending of *Magnificence* weak. He saw the main part of the play as topical satire, which turns in the end to 'attempted prophecy'; 'partly vague warning, partly merely the conventional *dénouement* of every moral play'. The 'mysteries' of *Magnificence* could all be 'unlocked by a single key, – its political application', and contemporary spectators

must have instantly recognized in its central figure constant allusion to the open handed Henry with the wealth of his earlier years and the self-will that always remained his dominant trait, and in its 'vices' and 'virtues' the alleged qualities of the two parties that had been fighting bitterly almost since the reign began, – one the party of

young favorites and counsellors of whom Wolsey, now at the height
of his power, had become leader and chief representative, the other
the party of the old nobility headed by the Duke of Norfolk. (p. cviii)

It is important to consider the implications of the word 'recognized'. Calling something a mirror implies an invitation to look
into it. But was Skelton's a general invitation, or did he have a
particular individual or group in mind? Spectators are inclined
to identify characters in a play with contemporary figures
whether or not the author intends that, as Ben Jonson was aware
when he begged the audience of *Bartholomew Fair* not to conceal

> any state-decipherer, or politic picklock of the scene, so solemnly
> ridiculous as to search out who was meant by the Ginger-bread-
> woman, who by the Hobby-horse-man, who by the Costermonger
> . . .   (*Induction*, 138–42)

Wolsey did recognise himself in a play performed at Gray's Inn
in 1526:

> whiche was compiled for the moste part, by master Ihon Roo seriant
> at the law. xx. yere past. and long before the Cardinall had any
> aucthoritie, the effecte of the plaie was, that lord gouernance was
> ruled by dissipacion and negligence, by whose misgouernance and
> euill order, lady Publike wele was put from gouernance: which
> caused Rumor Populi, Inward grudge and disdain of wanton
> souereignetie, to rise with a greate multitude, to expell negligence
> and dissipacion, and to restore Publik welth again to her estate, . . .
> it was highly praised of all menne, sauying of the Cardinall, whiche
> imagined that the plaie had been diuised of hym, . . . This plaie sore
> displeased the Cardinall, and yet it was neuer meante to hym . . .[88]

A guilty creature sitting at a play. Written 'long before the
Cardinall had any aucthoritie', Roo's play was supposedly concerned with the vices of governors in general, yet Wolsey saw it
as being particularly directed at him. One wonders whether it
was 'neuer meante to hym'. Roo and his associates must have
realised whom 'lord gouernance' would suggest in 1526.
Authors of interludes always protested that their plays aimed
only to correct vice in general:

> But truly we meane no person perticularly,
> But only to specifie of such generally (*The Longer*, Aiiv)

Many interludes have been shown to have a political meaning.[89]

It is likely that political reference would have been found in *Magnificence*, since it deals with a misguided prince, whatever Skelton's intentions.

Ramsay argued that the action in *Magnificence* conformed to the historical situation in 1516; recent criticism[90] has tended to feel that the play is too early in date and too general in intention to contain satire of Wolsey. But as I have shown, the date is uncertain, though probably later than 1516.[91] Thus it is impossible to point out precise historical parallels. Anyway most of the events in the play are general enough to be made to fit many occasions between 1515 and 1523 and indeed many since. History repeats itself: 'an allegory intended to describe a given political situation will often fit a dozen other situations as well'.[92] At least three different political readings have been made of Chaucer's *Parlement of Fowles*,[93] and two different political settings have been seen behind Skelton's own *Parrot*.[94] Then there is the problem that historical 'truth', so far as that can be determined by an unbiased reading of contemporary sources, will not be the same as that seen by the inevitably biased Skelton.

There is the further difficulty that a work like *Magnificence*, intended for public presentation, is unlikely to contain open abuse of the kind that will allow us easily to identify any figure referred to. It is one thing to write virulent satire for private circulation, as Skelton did in *Parrot*, *Cloute* and *Why come*, and quite another to make a public show of it. Even in *Parrot*, Skelton proceeds covertly to begin with (he speaks of *allegoria* being his protection), only gradually becoming more outspoken, and in *Cloute* he says 'For no man haue I named:/ Wherfore sholde I be blamed?' (1113–14). This smacks of the conventional announcement at the beginning of novels that the characters have no relationship to real persons: the references to Wolsey in these poems are clear enough for there to be no need to name him. Mention is made, for example, of Wolsey's taking the great seal with him to Calais (*Parrot*, 310), his hand in the murder of the Duke of Buckingham (*Cloute*, 613–14, 629–30, 636, 1013–21), his purchase of splendid tapestries for Hampton

Court (*Cloute*, 942–70), and a brothel with the sign of the Cardinal's hat (*Why come*, 233–6). There is nothing so outspoken in *Magnificence*, where Skelton would have needed to be more discreet. This makes the task of a politic picklock hard, since something not too immediately obvious to a contemporary audience will be even less so to a modern one, and we might easily become so solemnly ridiculous as to search out allusions that were never intended.

When, for example, Countenance talks of a 'carter' becoming a 'courtier' (483), is this a reference to the upstart Wolsey, as Ramsay would have it, or merely a comment on upstarts in general? In *Cloute* Skelton says that Wolsey has 'Sodaynly vpstarte/From the donge carte' (646–7), and 'the carter of York' was one of the terms of abuse used by other satirists of Wolsey, such as Roy and Barlowe.[95] Yet, in an early poem, Skelton called some unknown individual, also an upstart at court, 'Thys docter Deuyas commensyd in a cart' (*Coystrowne*, 55). Skelton tended to use the same terminology of abuse throughout his writing, apparently only after about 1520 focusing it on Wolsey. 'The vocal opposition to Wolsey in England can be said to have begun and reached its sudden crescendo in the early years of the 1520's,'[96] after he had engineered the splendid extravagances at the Field of the Cloth of Gold (1520), and (supposedly) taken a part in the murder of the Duke of Buckingham (1521). If *Magnificence* were written after 1520 (as I feel it was), the audience would think of Wolsey when they heard the word 'carter', and Skelton would have intended them to do so. Since, however, the date of the play is uncertain we must consider this sort of 'evidence' as neutral for the moment.

We need to decide whether anything in the play seems clearly directed at Wolsey, date aside. There is one very pointed allusion, not mentioned by Ramsay. It was well known that Wolsey formed a liaison in about 1515 with a Mistress Lark.[97] In *Henry VIII*, when the nobles are listing their complaints against the cardinal, Surrey challenges

> let his grace go forward,
> And dare us with his cap, like larks.   (III.ii.281–2)

He goes on to mention Wolsey's notoriously lascivious habits:

> I'll startle you
> Worse than the sacring bell, when the brown wench
> Lay kissing in your arms, lord cardinal.   (III.ii.294–6)

'Larks' and 'the brown wench' refer to this lady. In *Magnificence*, using the same image as Surrey, Conveyance says, 'I have an hobby can make larks to dare' (1343), and when Abusion offers Magnificence a 'lusty lass' 'to acquaint you with carnal delectation' (1548) Magnificence cries

> I would hawk whilst my head did wark,
> So I might hobby for such a lusty lark.   (1564–5)

Compare this with Skelton's complaint to Wolsey in *Cloute*:

> For some say ye hunte in parkes,
> And hauke on hobby larkes,
> And other wanton warkes,
> Whan the nyght darkes.   (193–6)

Magnificence's wish to hobby for a lark is a direct reference to Wolsey's relationship with his mistress. (Note the pun in *carnal*, 1548, used also by Roy and Barlowe.[98]) This confirms Ramsay's conviction that the play contains satire of Wolsey, suggesting indeed that there are qualities of the cardinal in Magnificence himself. Lines from *Why come* give further support for this:

> The kynges courte
> Shulde haue the excellence;
> But Hampton Court
> Hath the preemynence,
> And Yorkes Place,
> With my lordes grace,
> To whose *magnifycence*
> Is all the conflewence.   (403–10; my italics)

Here also 'magnifycence' = Wolsey (owner of Hampton Court).[99] Wolsey is at the centre of the court to which all come, as Magnificence is in this play.

The identification of Magnificence with Wolsey was made long ago by E. S. Hooper,[100] but his evidence was rather thin, being based mainly upon a misinterpretation of the word 'niggard' (388) as meaning an upstart. Ramsay's suggestion that Magnificence was Henry VIII was widely accepted until recently. Yet Skelton never wrote a word against Henry; on the contrary, he was always trying to ingratiate himself with the king, and Magnificence is not 'always treated with considerable respect';[101] he is condemned for pride, wrath and lechery, and made to look a fool. 'Magnificence = Henry VIII' only on the level where wealth is interpreted as *financial* well-being:[102] we are to read it as a warning to the king that his exchequer is being abused.[103]

Yet the play is not simply a warning; it is also a demonstration of how magnificence can turn, and has turned, into pride, into the falsely magnificent. It deals with the fall of a proud prince from prosperity to adversity (in which the loss of riches is only a part) through his own folly and vice. If that prince had a contemporary equivalent it would be more likely to be Wolsey than Henry, considering Skelton's attitude to the two personalities. The phrase 'prince royal' need not necessarily imply sovereignty,[104] it may stand for any great leader, and it is significant that Magnificence is always called a prince and never a king. The title 'your grace' by which the prince is frequently addressed in the play is conferred on archbishops and dukes as well as kings: we see it used of Wolsey in the extract from *Why come* above, with the suggestion that Wolsey had a 'court' which he thought superior to that of the king.

Contemporary opinion was similar to Skelton's. In his *Report of England*, written in 1519, the Venetian ambassador says of Wolsey:

> He ruled both the King and the entire kingdom. On Giustinian's first arrival in England he used to say to him, 'His Majesty will do so and so.' Subsequently, by degrees, he went forgetting himself, and commenced saying, 'We shall do so and so.' He had then reached such a pitch that he used to say, 'I shall do so and so.'[105]

Similarly, in 1520, the next Venetian ambassador remarks, 'It would be well to make a present to this "individual", who might be styled King of England.'[106]

To see Wolsey in Magnificence also makes good sense in

relation to the form of the play. We can only read Magnificence as Henry on the literal or historical level of the play, as a prince who is corrupted by his courtiers. On the moral level, those courtiers, the Vices, are concrete manifestations of the hero's own vice, *his* fancy, *his* folly. Skelton would never suggest that Henry was prone to so many vices, and had *no* virtues to remain present and continue the battle after the departure of Measure. Ramsay pointed out that it was in the nature of the moral play that the Vices should personify different aspects of the one character Wolsey, rather than each represent a different member of Henry's court, but he did not see that it should follow from this that the hero stand for Wolsey as a whole: the Vices (and Virtues, when there are any), are aspects of the central figure in a moral play.

Of course Magnificence is not meant to be the exact equivalent of Wolsey, any more than Piers is Christ; he is an allegorical figure and his interpretation may vary as seems appropriate. Basically he stands for any proud prince, and at some points he may indeed be like Henry VIII. But once the audience had seen qualities of Wolsey in the hero, either through the hints about Mistress Lark, or because there were frequent complaints about the cardinal's 'magnificence', or simply because he was the obvious choice when a proud prince was in question, then they would see the Vices as representing (on one level) aspects of his personality, for Wolsey was accused of most of the vices portrayed in Magnificence. In Skelton's later poems, in the writings of contemporary detractors, and of those who wrote about him soon after his death, there are many parallels to the sort of complaints made in this play. Some of these comments occur in texts printed later than 1523 (the latest possible date for *Magnificence*)[107], but that the same sort of thing was being said earlier is evident from the remarks of the Venetian ambassadors as early as 1516; from an anonymous ballad dated 1521;[108] and from Skelton's own satires of 1521–22.

The closest parallels are inevitably found in Skelton's own writing. *Why come* is a satire clearly and only directed at Wolsey, which, as we have seen, refers to his 'magnifycence'. Like

Magnificence, this poem is called a 'mirror'. The prologue uses some of the concepts dramatised in the play, and sounds rather like a summary of its plot:

> Than without collusyon,
> Marke well this conclusyon,
> Thorow suche abusyon,
> And by suche illusyon,
> Vnto great confusyon
> A noble man may fall, (17–22)

The complaint in *Magnificence* that 'will hath reason so under subjection' (19) is repeated:

> wyll dothe rule all thynge,
> Wyll, wyll, wyll, wyll, wyll,
> He ruleth alway styll. (102–4)

Later in the poem Skelton refers to the loss of 'circumspection' and 'sad direction' when the realm is ruled by one man. He speaks of control being gained by false flatterers 'with madde foly' and cries

> Than farewell to the,
> Welthfull felycity! (857–8)

Here a state of affairs described in very similar terms to that in *Magnificence* is openly blamed on Wolsey. Though 'abusion/confusion' occurs in *Against venemous tongues*, which may have no connection with *Magnificence* or Wolsey,[109] and statements about control of reason by will appear right from Skelton's earliest poem,[110] the full force of his satiric vocabulary brought to bear on Wolsey in *Why come*, and to a lesser extent in *Parrot* and *Cloute*, contains many more parallels to *Magnificence* than the earlier works, and these are bunched together in such a way as to confirm that *Magnificence* is closer in intention (and in date) to these satires specifically of Wolsey than to the earlier, more general complaints. Objections to the ruling of 'will' are made in all three poems (see *Parrot*, 414–17; *Cloute*, 1192–3, and the lines from *Why come* cited above); the proverb 'Measure is treasure' which sums up the theme of *Magnificence* is quoted in *Parrot* (64); both *Parrot* and *Why come* contain similar recitals of

excess[111] to Liberty's speech about *totum in toto* (2088 ff.; cf. also
Abusion's 'He doth abuse | Himself too too' and Fancy's 'Some-
time too sober, sometime too sad'). In *Why come* Skelton says of
Wolsey, 'He dothe . . . brall, | Lyke Mahounde in a play'
(593–4), and Magnificence's ranting speech closely resembles
those of tyrants like Herod in the miracle plays, who frequently
swore by 'Mahound'.[112]

Skelton was not the only one to call Wolsey a 'Tyrant'.[113]
Wolsey was notorious for shortcomings frequently mentioned
by the Vices in their soliloquies: corruption in the Church;
extravagance in dress and manners; upstart behaviour. A 'proud
prelate', 'hauyng more respect to the worldly honor of hys
person | than he had to his sperytuall profession',[114] he 'sett nott
by the gospell a flye'.[115] His magnificence in display, his
extravagance of dress and bearing, were frequently noted: he

> wold issue owt . . . apparelled all in red in the habytt of a Cardynall
> w^che was other of fynne skarlett or elles of crymmosyn Satten |
> Taffeta Dammaske | . . . the best that he could gett for mony | and
> vppon hys hed a round pyllion w^t a nekke of blake velvett set to the
> same in the Inner side | he had also a tippett of fynne Sables a bought
> his nekke | holdyng in his hand a very fayer Orrynge . . . There was
> also borne byfore hyme first the great Seale of Englond | And than his
> Cardynalles hatt . . . w^t ij great Crossis of Syluer borne byfore hyme
> w^t also ij great pillers of syluer | . . . Than his gentilmen vsshers cried
> and sayd | on my lordes & maysters | make way for my lordes grace |
> . . . And whan he came to the hall doore ther was attendaunt for
> hyme his mewle trapped all to gether in Crymmosyn velvett . . .[116]

He was accused of being an upstart because he came of lowly
origin: a 'poore mans Sonne borne in Ipsewiche';[117] reputedly
the son of a butcher: 'Carter of Yorcke | the vyle butchers
sonne'.[118] Individual qualities of the Vices are also paralleled by
contemporary comments on the activities and qualities of the
cardinal. His 'Abusyon', 'Collusyon' and conveying are spoken
of by the ballad writers.[119] Like Countenance, he indulged in
'Counterfeit matters in the law of the land' (431):

> It was indeed significant to see this fellow, ignorant of law, sitting in
> court and pronouncing judgement; although at first he was assisted
> by the lawyers who by ancient custom were his assessors, he began to

hear and dispose of many cases which were neither finished nor properly conducted; he forbade other cases, in which there was no doubt about the law, being taken to judgement . . .[120]

Like Crafty Conveyance he 'By sotell pretens all things conveyethe, | & Craftely hathe contryvyd';[121] 'by craftie suggestion gatte into his handes innumerable treasure'.[122] Like Cloaked Collusion he went in for 'Double-dealing' (696): 'In open presence he would lye and say vntruth, and was double both in speche and meanyng'.[123] Both Collusion and Wolsey are said to have the hypocritical 'two faces in a hoode'.[124] Like Abusion he spared for no cost in his clothes, as Cavendish shows, and he seems to have followed Abusion's instructions, just as Magnificence did, in using trouble with his stomach to get rid of tiresome business. 'Call for a caudle, and cast up your gorge, With . . . "Ah, how my stomach wambleth!"' (1615–18), suggests Abusion, and Magnificence is surprised at his intuition:

> I am panged ofttimes of this same fashion.   (1735)

So was Wolsey; frequently 'indisposed' when it did not suit him to give audience.[125] The Venetian ambassador notes, 'Cardinal Wolsey had been indisposed with fever; were unable to speak to him.'[126] An interview between Henry VIII and the emperor Charles V was delayed because 'Cardinal Wolsey was somewhat indisposed with colic'.[127] (Compare Fancy's accusation to Magnificence that 'colica passio hath groped you by the guts' (291).)

When Folly brings in the dog 'some good poor man's cur' (1129), which 'will in at every man's door' (1130), there seems to be pointed reference to Wolsey, for 'cur' was one of the most popular abusive epithets for the cardinal. Roy and Barlowe called him 'The mastif Curre bred in Ypswitch towne', and in the centre of the parody of Wolsey's arms that prefaces their text is a bandog' 'Gnawynge with his teth a kynges crowne'.[128] The ballad of 1521 had also repeatedly called Wolsey 'A Bocher's Curre'; the common people called him a 'Bochers dogge'.[129] By having Grime led in by Folly, Skelton may be suggesting that some of Wolsey's qualities are even lower than those of a fool. I

suspect that the same sort of reference is intended by Fancy's
hawk. Here I have only found parallels in Skelton's own works,
although the hawk image is implied in 'hobbying' for Mistress
Lark. Skelton calls the cardinal a 'faucon' (*Why come*, 772).
Fancy's hawk 'hath a great head' (1047), and Skelton says of
Wolsey that 'Hys woluys hede, wanne, bloo as lede, gapythe
over the crowne' (*Parrot*, 428). The hawk is compared to a
butterfly (1049); Skelton calls Wolsey a butterfly in *Cloute*
(336–42).[130] These images are obscure, but no more so than the
biblical imagery used to cover Wolsey's activities in *Parrot*.[131]
Skelton also makes puns, in *Parrot* and *Cloute*, on Wolsey's
name:[132] it is quite possible he intended an anagram on the
beginning of Wolsey in having the hawk mistaken for an owl.[133]
This sort of cryptic allusion is typical of Skelton's writing,[134]
especially in *Parrot*, where when most of the mysteries are
unlocked Wolsey is discovered inside. The dog and hawk were
almost certainly intended to be more than comic props.

Ramsay's suggestion that the vagueness of the end of the play
is due to its political application may still have point, though he
read the message differently. Skelton could prophesy Wolsey's
fall, and indeed did so very colourfully in *Colyn Cloute*:

> Fortune may chaunce to flyt,
> And whan he weneth to syt,
> Yet may he mysse the quysshon:
>> (996–8; see also 475–7, 667–72)

But he could not have alluded to events which occurred just
after his own death, and some years after the writing of
Magnificence. Yet after Wolsey's death his 'fall' was described in
terms very similar to those used in the epilogue to *Magnificence*:

Who lyste to Rede . . . this history may behold the wonderouse
mutabilite | of vayn honours | the brytell Assuraunce of haboun-
daunce | the oncertyntie of dignytes the fflateryng of fayned frendes |
And the tykkyll trust to worldly prynces | wherof thys lord Cardynall
hathe felt bothe of the swette & the sower . . . As fletyng frome
honors | losyng of Riches | deposed frome Dignytes | . . . Of all w^che
thynges he hathe had in this world the full felycyte as long as
that ffortune smyled vppon hyme | but when she began to frown

how sone was he depryved of all thes dremyng Ioyes And vayn pleasures . . .[135]

Magnificence shows 'How none estate living of himself can be sure' (2553); that 'in this world there is no earthly trust' (2540):

> Suddenly advanced and suddenly subdued;
> Suddenly riches, and suddenly poverty; . . .
> Suddenly thus Fortune can both smile and frown,
>
> (2522–3, 2525)

Wolsey's life and death were narrated in the series of examples in the *Mirror for Magistrates* in just the way that the life and fall of Magnificence were used by Skelton as 'A plain example of worldly vainglory'.

This similarity is partly a result of the Tudor habit of seeing the lives of eminent persons in a conventional rise/fall pattern, but occurs also because Wolsey's life 'conformed to a kind of stream-lined model of the familiar tragic pattern in which an eminent man is ruined by a downward turn of Fortune's wheel'.[136] If *Magnificence* is partly concerned with Wolsey that may explain the movement towards tragedy the play seems to make, only to stop short because he had not yet died.

We must remember, though, that *Magnificence* is not a tragedy but a *moral* play, in which the hero represents mankind. He cannot be said to stand *only* for a particular individual; be equated *simply* with a contemporary personality. On the allegorical level Magnificence represents *any* proud prince, even if Skelton does more than hint that a particular one is to be fitted into the slot. The mysteries of *Magnificence* cannot, as Ramsay thought, *all* be unlocked by a single key: Skelton 'takes as his subjects matters of which the accidents may be peculiar to his times but the substance is common to all, and not least to our own'.[137]

(c) *Staging*

Like many interludes, *Magnificence* was intended for performance in one of the Tudor halls as an entertainment to accompany some special banquet.[138] That it was one of the London halls is suggested by topical references to Tyburn (423, 909), 'the Half Street' (2264), Tower Hill (2141), and the Taylor's Hall (1405). This last reference, to the Hall of the Guild of the Merchant Taylors, in Threadneedle Street, is particularly interesting, for it is made in a manner that would have been a particularly pointed 'in' joke had the play actually been performed in that hall. Liberty says to Felicity:

> What will ye waste wind and prate thus in vain?
> Ye have eaten sauce, I trow, at the Taylor's Hall (1404–5)

which sounds like a reference to the noisy audience dining in the hall.[139] The comment 'Measure is meet for a merchant's hall' (382) would have particular point were it in a merchant's hall that the play was performed.[140] Unfortunately the Merchant Taylors' archives for the years 1485–1544 have been lost, though there are records for entertainments at the hall both before and after this (notably one given for James I in 1607 which included verses specially commissioned from Ben Jonson).[141] *Magnificence* is too long to have been presented during the intervals between courses, as *Fulgens and Lucrece* was, for example;[142] its full playing time must have been at least three hours, and it is not divided into two parts like *Fulgens* and *Nature*. There is no moment when the playing area is completely empty, though a break could have been made about half-way through the play, after Conveyance's soliloquy, before Magnificence comes back corrupted. Conveyance might sit and wait (or have a drink) in the acting area, or chat with the spectators, during the 'interval', and continue with his dialogue when Magnificence returns. References to 'this night' (365, 670) suggest that the play takes place during the evening, and some sort of banquet may be going on, for Fancy refers to the audience as 'this press | Even a whole mess'[143] (994–5). When Poverty goes to beg food for Magnificence he might collect it from members of the audience. Servants might be moving about during the performance, standing to watch when they were not needed. Collusion's request 'Give this gentleman room, sirs; stand utter!' (753) suggests that at least some of the spectators stood.[144] In a hall performance space would be cleared between the dining tables in front of the dais, and actors would come in and out through the two doors in the screen dividing the hall from the kitchen, or perhaps sometimes emerge from among the audience, like the servants A and B in *Fulgens*. *Magnificence* shows evidence of having been performed under these conditions. As we would expect if the acting took place in a space cleared on the hall floor, no setting or scenery is used: all the action occurs in the 'place', some undefined area at a distance from Magnificence's court.[145] Two entrances/exits were used: at 395 Magnificence goes out without seeing Collusion come in, and at 2325 Good Hope comes in at one side while Despair and Mischief rush out at the other. It would be possible to use the exits and entrances symbolically; the left (whence evil comes) always for the Vices in their 'natural' state; the right for the Virtues, or those going to or coming from the court. When Measure is forcibly removed by Abusion he cries, 'Hence, thou hainiard! Out of the doors, fast!' (1726), and though he might mean just 'get out',[146] comparison with a line in *Nature* suggests that Abusion probably refers to the double doors in the hall screen.[147] When no entrance or exit is given for a character it may mean that he comes from or joins the audience. At the beginning of the play Felicity might start his speech by getting up from a table at the back of the hall, and continue it as he walks down between the tables, to meet Liberty coming from another direction. When Poverty leaves Magnificence he might go round taking a collection from the audience while Magnificence *dolorously maketh his moan*. The actors wandered up and down between the tables during their soliloquies: Collusion (before whose speech the direction *Hic deambulat* occurs) says he talks 'to occupy the place', and describes his movements as 'up and down to trace'. The 'place' must have been large enough to allow differentiation of area within it: when Conveyance comes back to collect Collusion he must remain at some distance from Collusion and Abusion, for the latter asks, 'Who is *yond* that for thee doth call?' (779). Magnificence lies in the place for some time without being noticed by Liberty. When he speaks, Liberty, surprised, asks, 'What brothel, I say, is *yonder*, bound in a mat?' (2107). When someone blows a horn from the back, Liberty says, '*Yonder* is a whoreson for me doth rechate' (2152). The word *yonder* is used in lines intended to turn the audience's attention in a different direction, particularly to make them notice some new character as he approaches.[148] When Adversity appears Magnificence cries, 'Alas, who is *yonder* that grimly looks?' (1874), and the audience turn from watching the main area from which Fancy is now hurrying away, to see the grim figure approaching.

The play frequently takes advantage of its proximity to the audience. There are appeals for information or corroboration:

> This was properly prated, sirs; what said a? (746)

> Hear you not how this gentleman mocks? (32)

The audience are scrutinised by the actors:

> Now let me see about
> In all this rout
> If I can find out
> So seemly a snout
>
> Among this press, (990–4)

Digs are made at them:

> I trow some of you be better sped than I
> Friendship to feign and think full litherly. (722–3)

> they that come up of nought,
> (As some be not far and if it were well sought); (1242–3)

The audience perhaps even provide props. When Magnificence calls for 'a bowl or a basin' in which to vomit his rage, he could easily be given one from one of the tables. Through such devices the audience are lulled into a sense of security and closeness to the actors which makes the dramatic impact of surprise, when it is used, all the more effective. When Magnificence *would slay himself with a knife* (2323.1) and Good Hope *suddenly* snatches it from him, the audience would be as startled as Magnificence himself.

The minimum of props are used: except for the bed[149] on which Poverty places Magnificence, which could have been some couch permanently in the 'place', used occasionally by the actors, and understood to be a bed from the 'coverlet' which is placed over Magnificence, there are only the various objects which characters carry with them, and which are properly part of their costumes, being symbolic of their rôles. Costume also seems to have been kept fairly simple, except in the case of Courtly Abusion, who (perhaps specially to interest the tailors?) is dressed in a parody of the latest fashion: Afro-style haircut (834–5); high-laced boots (755, 852–4); very full sleeves (848–9). Folly would presumably be dressed in the usual fool's costume of motley, cap and bells, and carries with him a collection of objects commonly used by fools: a bauble (1041.1), a purse (1102), and a book (the fool's Bible).[150] In the scene between Fancy and Folly, Fancy is also dressed as a fool, and carries a purse. The two fools are accompanied by the hawk and the dog, which may have been live (though the risk of their misbehaving and spoiling the dinner would be great).[151] Cloaked Collusion, in accordance with his name, wears a 'cope', a long cloak or cape of a clerical nature, and a *biretta*.[152] There is not much to be gleaned about the costume of Conveyance (he has a 'gown', and also carries a purse), or Countenance, who presumably wore some sort of mask, symbolic of his name. Little is said about the costuming of the Virtues: Good Hope refers to himself as a 'potecary', and probably brought with him various medicines to display at appropriate points: 'rhubarb of repentance', 'drams of devotion', 'gums ghostly', somewhat in the manner of the doctor in mummers plays. 'Brother' Perseverance may be dressed as a friar, as perhaps he is in *Hickscorner*.[153] The appearance of figures like Adversity, Poverty, Despair and Mischief may be readily imagined.[154] Adversity looks 'grimly', and the 'clokes' (1875), 'clutches or claws' to which Fancy refers may be literally there. Poverty is 'ragged and rent', and Mischief bears the knife and halter symbolic of his connection with suicide. Magnificence himself is in 'rich array' (2011), then is *spoiled from . . . his raiment* (1876.1) and appears as a beggar until he is given a new garment by (appropriately) Redress.

Because of the doubling of parts, the costumes used are of the kind which can be quickly changed. The characters would need to be easily distinguishable by their costumes, since a figure could not be identified by the actor's *face*. (This is one reason why symbolic objects are carried.) The eighteen parts can be easily divided among five actors, a troupe of four men and a boy.[155] (There are no women, though the 'boy' would play them if there were.) In the first part of the play, before the re-entry of Magnificence, the doubling arrangement is fairly tightly worked out. The actors playing Felicity, Liberty and Measure must play Collusion, Countenance and Conveyance respectively. (Felicity and Liberty cannot play Conveyance because these three characters are in the 'place' together at 1376; Liberty cannot *easily* play Collusion as at one point there are only seven lines between the exit of one and the entrance of the other (2154–60).) Most of the new rôles in the latter part of the play, however, could be assigned in sequence to any of the three men actors not playing Magnificence. That Fancy was played by a boy (or possibly a dwarf), is clear from the frequent references to his small size, as well as the continuous joke in his using 'Largesse' as his counterfeit name.

The most convenient distribution of parts seems to be as follows:

A. Magnificence.
B. Felicity, Collusion, Folly, Poverty, Good Hope.
C. Liberty, Countenance, Abusion, Redress, Perseverance.
D. Measure, Conveyance, Adversity, Mischief, Circumspection.
E. Fancy, Despair.[156]

The doubling of parts inevitably affects the structure and content of *Magnificence*. No battle between Virtues and Vices, such as we find in moral plays like *The Castle of Perseverance*, can be dramatised when Virtues and Vices are played by the same actors, nor is it possible to see more than four of the six court

Vices together at the same time. Measure and Felicity cannot
return at the end of the play because the actors who played their
parts are needed for Good Hope and Circumspection. Soliloquies are made lengthy to allow other actors time to change:
while Collusion gives an account of his activities, Countenance
is putting on the elaborate costume of Abusion.

Doubling also explains the emphasis placed in the play on
repeating the characters' names. Exchanges like

> What, Counterfeit Countenance!
> What, Crafty Conveyance!   (494–5)

introductions:

> By God, sir, this is Fancy small-brain,
> And Crafty Conveyance, know you not him?   (583–4)

sudden 'discoveries':

> Cock's heart, it is Cloaked Collusion!   (596)

all help the audience to be quite clear which character is which.
It is obvious too that there is a practical element in the choice of
the kind of vice portrayed: Counterfeit Countenance can easily
change his rôle from that of Liberty by assuming a symbolic
mask; Cloaked Collusion need only put on his 'cope' to hide
Felicity's costume, and later Folly's.

The audience would appreciate that the same actors were
playing different parts, and so the possibility of 'in' jokes exists
here too. The forged letter supposed to have come from Circumspection is actually 'conveyed' by Conveyance, and the
same actor plays both parts. When Fancy tells Countenance

> And yet in faith man, we lacked thee
> For to speak with Liberty.   (538–9)

there is a joke in that Countenance *could* not speak to Liberty, as
Liberty is being played by himself. When Abusion asks under
whom Liberty was 'abiding' (937) he probably has at least part
of Liberty's costume on under his own.[157]

The necessity of costume change imposed by doubling is
turned to advantage in the play, for the shifting of rôles has an

important function in relation to the allegory. As on one level the characters represent aspects of Magnificence himself, their changing from virtue to vice and from one kind of vice to another is representative of his own inconstancy. For this reason, too, it is essential that the same actor play Magnificence throughout. The fluctuations in his own mental state are represented by a symbolic use of costume change, in a manner common in Tudor interludes.[158] The despoiling of his rich array by Adversity represents his loss of 'wealth' through lack of measure, and his reclothing by Redress shows him once again in a stable state of mind. The emergence of Fancy in his true colours[159] as a fool is a similar symbolic use of costume (and it is also practical that this kind of 'changing' is confined to characters played by actors who have only one, or mainly one, rôle).

The moving in and out of rôles also creates an effect similar to that of dance: the stately movements of Felicity, Liberty and Measure give way to the Gilbert and Sullivan-like cavortings of the Vices, and these to the slow procession of figures which winds up with a return to Magnificence's court. The stage directions lay great emphasis on the sort of movements to be made, as well as the manner in which they are to be made: *on tiptoe* (324.1), *strolling up and down* (572.2), *pointing with his finger* (778.1), *doing reverence and courtesy* (1515.1), *hurriedly* (493.1), *with a haughty expression* (572.1), *ironically* (748.1), *dolorously* (2048.1), *despairingly* (2038.1). These movements also help to make the characters' rôles clear to the audience: the whispering of Countenance emphasises his surreptitious activities, and the limping of Poverty his dejected state. The action was probably accompanied by a good deal of music: Countenance and Abusion are directed to come in singing; Abusion is asked if he can sing 'Venter tre dawse' and no doubt demonstrates his skill; some of the soliloquies, particularly that of Countenance, resemble a sort of patter song; Liberty is probably singing a lyric when he returns to find Magnificence 'bound in a mat' (and incidentally all this singing is done by actor C, who takes all these three parts). There are also various entertaining tricks and games: the game of vapors or verbal quarrelling[160]; the swapping of bird and dog and the exchange of purses in which Folly tricks Fancy; Folly's laughing Conveyance out of his coat; Folly's pretending to be deaf, and the riddles with which he confuses Magnificence. The various games and bits of comic business in the play are not just gratuitous entertainment, however. They form part of its total meaning, often being used to point up a contrast with the serious matter, or to parallel or parody it: the quarrelling of the Vices contrasts with the serious debate between the Virtues at the beginning of the play; when Conveyance, Collusion and Fancy join hands to consolidate their conspiracy, there is a parody of the 'linked chain' of love between Magnificence and the Virtues, which they thought could not be unbound; Fancy's getting an empty purse from Folly parallels Magnificence's loss of wealth; Abusion's 'cures' for Magnificence's sickness contrast with the real cures of the 'potecary' Good Hope, and Folly's removal of Conveyance's gown contrasts with Redress's putting *on* of Magnificence's garment. Sometimes an important point is made by contrasted activities within the same 'scene'. While Magnificence remains still and is *silently* reading the letter from 'Circumspection', Countenance comes in prancing about on tiptoe, making a lot of noise singing. Fancy hushes him up, showing the audience that all is not well with the letter. When Magnificence lies silent and still, Liberty comes in singing and dancing: two different examples of what Magnificence's lack of measure has led to.

(d) *Language and versification*

The same principle of contrast informs the use of language in the play. While the Virtues, and Magnificence when he is on their side, tend to speak in dignified, Latinate phrases, lengthy sentences with intricate syntax, the conversation of the Vices is racy and colloquial. The difference in tone and style is felt immediately upon Fancy's entry. From the sonorous tones of

> In joy and mirth your mind shall be enlarged,
> And not embraced with pusillanimity;

> But plenarly all thought from you must be discharged
> If ye list to live after your free liberty.
> All delectations acquainted is with me;[161]   (205–9)

we move to the down to earth pronouncement from Fancy:

> But covetise hath blown you so full of wind
> That *colica passio* hath groped you by the guts.   (290–1)

Much of the vocabulary of the Virtues consists of aureate words like *advertence, attemperance, contrived, consideration, demonstration, disputation*, while that of the Vices contains slangy expressions like *bleared, butts, hugger-mugger, knuckleboniard, pretty prong, yark*. Their different preoccupations are expressed also by the contexts from which their language is drawn. The Virtues, concerned with measure and reason, draw many of their terms from legal or scholarly debate: *argument, cause, debate, effect, infer, offence, privileged, probate, proved*. The speech of the Vices is studded with images of snaring and catching: *catched in a fly net, eat a fly, hawketh for a butterfly, ratches to run an hare*. The Virtues tend to use *sententiae*, the Vices proverbs.[162]

This difference, which is to be found in most Tudor interludes, partly results from the teaching of the rhetoricians about the use of appropriate style, high style for dignified characters, low style for villains and buffoons. Such differentiation, though, inevitably leads to assumptions about the moral qualities of the characters speaking, and so variations in language can be used to indicate changes in the state of mind of the hero, in a similar manner to changes in his dress. Magnificence's reaction to the language of the Vices changes as he does. Originally he disapproves strongly of Fancy's way of talking:

> Though Largesse ye hight, your language is too large.   (295)

He wants to send Fancy packing because of his cheek:

> You are nothing meet with us to dwell,
> That with your lord and master so pertly can prate.   (304–5)

Magnificence's objection to Fancy's language as too free and uncontrolled is similar to Measure's feeling when the discussion between Liberty and Felicity started to get out of hand:

> Your language is like the pen
> Of him that writeth too fast.   (90–1)

Magnificence's sense of proper dignity in language is lost when he becomes corrupted. He returns using Fancy's own words,[163] and is delighted with the conversation of Courtly Abusion:

> with pleasure I am surprised
> Of your language, it is so well devised;
> Polished and fresh is your ornacy.   (1530–2)

'Pleasure' has said nothing particularly elegant, only that he would be 'right glad' to do anything to please Magnificence. The prince has mistaken flattery for properly polished language. Courtly Abusion goes on to describe in highly artificial terms what is, after all, a whore:

> That quickly is envived with ruddies of the rose,
> Inpurtured with features after your purpose,
> The strains of her veins as azure indy blue,
> Enbudded with beauty and colour fresh of hue,
> As lily white to look upon her lere,
> Her eyen relucent as carbuncle so clear . . .   (1552–7)

Magnificence is so concerned with the fact that she is 'a baby to brace and to buss' that he does not notice that 'Pleasure' is mocking him with outrageous 'ornacy' totally inappropriate to the context. The catalogue of ladies' delights compared to jewels had been used quite conventionally by Skelton himself in an early poem,[164] but here the mixture of commonplace words such as 'merry' or 'lusty lips ruddy as the cherry' shows up the false sentiment inherent in the archaic 'lere' and 'eyen' as well as the aureate terms 'envived', 'enbudded', 'relucent'. Nor does he recognise the falseness of 'Sober Sadness's' plea that he should remember Measure:

> Please it your grace, at the contemplation
> Of my poor instance and supplication,
> Tenderly to consider in your advertence—
> Of our blessed Lord, sir, at the reverence—   (1634–7)

He is deluded by 'counterfeit language' (441).

Contrasting tones and speech-styles are created in the play by variations in versification as well as in language, and in this Skelton's method is far superior to that of many writers of interludes, who are content often to use long lines for Virtues and short ones for Vices. Skelton achieves a number of different effects by different rhyme patterns and line lengths. (Although lines have basically either two stresses or four, variations in the numbers of unstressed syllables can alter the speed of a line quite considerably.) The rhyme-royal stanza, with four-stress lines and a heavy caesura, is used particularly for the debate of the Virtues at the beginning, and the didacticism at the end of the play:

> Áll things contríved by mán's reáson,
> The wórld envíron, of hígh and low estáte,
> Be it eárly or láte, weálth hath a seáson.
> Weálth is of wísdom the very trué probáte.
> A foól is he with weálth that fálleth at debáte;
> But mén nówadays so unháppily be úred
> That nóthing than weálth may wórse be endúred.　　(1–7).

This is a highly controlled form and its use at the beginning and end of the play shows that it literally represents the 'measure' which is lost and regained. 'When measure lacketh, all thing disordered is' (122) applies to the verse too, which takes off in different directions from the rhyme-royal form and eventually returns to it, or is resolved into it. The form tends to use alliteration on some of its stressed syllables ('But if *p*rúdence be *p*róved' (16); '*W*éalth might be *w*ón' (17)). In the passage in which Magnificence gives his bombastic soliloquy alliteration is heavily present:

> For Í am *p*rince *p*eérless *p*róved of *p*órt,　　　　　　　　(1472)

> Í am the *d*íamond, *d*oúbtless, of *d*ígnity;　　　　　　　　(1478)

> I *r*eígn in my *r*óbes, I *r*úle as me líst,
> I *d*ríve *d*own these *d*ástards with a *d*ínt of my físt.　　(1486–7)

> For of all *b*árons *b*óld Í *b*ear the *b*éll;
> Of all *d*oúghty I am *d*oúghtiest *d*úke, as I *d*eém;　　(1499–1500)

An archaic feeling is produced by the over-use of this device, suggesting a note of falsity similar to that of Abusion's 'ornacy'. We notice that the most heavily alliterated lines are those in which Magnificence is speaking of himself, and how often the stress is on the word *I*, sometimes rather than the alliterated word. He cannot always keep it up. The irregularity of lines like 'Álexánder, of Mácedony king' (1467); 'Chárlemagne, that maintaíned the nóbles of Fránce' (1502), and especially the frequent lack of a caesura, show how he is being carried away by his own importance into a *literal* loss of 'measure'. The rhyme-royal form is used by the Vices in places where they pretend to dignity, as in the passage from Collusion already quoted, and in the soliloquies of Collusion and Conveyance. The audience would be aware of the indecorum of letting ruffians use this 'measured' speech. On the other hand, an effect of frivolity is achieved by the use of two-stress lines half the 'proper' length in the soliloquies of Abusion and Fancy.[165] The pattern of rhyme in Abusion's speech is that of rhyme-royal, suggesting a deliberate perversion or 'abusion' of proper measure by the use of two stresses instead of four. Fancy moves from leashes of four two-stress lines into couplets, suggesting the kind of inconsistency of which he accuses himself ('Now I will this and now I will that'). Countenance, who describes his speech as 'bastard rhyme, after the doggrel guise' (408), uses leashes of seven four-stress lines, another sort of perversion, or bastardisation, as he suggests, of the seven lines and four stresses in rhyme-royal.

The four-stress rhyming couplet (properly contained in rhyme-royal as the concluding two lines of each verse) is used for the latter half of Fancy's soliloquy, again with traces of alliteration ('Sómetime too sóber, sómetime too sád' (1008); 'I blúnder, I blúster, I blów and I blóther; I máke on the óne day and I már on the óther' (1036–7)). This form is most frequently used for dialogue, where, especially when alternate lines are taken by speakers, it can create a speedy, stichomythic effect:

Collusion   Hold thy hand, dáw, of thy dágger, and stínt of thy dín,
               Or I shall fálchion thy flésh, and scrápe thee on the
               skín.

Conveyance Yea, wílt thou, hángman, I sáy, thou cável,
Collusion Nay, thou rúde rávener, ráin-beaten jável!
Conveyance What, thou Cólin Cóward, knówn and triéd!
Collusion Nay, thou fálse-hearted dástard, thou dáre not abíde!
                                                    (2189–94)

Frequently in these exchanges extra syllables are added at the beginning of the line (as 'Hold thy hand', 'Yea', 'Nay', 'What', here), often exclamations like 'In faith', or imprecations:

Conveyance (By God,) we have máde Mágnificence to eát a fly.
Countenance How coúld ye do thát, and wás awáy?
Fancy (By God, man,) both hís págeant and thíne he can pláy.
                                                    (503–5)

The stress is that of ordinary speech rhythm, and the addition of the extra syllables adds to the colloquial effect, making it sound almost like prose.

There is not space here for a lengthy account of Skelton's skill in writing different kinds of dramatic language, which will be apparent from reading the play, but a few points may be mentioned. In the scene between Magnificence and Fancy, where the prince is persuaded of the importance of largesse, the narrative of Fancy's experiences 'at the sea side', given in a series of quick statements connected by conjunctions ('And another bade put out mine eye . . . And boys to the pillory gan me pluck, And would have made me Friar Tuck') is interspersed by half-hearted questions and remarks by Magnificence ('How so?'; 'By your sooth?'; 'Marry, sir, ye were affrayed.') which show he is not really listening, but musing on the contents of the letter. As Fancy continues the emphatic tone of his remarks ('And indeed sir'; 'With yea sir'; 'Yea sir') contrasts with Magnificence's hesitation, expressed in questioning inversion ('And say they so') and contradictory thought ('*Yet* measure is a merry mean'), which, when the prince is convinced, turn into emphasis ('In faith') and command ('Let us depart'). Another manner of expressing different moods is shown in the scene between Poverty and Magnificence. Poverty conveys the difference between Magnificence's former state and his present condition in a series of balanced antitheses:

That was wont to lie on feather beds of down;
Now must your feet lie higher than your crown.
Where you were wont to have caudles for your head,
Now must you munch mammocks and lumps of bread;   (2007–10)

This unemotional, rather factual series of statements is the cue for Magnificence's *ubi sunt* lament:

Where is now my wealth and my noble estate?
Where is now my treasure, my lands, and my rent?
Where is now all my servants that I had here a late?   (2056–8)

where the rhetorical questions and the *traductio* (the continued repetition of the same phrase) give the prince's speech, which is basically conveying the same *information* as that of Poverty, a highly charged emotional quality.

As we would expect from the writer of *Against Garnesche*, much of the comedy in the Vice scenes arises from their speedy exchange of insults, and their swearing (as in the lines between Collusion and Conveyance already quoted), but one of the most interesting features of the Vices' language is their use of indirect speech. This shows versatility when it appears in their soliloquies, as in Countenance's or Conveyance's mimicry of conversations between a mistress and her lover (456–61, 1348–53). But perhaps most successful is Abusion's imitation of an angry fellow whose example he suggests Magnificence should follow:

Call for a caudle and cast up your gorge,
With: 'Cock's arms, rest shall I none have
Till I be revenged on that whoreson knave!
Ah, how my stomach wambleth! I am all in a sweat.
Is there no whoreson that knave that will beat?'   (1615–19)

This highly exaggerated portrait is taken for a marvel by Magnificence, and he follows Abusion's instructions when dealing with Measure. To have Abusion use reported speech, instead of giving these lines to Magnificence, provides several extra effects: contrast with 'Pleasure's' earlier ornate language, amusement at Magnificence taking the exaggerated report for a true picture, and then expectation satisfied when Magnificence finally does burst out.

(e) *Productions*

Nothing is known about the original production of *Magnificence*, apart from what can be deduced from the text itself, discussed under section (c) above. What seems to be a reference to the play in Udall's *Respublica* (1553) suggests that it was still known some years after it was written, though perhaps from the printed text rather than performance. Discussing the causes of the ruin of the commonwealth, the Prologue states:

> But though these vices, by *cloaked colusion*
> And by *counterfeit* names hidden their *abusion*,
> Do reign for a while, to commonweals' prejudice,
> Perverting all right and all order of true justice,
> Yet time trieth all, and time bringeth truth to light,
> That wrong may not ever still reign in place of right.
>
> (23–8; my italics)

Udall apparently refers to some of the Vices of Skelton's play.

After this, no doubt partly because of Skelton's reputation, there appears to have been no interest in *Magnificence*, and no production of it, for about four hundred years. The earliest revival seems to have been an amateur performance given by the Poetry Society of the Instituto Britânico em Portugal, which took place in Lisbon on 17 December 1939.[166] W. H. Auden and Noah Greenberg began an adaptation in the early 1950s, but did not complete it.[167] In November 1962 the play was produced by John Carrington in the chapel of Jesus College, Cambridge. Then two major productions occurred almost simultaneously, in 1963. In May of that year the Tavistock Repertory Company performed a shortened version at the Tower Theatre, Canonbury, under the direction of Michael Imison.[168] The stage was kept bare, with simply a stylised tree in the centre, the focus being on costumes, as it would have been in the original production. Some doubling was attempted, though nine actors were used, rather than five. The director concentrated on the general relevance of Skelton's message:

> the moral it offers is not political or topical. Though the allegory centres on the question of who shall be master of the court of

Magnyfycence, the matter is treated in the most general way. The virtues Skelton recommends—Measure or moderation and thought or Sober Circumspection—are desirable in anyone with money to spend.[169]

In contrast, the O.U.D.S. 1963 summer production in New College Gardens (part of a double bill with *Prometheus Bound*!), directed by John Duncan, focused on the political and topical references in the play, updating it with contemporary gags, and making the characters more familiar; for example, the Virtues at the end of the play were costumed as a physiotherapist, a nurse, a surgeon, and a member of the Salvation Army. In the words of the director, the production was 'a cock-up', and he found the rival version 'extremely boring'. Undeterred, John Duncan directed another production of *Magnificence* by the National Youth Theatre at the Shaw Theatre in August 1974, accompanied by new music from the National Youth Jazz Orchestra. This time topical reference was eschewed, and the play was set 'nowhere, anywhere, and everywhere simultaneously'.[170] Emphasis was as much on the serious moral as the comedy. The transition from vice to sin was given further attention by the introduction of a very successful masque sequence based on the words of *Elinor Rummyng*, showing Magnificence succumbing to lusty lasses, and by the appearance of Christ repeating the words of *Woefully Arrayed* at the moment of Magnificence's fall. Though the reviews were not of the best ('No. This will not do,' *Guardian*, 21 August 1974; 'Could do better,' *Times*, 21 August 1974), the audience evidently enjoyed the play very much.

Bob Godfrey produced the play at Stockwell College, London, in November 1974. In February 1975 there was a performance of *Magnificence* by the Poculi Ludique Societas (affiliated to the Centre for Medieval Studies at the University of Toronto), directed by Daniel De Matteis. The play was staged in conditions as close as possible to those of Tudor interludes, appropriately in the Debates Room of one of the university residences, and with five actors dividing the parts according to Ramsay's plan. The emphasis was on showing the play to be 'a brilliantly conceived satire on the use of power'.[171]

A recording of part of *Magnificence*, adapted by John Barton, and read by members of the Royal Shakespeare company, is available in the U.S.A.[172]

NOTES

1 *Epistle to Augustus*, 38.
2 *The Arte of English Poesie*, ed. G. Willcock and A. Walker (1936), p. 84.
3 T. Warton, *The History of English Poetry* (1778), II, pp. 360–1. This play is almost certainly a fabrication of Warton's. See Ramsay, pp. xviii–xix.
4 See R. S. Kinsman and T. Yonge, *John Skelton: Canon and Census*, Renaissance Society of America Bibliographies and Indexes, no. 4 (1967), pp. xiv–xv; G. L. Frost and R. Nash, *'Good Order*, a Morality Fragment', *Studies in Philology*, XLI (1944), pp. 483–601; Pollet, pp. 260–1.
5 Pollet, p. 6. For information on some of these Skeltons see I. A. Gordon, *John Skelton* (1970), pp. 11–14.
6 *Caxton's Eneydos*, ed. W. T. Culley and F. J. Furnivall (E.E.T.S., 1890), p. 4.
7 See, e.g., *Garnesche*, IV, 80–4; *Calliope*.
8 See Nelson, p. 62, pp. 161 ff.
9 Dyce, I, p. xiii.
10 Pollet, p. 10.
11 Translated in Nelson, p. 72.
12 *Ibid.*
13 It has been suggested that Skelton may have been tutor to Prince Arthur, Henry VII's older son, as well, and so perhaps joined the court earlier. See F. M. Salter, 'Skelton's "Speculum Principis"', *Speculum*, IX (1934), pp. 30–3. But Nelson doubts this; see pp. 64–5.
14 Translated in Nelson, p. 76.
15 J. A. Froude, *Life and Letters of Erasmus* (1894), p. 97.
16 *Lives of the Queens of England* (1840–8), IV, p. 104.
17 Dyce, I, p. xxii.
18 Nelson, p. 77.
19 Nelson, p. 81.
20 *Ibid.*
21 Dyce, I, pp. xx–xxi.
22 Dyce, I, p. lxi.
23 *Ibid.*
24 Translated in Nelson, p. 116.
25 *Ibid.*, p. 117.
26 Dyce, I, p. xxvii.
27 Nelson, p. 118.
28 *Ibid.*, p. 120
29 For a detailed account of the Grammarians' War, see Nelson, pp. 148–57.
30 Quoted in Dyce, I, p. xxxviii.
31 Some of these coincidences have been pointed out by Glassco, pp. 152–5.
32 Nelson, p. 115.

33 Ramsay, pp. cxxvi–viii; Nelson, pp. 210–11.

34 See below, p. 37 ff.

35 Dyce, I, p. xlvi.

36 *Ibid.*, p. lxxii.

37 Hall, p. 657.

38 See below, p. 34 ff.

39 Dyce, I, p. xlix.

40 See *Parrot*, 147 ff.

41 *Ibid.*, 158–9.

42 See, e.g., *Sparowe*, 774 ff.

43 See F. M. Salter, 'John Skelton's Contribution to the English Language', *Transactions of the Royal Society of Canada*, 3rd Series, Section II, XXXIX (1945).

44 For a study of Skelton's use of different *personae* in his writing, see S. E. Fish, *John Skelton's Poetry* (1965).

45 Quoted in Dyce, I, p. xxx.

46 W. W. Greg, *A Bibliography of the English Printed Drama to the Restoration*, Vol. I (1939), p. 87. According to Warton (*History of English Poetry*, Vol. II (1778), p. 336), the play was printed by Rastell in 1533, though in the revised edition of this work (London, 1840), Warton says it was printed by Rastell, without date (p. 511).

47 A note by Steevens in this copy also attributes the printing of it to Rastell.

48 See Collation, 319, 329, 633, 1874, 1880, 1884, 2015.

49 Dobson, II, 827–925 *passim*.

50 This can have the force of a comma, semicolon, or full stop, and is modernised accordingly.

51 See Dyce, II, p. 236.

52 See *ibid.*, pp. 366–7.

53 See Ramsay, pp. xxi–v.

54 *Ven. Cal.* II, no. 52, p. 22.

55 *Ibid.*

56 J. J. Scarisbrick, *Henry VIII* (1968), p. 74.

57 *Ven. Cal.* II, no. 1287, p. 558.

58 If 'Pluck down lead' (1025) were meant to refer to Wolsey's dissolution of certain nunneries in 1521, this would of course provide a much later *terminus a quo*. But it may not. (See note on 1025).

59 These matters are discussed in section 4(b).

60 Southern has recently suggested the definition 'a show given at an interval in, or as an accompaniment to a feast' (p. 307). This definition is derived from what is known about the presentation of these plays, and avoids any question of their subject-matter. Craik says, 'Tudor plays called interludes by their authors and publishers normally employed allegorical methods to a didactic purpose' (p. 1), but the term was also used of non-allegorical didactic plays, such as *Fulgens and Lucrece*, and of comedies neither allegorical nor didactic, such as *Ralph Royster Doyster*.

61 E. N. S. Thompson, 'The English Moral Plays', *Transactions of the Connecticut Academy of Arts and Sciences*, XIV (1908–10), p. 315.

62 In both plays Mischief offers the hero a rope to hang himself. This personification does not appear in any other extant moral play.

63 See Paula Neuss, 'Active and Idle Language: Dramatic Images in *Mankind*', *Stratford-upon-Avon Studies XVI* (1973), p. 44.

64 Ramsay, pp. xxxii–iii.

65 Harris, pp. 139 ff.

66 See note on 1.

67 See notes on 119, 121, 710, 1467 ff.

68 Ed. Robert Steele (E.E.T.S., 1894), pp. 24–5.

69 See the Introduction to Lester Born's edition of *The Education of a Christian Prince* (1936), *passim*.

70 In the next line, however, Adversity does associate himself particularly with the great (1884).

71 This speech has been constantly misunderstood because the opening line was misread. See note on 1.

72 Clearly Skelton does not identify Magnificence with perseverance as Caxton does in his translation of *Somme le roi*, since Perseverance is a separate character.

73 See below, pp. 53–55.

74 *Three Prose Versions of the Secreta Secretorum*, ed. R. Steele (E.E.T.S., 1898), p. 52.

75 *Diodorus*, I, p. 359.

76 See 1026, 1185.

77 A frequent habit of Vices in the interludes. See Craik, pp. 87 ff.

78 For Ramsay's view that Fancy was dressed as a fool from his first entry, see below, note 159.

79 See 1866 ff.

80 *O.E.D.* III. 7, etc.

81 See 1172.

82 Compare 572.1 and 1693.1. Collusion enters *cum elato aspectu*, and Magnificence is *aspectante vultu elatissimo*. See Collation.

83 Cf. 251, 1380.

84 See note on 1458 ff.

85 Willard Farnham, *The Medieval Heritage of Elizabethan Tragedy* (1956), p. 216. Harris, however, argues that the ending of *Magnificence* is essential to what he sees as its demonstration of the cardinal virtue of Fortitude and its 'two part morality structure'.

86 See below, p. 48, for a partial explanation of this.

87 See, e.g., 2326, 2340. With his various medicines, Good Hope is reminiscent, too, of the restoring 'Doctor' in Mummers' plays. See below, p. 46.

88 Hall, p. 719.

89 See David Bevington, *Tudor Drama and Politics* (1968); T. W. Craik, 'The Political Interpretation of Two Tudor Interludes', *R.E.S.*, IV (1953), pp. 98–108.

90 Especially Harris, who argues that Ramsay's equation of Measure with Norfolk and Fancy and the other Vices with Wolsey must be wrong because Norfolk and Wolsey were not in opposition in 1516 (pp. 12–45). Cf. Heiserman, pp. 66–125. But for a different opinion, see Glassco, p. 177: 'no matter how energetically Harris attempts to remove Wolsey from *Magnifycence*, one cannot escape the impression that the play is an indictment of all the Cardinal represents'.

91 See Section 3, above.

92 Nelson, p. 160.

93 See Donald C. Baker, 'The Parliament of Fowls', in *Companion to Chaucer Studies*, ed. B. Rowland (1968), p. 357.

94 Fish, *op. cit.*, p. 139.

95 *Rede me*, p. 20.

96 Harris, p. 16; cf. R. J. Schoeck, 'Satire of Wolsey in Heywood's "Play of Love"', *Notes and Queries*, CXCVI (1951), pp. 112–14. He says 'Wolsey's unpopularity began about 1521' (p. 114). But disparaging remarks from Venetian ambassadors occur as early as 1516 (see below, note 106). Cf. Glassco, p. 164.

97 Pollard, p. 306; Kinsman, *Poems*, p. 183. She was the mother of his illegitimate son, Thomas Wynter.

98 *Rede me*, p. 39, 'some men call hym Carnall' (suggesting a contraction of 'cardinal').

99 Roy and Barlowe also called Wolsey 'this spretuall magnificence' (*Rede me*, p. 50).

100 In 'Skelton's "Magnyfycence" and Cardinal Wolsey', *M.L.N.*, XVI (1901), pp. 426–9.

101 Ramsay, p. cviii.

102 See above, p. 24.

103 Cf. Heiserman, p. 82 ('but one exchequer was being wasted').

104 See *O.E.D.* royal a. 8, 9. It is true that 'royal' is more often used of sovereigns, however.

105 *Ven. Cal.*, II, no. 1287, p. 560.

106 *Ven. Cal.*, III, no. 1, p. 1 (1520). Cf. also *Ven. Cal.*, II, no. 732, p. 302 (1516); Hall, p. 593 (1518); *Parrot*, 430.

107 Or at least for the version of the play mentioned in *Garlande*. As I have already pointed out (p. 15 above), Skelton could have revised the play between this reference to it *c.* 1523 and its printing *c.* 1530.

108 *Ballads*, pp. 331–5.

109 For a different opinion, see Pollet, p. 83.

110 *Northumberlande*, 52–6.

111 Wolsey is also accused of being without measure in the ballads: 'hyt ys to hye, with-owte mesure; / hys pryde hathe wastyd mvche of your Tresure' (*Ballads*, p. 333, ll. 23–4); Wolsey's ministers 'haue Made A wonderfull Colleccion / of Substaunce owte of Measure' (*Ballads*, p. 354, ll. 71–2).

112 'I xal horvle of yower hedes, be mahondes bones, / as I am trew kyng to mahond so fre' (*Mary Magdalene*, 142–3). After saying this Herod condemns any who 'werkyn ony wondyr a-ȝens my magnyfycens' to be cast into 'carys cold'.

113 Cf. 'Nero nor herod / wer never so noyus certayne' *Rede me*, p. 115.

114 Cavendish, p. 182.

115 *Rede me*, p. 46.

116 Cavendish, p. 23.

117 *Ibid.*, p. 4.

118 *Rede me*, p. 20.

119 *Ballads*, p. 334, l. 42; p. 353, l. 38, 44. See also *Rede me*, p. 54.

120 *The Anglica Historia of Polydore Vergil*, ed. and trans. Denys Hay (1950), p. 231.

121 *Ballads*, p. 355, ll. 104–5.

122 Hall, p. 774.

123 *Ibid.*

124 *Magnificence*, 710; *Rede me*, p. 76. This is proverbial however; see note on 710.

125 He was, however, often genuinely ill, and in fact died of a flux, as Cavendish reports.

126 *Ven. Cal.* II, no. 655, p. 266.

127 *Ven. Cal.* III, no. 43, p. 12. Matters got moving when Wolsey 'was in better health than usual' (*Ven. Cal.* III, no. 47, p. 13).

128 *Rede me*, p. 20.

129 Hall, p. 704 (1525). Shakespeare draws on this in *Henry VIII*: 'This butcher's cur is venom-mouth'd, and I / Have not the power to muzzle him' (I.i.120–1). Cf. also *Parrot*, 321–2, 480; *Why come*, 293–6—in the lines from *Parrot* Wolsey is called 'mangey', as is Grime.

130 Thus when Folly says that the hawk 'is less a great deal / Than a butterfly of our land' (1051–2) 'butterfly' may refer to the cardinal. Magnificence himself is compared to a butterfly twice: 403, 575.

131 For a thorough discussion of this, see Fish, *op. cit.*, pp. 135–76.

132 *Parrot*, 428 ('woluys hede'), *passim* 'Lyacon'; *Cloute*, 128 ('A Webbe of lytse wulse'), Latin epilogue ('*maris lupis*'= 'wolf-of-the-sea').

133 Other detractors of Wolsey also indulged in word play: 'But nowe ye are soo stoppyd with *wolle*, / ye Can not Barke' (*Ballads*, p. 334, 45–6). North's effusive (and ironic) *Praise of Wolsey* contains an acrostic reading 'God preserve Thomas lord legate and cardynal' in the first letter of each line (Pollard, p. 226).

134 See above, p. 2.

135 Cavendish, pp. 187–8.

136 P. L. Wiley, 'Renaissance Exploitation of Cavendish's *Life of Wolsey*', *Studies in Philology*, XLIII (1946), p. 123.

137 W. H. Auden, review of Philip Henderson's *The Complete Poems of John Skelton*, *The Criterion*, XI (January 1932), p. 319.

138 See above, note 60.

139 'To eat sauce' is proverbial, however (see note on 1405).

140 See also 1575.

141 *Memorials of the Guild of Merchant Taylors* compiled by C. M. Glode, (1875), p. 154.

142 See Craik, pp. 2–3.

143 I.e. 'Company of persons eating together' (*O.E.D.* sb. 4).

144 Cf. the reference in *Mankind* to 'ye souerens that sytt and ye brothern that stonde ryght wppe.' (29).

145 For the meaning of 'place', see note on 239.1.

146 See *O.E.D.* door 5.

147 See Southern, pp. 194–5.

148 Southern discusses in some detail the use of the 'heralded' entry in *Magnificence*; see pp. 189–94.

149 If it *is* a bed. See note on 1967.2.

150 On fool's costume, see F. Douce, *Illustrations of Shakespeare* (1807), II, p. 317 ff.; Enid Welsford, *The Fool* (1968), pp. 121–2.

151 Performing dogs were used in the theatre, however, from medieval times. See R. Axton, 'Popular Modes in the Earliest Plays', *Stratford-upon-Avon Studies*, XVI (1973), p. 18.

152 See notes on 601, 602, 748.1

153 Dodsley, I, p. 179.

154 Craik suggests that Despair and Mischief were dressed as devils (p. 52). But see note on 2325.

155 See D. M. Bevington, *From Mankind to Marlowe* (1962), p. 68 ff.

156 This is not the same as Ramsay's arrangement (see pp. xlix–l), but the only significant difference is that he suggests the same actor should play Folly and Courtly Abusion. This would necessitate two changes of the two most elaborate costumes. If B plays Collusion and Folly he has plenty of time to don his fool's costume between Collusion's exit at 823.1 and Folly's entrance at 1041.1. To become Collusion again he need only resume his 'cope', which he can easily remove during Magnificence's six-line soliloquy (1798–1803), after which B returns as Folly. It is also easier if the part of Despair is assigned to the 'boy' rather than B, C, or D, since there are only seven lines between their exits and his entrance. It is symbolically appropriate, too, for Despair to appear shrunken in size.

157 See also note on 1599.

158 See Craik, p. 73 ff. (*Magnificence* is discussed on p. 87).

159 Ramsay deduced from Fancy's remarks about his treatment by the crowd at Calais (on the possible loss of his ears, and the tonsuring of his head), that he was in Fool's costume at his first entrance (see p. xcviii ff). But if so there would be no reason for Folly to be surprised at seeing him 'in a fool's case' (1045). He might have been wearing his fool's costume under that of 'Largesse', occasionally visible to the audience. Besides being appropriate to the allegory, this would be practical, as it would be easier for him to change. Cf. the behaviour of Flatterie, Falset and Dissait in Bale's *King John*, on which Craik comments (p. 70).

160 See note on 811.

161 Liberty is speaking, at this stage still with the Virtues. He sounds very different when he returns after Magnificence's fall. See 2065 ff.

162 Cf. Kinsman, 'Old Sayde Sawe', pp. 115–16 and *passim*. (There are in fact over 100 proverbs in the play.)

163 See above, note 83.

164 See note on 1552 ff.

165 This point was discussed by Allan B. Fox in 'Rhyme, Rhythm and Unreason in Skelton's *Magnificence*', a paper presented at the 1974 Conference on Medieval Studies at Kalamazoo, Michigan.

166 I am indebted to S. George West for this information.

167 See Harris, p. vi.

168 My attention was originally drawn to this by Harold Brooks.

169 Extract from the programme note by Michael Imison.

170 Extract from the programme note by John Duncan.

171 Extract from the programme note by Daniel De Matteis. See p. 134.

172 *English Drama from its Beginnings to the 1580s as presented by the B.B.C.*, *The First Stage*, Dover Publications. Library of Congress No. R68–3183.

MAGNIFICENCE

A goodly interlude and a
merry, devised and made by
Master Skelton, poet laureate
late deceased.

Title-page. From the first (undated) edition (see frontispiece)
goodly] excellent. Perhaps also 'notable or considerable in respect of size'
(*O.E.D.* a. 2).

These be the names of the players.

Felicity	Cloaked Collusion	Good Hope
Liberty	Courtly Abusion	Redress
Measure	Folly	Circumspection
	Adversity	Perseverance.
Magnificence	Poverty	
	Despair	
Fancy	Mischief	
Counterfeit Counte[nance]		
Crafty Conveyance		

---

the names of the players.] This list appears after the end of the play in F (f. xxx). The characters are listed in order of appearance, and are separated into four groups: Virtues; the hero; Vices; more Virtues. See Intro., section 4(c), where the number of actors and probable distribution of parts is discussed.

Felicity] happiness, prosperity. His full name is Wealthful Felicity, sometimes abbreviated to Wealth. See note on 23.

Liberty] power to do as one likes. See note on 21.1.

Measure] moderation, temperance; also 'due proportion' (*O.E.D.* sb. 11 a).

Magnificence] cannot be simply glossed: one of the functions of the play is to examine and define the possible meanings of the term. See Intro., pp. 25–6.

Fancy] caprice, whim.

Counterfeit Countenance] (1) simulated self-restraint; (2) deceitful demeanour. See note on 44.

Crafty Conveyance] (1) crafty conduct; (2) skilful stealing.

Cloaked Collusion] disguised deceit.

Courtly Abusion] evil perversion of gentlemanly behaviour.

Despair] See notes on 2285, 2337.

Mischief] harm, evil. See note on 2309.1.

Redress] reparation. As Redress gives Magnificence new garments (see 2406), there is a pun on 'reclothe', or rather on the noun relating to this: 'clothing again' (though *O.E.D.* cites no instance of this sense before 1739).

Circumspection] care, heedfulness. Usually called by his full name: Sad (i.e. serious) Circumspection. See note on 16.

[*Enter* FELICITY.]

Felicity. All things contrived by man's reason,
     The world environ, of high and low estate,
     Be it early or late, wealth hath a season.
     Wealth is of wisdom the very true probate.
     A fool is he with wealth that falleth at debate;   5
     But men nowadays so unhappily be ured
     That nothing than wealth may worse be endured.

0.1.] *Ramsay.*   1. things] thyngys *F;* thyng ys *Ramsay.*   2. world environ, of] *this ed.;* world enuyronnyd of *F;* world, enuyronned of *Ramsay.*

0.1.] Felicity may 'enter' by emerging through the screen doors, or he may already be 'on stage', beginning his speech when the audience becomes silent.

1–21.] It is unfortunate that the play's opening speech should be its most obscure. Felicity's statement may be summarised thus: 'Prosperity comes sometime in his life to every reasonable man. Prosperity is not a stable state, but liable to change, yet the exercise of prudence may help prosperity to last. Nowadays, however, will has taken charge over reason, so there is very little prosperity.'

1.] 'When everything is (lit. 'everything being') directed by man's reason'; an absolute participle construction analogous to that of Latin, frequently used by Skelton especially in *Diodorus*, and quite common in contemporary usage: see Visser, I, p. 367 ff. *Contrived* here seems to combine the senses 'devised' and 'managed' (*O.E.D.* v.[1] 1, 6): Skelton suggests that men can (and should) use their reason to achieve prosperity and to maintain themselves in it. Ramsay's rendering of this line as 'All things are effected or brought to pass by the intelligence' is obviously incorrect, since the final point of Felicity's speech is that 'nowadays' they are *not*. Cf. 'By witte of man al thyng that is contryved, / Standith in proporcion, plainly to conclude' (Lydgate, 'Song', 1–2). See Intro., pp. 19–20.

2. *The world environ*] the world round, all over the world. Skelton's frequent use of this phrase in *Diodorus* (p. 6, l. 9, p. 10, l. 35, p. 13, l. 13, etc.), and its occurrence in *The Four Elements* (Dodsley, I, p. 6), show F's *enuyronnyd* to be an error. See note on 1328.

of high and low estate] by men of all conditions (*of* follows *contrived*, 1).

3. *wealth*] well-being, prosperity.

season] due time.

4. *probate*] evidence. Prosperity is proof of a man's wisdom, since he must have gained it by exercising his reason.

5.] Proverbial; Whiting F426.1.

6. *so unhappily be ured*] have such unfortunate habits. Cf. *O.E.D.* ure sb. III. 4: 'custom or habit.' *O.E.D.* cites no verb 'ure' in this sense, and enters this example under 'eure' v: to destine, which I think incorrect. Skelton often uses this phrase of those he despises; e.g. *Albany*, 126, *Replycacion*, 95.

7.] 'That they find nothing more unbearable than prosperity', i.e. they are fools (see 5).

To tell you the cause meseemeth it no need;
The amends thereof is far to call again.
For when men by wealth, they have little dread   10
Of that may come after experience true and plain;
How after a drought there falleth a shower of rain
And after a heat oft cometh a stormy cold.
A man may have wealth, but not as he would,

Ay to continue and still to endure,   15
But if prudence be proved with sad circumspection;
Wealth might be won and made to the lure
If nobleness were acquainted with sober direction;
But will hath reason so under subjection,
And so disordereth this world over all,   20
That wealth and felicity is passing small.

[*Enter* LIBERTY.]

11. after experience] *this ed.;* after; experyence *Dyce.*   15. endure,] *this ed.;*
endure; *Dyce;* endure. *Ramsay.*   16. circumspection;] *this ed.;* circumspec-
cyon, *Dyce.*   21.1.] *Ramsay.*

9. *far to call again*] i.e. a long way off.

10. *by wealth*] (1) experience prosperity (*O.E.D.* aby v. 5; wealth 1); (2)
purchase riches (*O.E.D* aby v. 1, also buy v. 1, (the two forms were often
confused); wealth 3).

11. *that*] what.

12.] Proverbial; Tilley D621.

13.] Proverbial; Whiting H305.

15. *still*] continually.

16. *But if*] unless.

proved] demonstrated in action.

sad circumspection] wise caution, serious attentiveness. The personification
Sad Circumspection, the purported author of Fancy's forged letter (see 311–2),
appears at the end of the play (2419 ff.); here the quality, rather than the
'character', is intended.

17. *made to the lure*] trapped. The metaphor is from falconry.

18. *sober*] serious, wise.

20. *over all*] everywhere.

21. *felicity*] prosperity.

passing] extremely.

21.1.] Liberty is probably making his way forward during Felicity's speech. It
is appropriate for him to 'enter' (i.e. appear in the main acting area, or 'place':
see note on 239.1) soon after the mention of 'will', of which he is partly a

But where wones Wealth, and a man would wit?
For Wealthful Felicity, truly, is my name.

Liberty. [*Approaching him*] Marry, Wealth and I was
    appointed to meet,

And either I am deceived, or ye be the same.   25

Felicity. Sir, as ye say. I have heard of your fame:
    Your name is Liberty, as I understand.

Liberty. True you say sir. Give me your hand.

                                [*They shake hands.*]

Felicity. And from whence come ye, and it might be
    asked?

Liberty. To tell you, sir, I dare not, lest I should be
    masked   30

    In a pair of fetters, or a pair of stocks.

Felicity. [*To audience*] Hear you not how this
    gentleman mocks?

Liberty. Yea, too knacking earnest what and it preve?

26. ye say. I] *Ramsay;* ye say, I *Dyce.*

---

personification. See also note on 2064.1. Felicity is unaware of Liberty's presence until he speaks.

22. *wones*] lives.

and a man would wit?] if one wanted to know? (Perhaps this line should be
given to Liberty. But it can be considered a rhetorical question addressed partly
to the audience).

23.] 'For in fact *my* name is Wealthful Felicity.' Felicity is being pedantic, for
Wealthful Felicity and Wealth are one and the same, as is clear from Liberty's
opening remarks.

26. *fame*] reputation.

29. *and*] if.

30. *masked*] caught up, entangled.

30–1.] This comment is enigmatic. Liberty seems to be implying that he has
escaped from prison (cf. 35), and is afraid of being caught and locked up again. It
is quite common for Vices in interludes to announce that they have escaped
imprisonment or hanging: Riot in *Youth*, e.g., says, 'I come lately from Newgate' (Dodsley, II, p. 14). But Liberty's remark here seems inconsistent with the
suggestion in 144 and 221–2 that recently Liberty has been *too* free. Perhaps he
simply means that he has been somewhere he shouldn't, or possibly the point is
that if the authorities learn 'whence' Liberty comes, they will be able to get hold
of him and lock him up.

33.] 'Yes, but what if it prove to be all too true?' F *preue* is retained in a
regularised form here not merely for the rhyme but also because it seems

Felicity. Why, to say what he will Liberty hath leave.

Liberty. Yet Liberty hath been locked up and kept in
    the mew.   35

Felicity. Indeed, sir, that liberty was not worth a cue!
    Howbeit liberty may sometime be too large
    But if reason be regent and ruler of your barge.

Liberty. To that ye say I can well condescend:
    Show forth, I pray you, herein what you intend.   40

Felicity. Of that I intend, to make demonstration
    It asketh leisure with good advertence.
    First I say we ought to have in consideration
    That liberty be linked with the chain of countenance,
    Liberty to let from all manner offence;   45
    For liberty at large is loath to be stopped,
    But with countenance your corage must be cropped.

Liberty. Then thus to you—
Felicity.   Nay, suffer me yet further to say,

42. advertence] aduertence *Ramsay;* aduertysment *F*.   44, 47. countenance]
countenaunce *F;* Continence *Ramsay*.

---

deliberately chosen by Skelton. Normally he uses *proue*. For the intensifier
knacking, 'downright', cf. 'the party is in good knacking earnest' (*Ralph Royster
Doyster*, III. ii [58], Dodsley, III, p. 100).

    35. *in the mew*] cooped up.

    36. *cue*] 'The sum of half a farthing, formerly denoted in College accounts by
the letter q, originally for *quadrans*' (*O.E.D.* sb.[1] 2). ·

    37. *large*] free, uncontrolled.

    38. *your barge*] i.e. the ship of your soul. The metaphor is taken up again at the
end of the play (see 2555–8), and is popular with Skelton, being the main motif
of *Bowge*, and occurring in *Cloute*, 1253 ff.

    39. *condescend*] acquiesce.

    40. *intend*] mean.

    42. *advertence*] attention.

    45. *let*] hinder.

    manner offence] kind of injury.

    47. *countenance*] continence, self-restraint. (*Continence* is a doublet of *counte-
nance*: it seems best to retain the F form here in view of its associations with
Counterfeit Countenance, who, far from 'cropping' Liberty's 'corage', helps
him to freedom).

    corage] boldness.

    cropped] removed, cut off.

And peradventure I shall content your mind.
Liberty, I wot well, forbear no man there may,   50
It is so sweet in all manner of kind.
Howbeit liberty maketh many a man blind;
By liberty is done many a great excess;
Liberty at large will oft wax reckless.

Perceive ye this parcel?   55
Liberty. Yea, sir, passing well.
    But and you would me permit
    To show part of my wit,
    Somewhat I could infer
    Your conceit to debar,   60
    Under supportation
    Of patient toleration.
Felicity. God forbid ye should be let
    Your reasons forth to fet;
    Wherefore at liberty   65
    Say what ye will to me.

Liberty. Briefly to touch of my purpose the effect:
    Liberty is laudable and privileged from law;
    Judicial rigour shall not me correct—
Felicity. Soft, my friend; herein your reason is but raw.   70
Liberty. Yet suffer me to say the surplus of my saw,

---

50. *forbear no man there may*] no one can do without.
51. *all manner of kind*] every way.
55.] 'Do you understand this part [of my argument]?' (*O.E.D.* parcel sb. I.1).
59–60.] 'I could put forward some arguments to hinder your conception' (*O.E.D.* infer v. 2; conceit sb.1).
61–2.] Cf. *Hauke*, 31–2.
61. *Under supportation*] with the assistance.
63. *let*] prevented.
64. *fet*] bring.
67.] 'To touch briefly on the drift of my argument' (*O.E.D.* purpose sb. 4; effect sb. 2b).
71. *the surplus of my saw*] the rest of my speech.

What wot ye whereupon I will conclude?
I say there is no wealth whereas liberty is subdued.

I trow ye cannot say nay much to this:
To live under law, it is captivity;   75
Where dread leadeth the dance there is no joy nor
    bliss.
Or how can you prove that there is felicity
And you have not your own free liberty
To sport at your pleasure, to run and to ride?
Where liberty is absent, set wealth aside.   80

Here enters MEASURE.

Measure. Christ you assist in your altercation!
Felicity. Why, have you heard of our disputation?
Measure. I perceive well how each of you doth reason.
Liberty. Master Measure, you be come in good season.
Measure. And it is wonder that your wild insolence   85
    Can be content with Measure presence!
Felicity. Would it please you then—
Liberty. Us to inform and ken—
Measure. Ah, ye be wonders men!
    Your language is like the pen   90
    Of him that writeth too fast.
Felicity. Sir, if any word have passed

80.1.] Hic intrat Measure. *F.*   81. altercation] altrycacyon *F.*

---

72. *What wot ye*] How do you know.
73. *whereas*] where, when.
subdued] made submissive.
81. *Christ you assist*] may Christ assist you.
84. *season*] time.
85. *wonder*] wonderful.
86. *Measure presence*] Measure's presence. For this uninflected genitive with
words containing a sibilant, cf. 1100, 1199.1, 1316, 2237.
88. *ken*] instruct.
89. *wonders*] wonderful (*O.E.D.* a. and adv.).
90–1.] i.e. 'your language is elliptical'.
92–3. *if any word hath passed / Me*] if I have skipped any word.

Me, other first or last,
　　To you I arect it, and cast
　　Thereof the reformation.　　　　　　　　　　95
Liberty. And I of the same fashion.
　　Howbeit, by protestation
　　Displeasure that you none take,
　　Some reason we must make.
Measure. That will not I forsake　　　　　　100
　　So it in measure be.
　　Come off therefore, let see,
　　Shall I begin or ye?
Felicity. Nay, ye shall begin, by my will.
Liberty. It is reason and skill　　　　　　　105
　　We your pleasure fulfil.
Measure. Then ye must both consent
　　You to hold content
　　With mine argument,
　　And I must you require　　　　　　　　　110
　　Me patiently to hear.
Felicity. Yes, sir, with right good cheer.
Liberty. With all my heart entire.

112. cheer] chere *F*.　　　113. entire] intere *F*.

---

93. *other*] either.

94. *to you I arect it*] I offer it to you [for correction]. Cf. 'Arrectinge vnto your wyse examinacion / How all that I do is vnder refformation' (*Garlande*, 410–11). *O.E.D.* gives *arect* as a late variant of 'aret'. The citations there do not include this sense, though under 3b the sense 'To commit a charge to, entrust, deliver' is explained as a misuse of Spenser's. Cf. *erected*, 2479.

cast] contrive, arrange.

97–8.] 'However, on the condition that you take no offence' (*O.E.D.* protestation 1b).

99.] This probably means 'we must engage in some argument' (*O.E.D.* make v. 57d, though this is usually used of legal contracts like marriage; reason sb. 1, 19, and cf. the use of the verb *reason*, 83); but it may mean 'we must make some sort of speech' (make v. 57g; reason sb. 1, 3), or even 'we must make some sort of satisfaction [for offending you]' (the equivalent of Fr. *faire raison*, see make v. 15).

100. *forsake*] refuse.

102. *Come off*] come on.

let see] '*absol*. prefixed to a request (= 'come', 'go to')' (*O.E.D.* see v. 15b).

105. *skill*] right, fitting.

Measure. Horacius to record in his volumes old:
    With every condition measure must be sought.   115
    Wealth without measure would bear himself too
      bold;
    Liberty without measure prove a thing of nought.
    In ponder, by number, by measure, all thing is
      wrought,
    As at the first original, by godly opinion;
    Which proveth well that measure should have
      dominion.   120

    Where measure is master, plenty doth none offence;
    Where measure lacketh, all thing disordered is;
    Where measure is absent, riot keepeth residence;
    Where measure is ruler there is nothing amiss.
    Measure is treasure. How say ye, is it not this?   125
Felicity. Yes, questionless, in mine opinion
    Measure is worthy to have dominion.

118. In ponder, by number,] *this ed.;* I ponder by number *F;* I ponder by
number, *Dyce;* I ponder by nomber; *Ramsay.*

---

114. *Horacius to record*] to repeat Horace. The reference is to the 'golden mean'
of the *Odes*, II, x. See Harris, pp. 139–44.
   115.] Cf. the proverb 'There is a measure in all things'; Tilley M806.
with every condition] in every situation, at all times.
   118. *ponder*] weight.
all thing] everything (see *O.E.D.* thing sb[1] 3: 'In early use sometimes *sing.* in
collective sense').
   119 *at the first original*] in the very beginning. The *godly opinion* is that of
Solomon: *omnia mensura et numero et pondere disposuisti* (Wisdom xi, 21). With
118–19 cf. Lydgate, 'Song', 3, 6 (quoted in Intro., p. 20); 'For God made all
things, and set it sure / In Number, Ponder and in Measure' (Thomas Norton,
Ordinall of Alchemy, p. 58, cited *O.E.D.* ponder sb. 1); 'in mesure god made alle
manere thynges, / And sette hit at a sertayn and at a syker numbre' (*Piers
Plowman*, C text, XXIII, 254–5), and see *O.E.D.* weight 2, where similar
sentiments are cited from Hampole's *Pricke of Conscience* and Henryson's
Preiching of the Swallow. Clearly proverbial, though not in Tilley or Whiting.
   121.] Cf. 'Where mesure fayleth, wrong wrought is in euery dede' (Lydgate,
'Song', 21).
   125. *Measure is treasure*] Proverbial; Tilley M805.
this] thus.
   126. *questionless*] without doubt.

Liberty. Unto that same I am right well agreed,
    So that liberty be not left behind.
Measure. Yea, liberty with measure need never dread.   130
Liberty. What, liberty to measure then would ye bind?
Measure. What else? For otherwise it were against kind;
    If liberty should leap and run where he list,
    It were no virtue, it were a thing unblest;

    It were a mischief if liberty lacked a rein   135
    Wherewith to rule him with the writhing of a wrest;
    All trebles and tenors be ruled by a mean.
    Liberty without measure is accounted for a beast;
    There is no surfeit where measure ruleth the feast;
    There is no excess where measure hath his health;   140
    Measure continueth prosperity and wealth.

Felicity. Unto your rule I will annex my mind.
Liberty. So would I, but I would be loath
    That wont was to be formest, now to come behind.
    It were a shame, to God I make an oath,   145
    Without I might cut it out of the broadcloth
    As I was wont ever at my free will.
Measure. But have ye not heard say that 'will is no skill'?

134. unblest] vnblyst *F.*   138. beast] beste *F.*   139. feast] feste
F.   141. continueth] contynwyth *F.*

   129. *So that*] on the understanding that.
   132. *it were against kind*] it would be unnatural.
   133. *list*] pleased.
   135. *mischief*] harmful thing.
   136. *writhing*] twisting.
   wrest] tuning key, with a pun on 'wrist' continuing the metaphor in *rein*.
   137. *mean*] 'A middle or intermediate part in any harmonised composition or
performance' (*O.E.D.* sb. 2).
   140. *health*] well-being.
   142. *annex my mind*] join my way of thinking, or inclination.
   144. *formest*] first. Cf. 'The formest was alway behynde' (*The Book of the
Duchess*, 890). More commonly 'The first shall be last', as in Matt. xix, 30, etc.
   145.] 'It would be a pity, I swear to God'.
   146. *broadcloth*] double width cloth. Cf. the proverb 'To cut it out of whole
cloth'; Tilley C433 (1546), (meaning 'to do something with free abandon').
   148. *'will is no skill'*] Proverbial; Whiting W273 (*skill* = 'reason').

Take sad direction, and leave this wantonness.
Liberty. It is no mastery—
Felicity.   Tush, let Measure proceed,   150
And after his mind hardily yourself address;
For without measure, poverty and need
Will creep upon us, and us to mischief lead;
For mischief will master us, if measure us forsake.
Liberty. Well, I am content your ways to take.   155

Measure. Surely I am joyous that ye be minded thus.
Magnificence to maintain, your promotion shall be.
Felicity. So in his heart he may be glad of us.
Liberty. There is no prince but he hath need of us three:
Wealth, with Measure and pleasant Liberty.   160
Measure. Now pleaseth you a little while to stand;
Meseemeth Magnificence is coming here at hand.

Here enters MAGNIFICENCE.

Magnificence. To assure you of my noble port and fame,
Who list to know, Magnificence I hight.
But Measure, my friend, what hight this man's name?
                    [*Indicates* FELICITY.]   165
Measure. Sir, though ye be a noble prince of might,
Yet in this man you must set your delight.
And sir, this other man's name is Liberty.
Magnificence. Welcome, friends, ye are both unto me.

150. It is] *Dyce;* It it *F*.   162.1.] Hic intrat magnyfycence *F*.

---

149. *sad*] serious.
wantonness] capriciousness.
150. *It is no mastery*] it needs no skill.
151. *after*] according to.
mind] judgement.
hardily] energetically, boldly.
address] direct.
153. *mischief*] harm, evil.
157. *maintain*] support, assist (in effect, 'serve').
161. *pleaseth*] may it please.
stand] stay where you are.
163. *port*] state, bearing.
164. *hight*] am called.

But now let me know of your conversation.   170
Felicity. Pleaseth your grace, Felicity they me call.
Liberty. And I am Liberty, made of in every nation.
Magnificence. Convenient persons for any prince royal.
  Wealth with Liberty, with me both dwell ye shall,
  To the guiding of my Measure you both committing: 175
  That Measure be master us seemeth it is sitting.

Measure. Whereas ye have, sir, to me them assigned,
  Such order I trust with them for to take
  So that Wealth with measure shall be combined,
  And Liberty his large with measure shall make.   180
Felicity. Your ordinance, sir, I will not forsake.
Liberty. And I myself wholly to you will incline.
Magnificence. Then may I say that ye be servants mine,

  For by Measure, I warn you, we think to be guided;
  Wherein it is necessary my pleasure you know: 185
  Measure and I will never be divided
  For no discord that any man can sow,
  For measure is a mean, nother too high nor too low,

173. royal] ryall *F*. 179. combined] conbyned *F*. 187. sow] sawe
F. 188. low] lawe *F*.

170.] 'But now let me become acquainted with you' (*conversation* may mean
'society', 'occupation', or 'behaviour' (*O.E.D.* 2, 4, 6)). Magnificence wants to
know what sort of people they are, but Felicity takes the request very literally,
and gives his name, which Measure, oddly, had neglected to do.

172. *made of*] highly valued (*O.E.D.* make v. 21 b).

173. *convenient*] suitable.

royal] F. ryall (stress on second syllable).

175.] 'Both submitting yourselves to the guidance of my Measure'.

176. *sitting*] proper, befitting.

177. *Whereas*] seeing that.

180.] This seems to mean 'Liberty shall take his freedom in moderation'; the
phrase 'make one's large' being analogous to 'be at large'. *O.E.D.* cites this
example under 'large' sb. C.3 ('freedom') with a query.

181. *ordinance*] decree.

184. *warn*] inform.

188. *Measure is a mean*] Cf. the proverb 'Measure is a merry mean'; Tilley
M804, which Magnificence quotes, 380.

nother] neither.

In whose attemperance I have such delight
That measure shall never depart from my sight.   190

Felicity. Laudable your conceit is to be accounted
For wealth without measure suddenly will slide.
Liberty. As your grace full nobly hath recounted,
Measure with nobleness should be allied.
Magnificence. Then, Liberty, see that Measure be your
        guide,   195
For I will use you by his advertisement.
Felicity. Then shall you have with you prosperity resident.

Measure. I trow good fortune hath annexed us together,
To see how greeable we are of one mind.
There is no flatterer nor losel so lither,   200
This linked chain of love that can unbind.
Now that ye have me chief ruler assigned
I will endeavour me to order everything
Your nobleness and honour concerning.

Liberty. In joy and mirth your mind shall be enlarged,   205
And not embraced with pusillanimity;
But plenarly all thought from you must be discharged
If ye list to live after your free liberty.
All delectations acquainted is with me;
By me all persons work what they list—   210

---

189. *attemperance*] moderation.
191. *conceit*] apprehension, judgement (*O.E.D.* sb. 2, 4).
192. *slide*] steal away, disappear.
196. *advertisement*] instruction.
198. *annexed*] joined.
199. *greeable*] compliant.
200. *losel so lither*] scoundrel so wicked.
205. *enlarged*] made free or liberal.
206. *embraced*] buckled in.
207. *plenarly*] entirely.
thought] anxiety, care.
209.] 'All pleasures are personally known to me'.
210. *list*] please.

Measure. Hem, sir, yet beware of 'had I wist'!

    Liberty in some cause becometh a gentle mind
    By course of measure, if I be in the way;
    Who counteth without me is cast too far behind
    Of his reckoning, as evidently we may   215
    See at our eye the world day by day:
    For default of measure all thing doth exceed.
Felicity. All that ye say is as true as the creed,

    For howbeit liberty to wealth is convenient,
    And from felicity may not be forborne,   220
    Yet measure hath been so long from us absent
    That all men laugh at liberty to scorn.
    Wealth and wit, I say, be so threadbare worn

213. By course] *this ed.*; Bycause course *F*.   214. counteth] countyth *Dyce;*
countyd *F*.   216. See at] Se at *Dyce;* So at *F*.

---

    211. *'had I wist'*] if only I had known [what would happen, I wouldn't have
done it] . 'Beware of "had I wist"' ('Beware of being wise after the event') is
proverbial; Tilley H8. See also 1396.
    212. *in some cause becometh*] under some conditions befits.
    gentle] noble, honourable.
    213. *By course of*] Through the habitual practice of (*O.E.D*. sb. 19). F. *Bycause
course* has *cause* repeated in error from the previous line.
    if I be in the way] as long as I am present (*way* punning on other meanings of
course).
    214–15.] 'Anyone who does his accounts without me will find himself way
below his estimate' (because he will have spent more than he should).
    216.] 'See clearly throughout the world continually'. (With *the world*, adver-
bial phrase without preposition, cf. *the world environ*, 2, *the world about*, 1328.)
    218. *true as the creed*] Proverbial; Tilley C819.
    219. *convenient*] consonant with the nature of.
    220. *forborne*] given up, parted with.
    222. The exact meaning of this line is unclear. If *liberty* is intended as object,
then two constructions have been combined: *laugh at liberty*, and *laugh liberty to
scorn*, and the sense is 'all men mock or deride liberty'. It seems more likely that
at liberty is an adverbial phrase (as in 735, 1319, 1780, etc.); *laugh to scorn* then
has no object, (which is unusual, but cf. *laughing to scorn*, 446), and the line
means 'that all men are free to behave mockingly'.
    223. *wit*] intelligence, understanding.

That all is without measure, and far beyond the
    moon.

Magnificence. Then nobleness, I see well, is almost
    undone   225

But if thereof the sooner amends be made;
For doubtless I perceive my magnificence
Without measure lightly may fade,
Of too much liberty under the offence.
Wherefore, Measure, take Liberty with you hence,   230
And rule him after the rule of your school.

Liberty. What, sir, would ye make me a popping fool?

Measure. Why, were not yourself agreed to the same,
    And now would ye swerve from your own ordinance?

Liberty. I would be ruled and I might for shame.   235

Felicity. Ah, ye make me laugh at your inconstance!

Magnificence. Sir, without any longer dalliance,
    Take Liberty to rule, and follow mine intent.

Measure. It shall be done at your commandment.

---

224. *far beyond the moon*] Cf. the proverb 'He casts beyond the moon'; Tilley
M1114 (1546).

228. *lightly*] easily.

229. *under the offence*] as a result of the fault.

232. *a popping fool*] One who blurts out his words suddenly and automatically
(as if they had been learnt parrot fashion). See *O.E.D.* pop v.[1] 5: 'to put
promptly, suddenly or unexpectedly', which cites 'porisshly forthe popped /
Your sysmaticate sawes' (*Replycacion*, 121–2). For *popping*, see also *Replycacion*, 39; *Why come*, 261. In each case a pun on 'popinjay' is likely.

234. *ordinance*] arrangement.

235. *and I might for shame*] if I could [do so] without disgrace.

236. *inconstance*] inconsistency.

237. *dalliance*] discussion (*O.E.D.* 1).

238. *intent*] aim, purpose.

239.1. the place] the playing area. 'Place', like its Latin equivalent, *platea*, is a
technical term in medieval and Tudor drama. 'With indoor Interludes the word
was . . . particularly applied to the floor of a Great Hall as a whole; that is to say,
for defining . . . an area where both audience and players were' (Southern, pp.
186–7).

So let MEASURE *leave the place with* LIBERTY,
and MAGNIFICENCE *remain with* FELICITY.

Magnificence. It is a wanton thing, this liberty: 240
 Perceive you not how loath he was to abide
 The rule of Measure, notwithstanding we
 Have deputed Measure him to guide?
 By measure each thing duly is tried,
 Think you not thus, my friend Felicity?   245
Felicity. God forbid that it otherwise should be.

Magnificence. Ye could not else, I wot, with me endure.
Felicity. Endure? No, God wot, it were great pain:
 But if I were ordered by just measure
 It were not possible me long to retain.   250

Here enters FANCY.

Fancy. [*To* FELICITY] Tush, hold your peace, your
 language is vain.
 [*To* MAGNIFICENCE] Please it your grace to take
 no disdain
 To show you plainly the truth as I think.
Magnificence. Here is none forseth whether you flete or
 sink.

239.1–2.] Itaque measure exeat locum cum lybertate et maneat magnyfycence cum felicitate. *F*. 250.1.] Hic intrat Fansy. *F*.

---

 241. *abide*] tolerate.
 244. *duly is tried*] is rightly judged, properly determined.
 248. *it were great pain*] it would be very difficult (*O.E.D.* sb.[1] 5).
 249. *ordered*] directed.
 250.1.] Fancy is 'disguised' as 'Largesse'. His true identity might be apparent to the audience, if his fool's costume is glimpsed under his courtier's attire. See Intro., note 159.
 251.] Cf. Magnificence's words, 1380, and see Intro., p. 29.
 252.] An extra rhyming line (making an eight-line stanza).
 Please it] may it please.
 253. *To show you*] if I show you.
 254. *forseth*] cares.
 flete] float. Cf. 'Him rekketh never wher she flete or synke' (*Anelida and Arcite*, 182); 'Nat wot I well wher that I flete or synke.' (*Parlement of Fowles*, 7); 'Sink or swim'; Tilley S485.

Felicity. From whence come you, sir, that no man looked
    after?   255
Magnificence. Or who made you so bold to interrupt my
    tale?
Fancy. Now, *benedicite*, ye ween I were some hafter,
    Or else some jangling Jack-of-the-Vale.
    Ye ween that I am drunken, because I look pale.
Magnificence. Meseemeth that ye have drunken more
    than ye have bled.   260
Fancy. Yet among noblemen I was brought up and bred.

Felicity. Now leave this jangling, and to us expound
    Why that ye said our language was in vain.
Fancy. Marry, upon truth my reason I ground:
    That without largesse nobleness cannot reign.   265
    And that I said once yet I say again:
    I say without largesse worship hath no place,
    For largesse is a purchaser of pardon and of grace.

Magnificence. Now I beseech thee tell me what is thy
    name.
Fancy. Largesse, that all lords should love, sir, I hight.   270
Felicity. But hight you Largesse, increase of noble fame?
Fancy. Yea, sir, undoubted.
Felicity.   Then of very right

---

255. *looked after*] anticipated.

256. *tale*] conversation.

257. *ye ween I were some hafter*] you imagine me to be some trickster.

258. *jangling*] chattering, noisy.

Jack-of-the-Vale] a contemptuous nickname, equivalent to 'fool'. Cf.
Margery, 6.

259.] Cf. 'The Millere, that for dronken was al pale' (*Canterbury Tales*, I.
3120), and Chaucer's description of the drunken Cook: 'ful pale and no thyng
reed' (IX.20). This proverbial expression appears more commonly in the form
in 260: 'He has drunk more than he has bled', Tilley D608.

265. *largesse*] liberality. Fancy's reply has nothing to do with the 'language' of
Felicity and Magnificence; see Intro., pp. 26–7.

267. *worship*] honour, dignity.

270. Fancy's assumed name contains a joke: he is very small. See Intro. p. 47.

272. *undoubted*] without a doubt.

With Magnificence, this noble prince of might,
Should be your dwelling, in my consideration.
Magnificence. Yet we will therein take good deliberation. 275

Fancy. As in that I will not be against your pleasure.
Felicity. [*To* MAGNIFICENCE] Sir, hardily, remember
    what may your name advance.
Magnificence. [*Musing*] Largesse is laudable, so it be in
    measure—
Fancy. Largesse is he that all princes doth advance;
    I report me herein to King Lewis of France. 280
Felicity. Why have ye him named, and all other refused?
Fancy. For sith he died, largesse was little used.

    [*To* MAGNIFICENCE] Pluck up your mind, sir; what
    ail you to muse?
    Have ye not wealth here at your will?
    It is but a madding, these ways that ye use. 285
    What availeth lordship, yourself for to kill
    With care and with thought how Jack shall have Gill?
Magnificence. What! I have espied ye are a carl's page.
Fancy. By God sir, ye see but few wise men of mine age,

278. be in measure] *Ramsay;* in measure be *F*.   288. carl's] carles *F*.

277. *hardily*] by all means.
280. *I report me*] I appeal for support (*O.E.D.* v. 6).
king Lewis of France] probably Louis XII. See Intro., p. 15.
282. *sith*] since, after.
283] 'Cheer up, sir; what troubles you that you reflect so?'
285. *a madding*] madness.
286. *What availeth lordship*] What use is it to [your] dignity.
286–7. *yourself . . . Gill?*] to worry yourself to death about trifling matters (?).
'Jack shall have Gill' is proverbial; Whiting J7. For 'to kill oneself with care', cf.
'Care will kill a cat'; Tilley C84 (1585).
288. *a carl's page*] a churl's servant, i.e. 'the lowest of the low'. That F *carles* =
'carl's' and not 'careless' is confirmed by 'carl's son' (897), where the context
'brought up of nought' indicates that 'churl's' is the intended meaning. There is
word-play on 'careless', following *care*, 287. Ramsay *glosses* 'careless', however.
289.] Fancy chooses to ignore the insult, taking 'page' to mean 'boy' rather
than 'servant'. (An 'in' joke, since he is played by a boy.)

But covetise hath blown you so full of wind   290
That *colica passio* hath groped you by the guts.

Felicity. In faith, brother Largesse, you have a merry
    mind.

Fancy. In faith, I set not by the world two Doncaster
    cuts.

Magnificence. Ye want but a wild flying bolt to shoot
    at the butts.

Though Largesse ye hight, your language is too large, 295
For which end goth forward ye take little charge.

Felicity. Let see this check if ye void can.

Fancy. In faith, else had I gone too long to school,
    But if I could know a goose from a swan.

Magnificence. Well, wise men may eat the fish when
    ye shall draw the pool.   300

Fancy. In faith, I will not say that ye shall prove a fool,
    But ofttimes have I seen wise men do mad deeds.

---

290. *covetise*] covetousness. (Fancy begins his attack on Magnificence's employment of Measure by suggesting that he is mean.)

291. colica passio] colic. (Wolsey frequently suffered from colic; see Intro.,
p. 40.

groped] seized (*groped you by the guts* probably means 'given you the gripe';
O.E.D. does not give this sense under 'grope' v., but see 'gripe' v.[1] 8).

293. *set by*] value.

cuts] (1) slashes (Doncaster daggers were proverbial; see Tilley B22, 1659); (2)
cunts (see *A Chaste Maid In Cheapside*, II.i, note 135; cf. 'kutte', *Ludus
Coventriæ* p. 205, l. 152).

294. *bolt*] arrow.

butts] (1) marks; (2) buttocks; (3) casks of ale (Fancy is supposed drunk).
Magnificence has in mind the proverb 'A fool's bolt is soon shot'; Tilley F515.

296] Proverbial; Tilley E130 (this example is not cited).

charge] account.

297.] 'Let us see if you can escape this rebuke' (for *let see* used with indirect
question see *O.E.D.* see v. 15b).

298. *else had I*] otherwise I should have.

gone too long to school] i.e. gone to school to no purpose = remained ignorant.

299.] Proverbial; Tilley G369.

300. *draw*] draw a net through. Magnificence means that Fancy is such a fool
that he will let others eat the fish he catches. Cf. the proverb 'Fools lade the water
and wise men catch the fish'; Tilley F538.

Magnificence. Go shake the dog, hey, sith ye will needs!

You are nothing meet with us for to dwell,
That with your lord and master so pertly can prate.   305
Get you hence, I say, by my counsel!
I will not use you to play with me checkmate.
Fancy. Sir, if I have offended your noble estate,
I trow I have brought you such writing of record
That I shall have you again my good lord.   310

To you recommendeth Sad Circumspection,
And sendeth you this writing closed under seal.
                              [*Gives him a letter.*]
Magnificence. This writing is welcome with hearty
       affection.
Why kept you it thus long? How doth he, well?
Fancy. Sir, thanked be God, he hath his hele.   315
Magnificence. Wealth, get you home and command me to
       Measure;
Bid him take good heed to you, my singular treasure.

306. counsel] counsell *F.*   314. well] wele *F.*

---

303. *shake the dog*] In *Dundas*, 28, and *Albany*, 159, the wording is 'shake *thy* dog', which may therefore be intended here, but cf. 'catch the doge' (*The Marriage of Wit and Wisdom*, 6r). It is simply a contemptuous expression. (As far as we know, Fancy does not own a dog at this point, though he later gets one from Folly in exchange for his hawk.)
   sith ye will needs] since you must.
   305. *so pertly can prate*] can chatter so cheekily.
   306. *counsel*] F *counsell* (stress on second syllable).
   308. *estate*] status, degree.
   309. *record*] repute.
   311.] 'Sad Circumspection recommends himself to you' (i.e. Magnificence's absent counsellor, who returns at the end of the play).
   312. *this writing*] The letter has been forged by Countenance (see 531 ff.). In *The Marriage of Wit and Wisdom* Fancy (in this case female) also gives the hero a counterfeit letter of introduction.
   315. *hele*] health.
   316. *command*] commend.
   317. *singular*] special.

Felicity. Is there anything else your grace will command
    me?
Magnificence. Nothing but fare you well till soon,
    And that he take good keep to Liberty.   320
Felicity. Your pleasure, sir, shortly shall be done.
Magnificence. I shall come to you myself, I trow, this
    afternoon.

                        [*Exit* FELICITY.]

    I pray you Largesse, here to remain
    Whilst I know what this letter doth contain.

    Here let him make as if he were reading the letter silently.
    Meanwhile let COUNTERFEIT COUNTENANCE *come on*
    singing, who on seeing MAGNIFICENCE *should softly*
    retreat on tiptoe. At the right moment, after a while, let
    COUNTERFEIT COUNTENANCE *approach again look-*
    ing out and calling from a distance, and FANCY *motions*
    silence with his hand.

Countenance. What, Fancy, Fancy!   325
Magnificence. Who is that that thus did cry?
    Methought he called 'Fancy'.

319. *Magnificence.*] Magnyfycence *F(BL)*; Magnyfycecen *F(CUL)*.
324.1–6.] *this ed.;* Hic faciat tanquam legeret litteras tacite: Interim superue-
niat cantando counterfet countenaunce suspenso gradum qui viso magnyfycence sensum retrocedat ad tempus post pusillum rursum accedat counterfet countenaunce prospectando et vocitando a longe et fansy animat silen-
tium cum manu. *F;* . . . *suspenso gradu, qui, viso* MAGNYFYCENCE, *sensim*
retrocedat; at tempus . . . Dyce.   327. 'Fancy'] Fansy *Dyce;* fanfy *F.*

---

    320. *keep to*] care of.
    324. *Whilst*] until.
    324.1–6.] 'The whole of this direction is of the greatest interest as being one of
the fullest and most minute acting-directions in all early drama' (Southern, p.
188). The piece of stage business alerts the audience to the fact that Fancy's
letter is not what it purports to be. As it was forged by Counteraunce, he is
naturally interested in its fate. Countenance is perhaps *singing* the first few lines
of his soliloquy, 410 ff. (cf. Fancy's *crying*, 910.1), which would help to identify
him. At this point, too, we learn the real name of 'Largesse'.
    who . . . while] My translation is based on the following emendation and
punctuation of F's Latin: *suspenso gradu qui viso Magnyfycence sensim retrocedat.*
Ad tempus, post pusillum, (see Collation).

Fancy. It was a Fleming hight Hansy.
Magnificence. Methought he called 'Fancy' me behind.
Fancy. Nay, sir it was nothing but your mind.   330
 But now sir, as touching this letter—
Magnificence. I shall look in it at leisure better;
 And surely ye are to him behold,
 And for his sake right gladly I would
 Do what I could to do you good.   335
Fancy. [*Aside*] I pray God keep you in that mood.
Magnificence. This letter was written far hence.
Fancy. By lakin sir, it hath cost me pence
 And groats many one or I came to your presence.
Magnificence. Where was it delivered you? Show unto me.   340
Fancy. By God, sir, beyond the sea.
Magnificence. At what place now, as you guess?
Fancy. By my troth sir, at—Pontesse:
 This writing was taken me there,
 But never was I in greater fear.   345
Magnificence. How so?

329. 'Fancy'] fansy *F(BL)*; fanfy *F(CUL)*.   334. would] wolde *F*.

---

328. *Hansy*] Hans. But a 'hansy' = a Fleming: the Revels Accounts for 1510 refer to the cost of '2 "hansy's hats," cloaks, and coats' (*L.P.* II, p. 1492), and a drunken Fleming called Hance appears in *Like Will to Like*. Flemings had a bad reputation (Courtly Abusion later comes in chanting in Flemish), and Fancy suggests that Countenance, as such, is to be disregarded.

330. *nothing but your mind*] only your imagination.

331. *as touching*] concerning.

333. *behold*] under obligation.

338. *By lakin*] By [our] Lady.

339. *or*] before.

341.] Fancy is being deliberately vague to allow himself time to think of a convincing place, for the letter was actually delivered to him by Conveyance (see 534).

342. *guess*] suppose.

343. *Pontesse*] Pontoise, near Paris. Probably this town just occurred to Fancy on the spur of the moment, but it may have held some particular significance for Skelton's audience. It appears in an apparently random list of places supposedly conquered by Manhood in *Mundus and Infans* (Dodsley, I, p. 251).

344. *taken me*] delivered to me (*O.E.D.* v. 60).

Fancy.   By God, at the sea side,
　　Had I not opened my purse wide,
　　I trow, by our lady, I had been slain,
　　Or else I had lost mine ears twain.
Magnificence. By your sooth?
Fancy.   Yea, and there is such a watch   350
　　That no man can scape but they him catch.
　　They bare me in hand that I was a spy,
　　And another bade put out mine eye;
　　Another would mine eye were bleared,
　　Another bade shave half my beard,   355
　　And boys to the pillory gan me pluck,
　　And would have made me Friar Tuck,
　　To preach out of the pillory hole

350a. *Magnificence.*] *Dyce;* Fansy *F.*   350b. *Fancy.*] *Dyce; not in F.*

---

347 ff.] Ramsay thought that Fancy's reference to his purse, ears, and 'tonsure' like Friar Tuck in this passage meant that he would be dressed as a fool. These are certainly hints as to his true nature, but I think that he does not appear in full fool regalia until later. See Intro., note 159.

351. *scape but they him catch*] escape without them catching him.

352. *bare me in hand*] asserted.

353–4. *another . . . another*] one . . . another.

354. *bleared*] dimmed, blurred; here apparently literally, though 'to blear the eye' is a common metaphor for 'hoodwink', as in *Darlyng dere*, 28.

356 ff.] With Fancy's experiences here, cf. those of Evil Counsel in *John the Evangelist*: 'I will no more go to Coventry, / For there knaves set me on the pillory, / And threw eggs at my head / So sore that my nose did bleed / Of white wine gallons thirty' (Farmer, *Tudor Plays*, pp. 360–1).

356. *pillory*] A contrivance for punishment similar to the stocks, with a hole through which the offender's head and hands were thrust. There is a pun on 'pill', whose past participle = 'bald'.

pluck] puns on 'pull' and 'strip'; Fancy implies 'they dragged me by the hair pulling it out as they went'.

357. *Friar Tuck*] The fat friar of the Robin Hood May games, with whom fools were traditionally associated (see E. K. Chambers, *The Medieval Stage*, 1903, I, pp. 195–8). Fancy's loss of hair would suggest the Friar's tonsure, but the character may have occurred to Skelton because he had written of Robin Hood elsewhere. Barclay, scornfully comparing his skill to Skelton's lack of it, comments, 'I wryte no Iest ne tale of Robyn hode' (*Ship*, II, p. 331). 'Skelton' himself plays the part of Friar Tuck in Munday's *The Downfall and Death of Robert Earl of Huntingdon* (1601).

Without an antetheme or a stole;
And some bade 'sear him with a mark':   360
To get me fro them I had much work.
Magnificence. [*Ironically*] Marry, sir, ye were affrayed.
Fancy. By my troth, had I not paid and prayed,
    And made largesse (as I hight),
    I had not been here with you this night;   365
    But surely largesse saved my life,
    For largesse stinteth all manner of strife.
Magnificence. It doth so, sure, now and then,
    But largesse is not meet for every man.
Fancy. No, but for you great estates   370
    Largesse stinteth great debates,
    And he that I came fro to this place
    Said I was meet for your grace;
    And indeed sir, I hear men talk,
    By the way as I ride and walk,   375
    Say how you exceed in nobleness
    If you had with you largesse.
Magnificence. And say they so, in very deed?
Fancy. With yea, sir, so God me speed.
Magnificence. Yet measure is a merry mean.   380
Fancy. Yea, sir, a blanched almond is no bean!
    Measure is meet for a merchant's hall,

361. work] warke *F.*   368. then] than *F.*

---

359. *antetheme*] text prefixed to a sermon.
stole] priest's robe.
360. *'sear him with a mark'*] 'brand him'.
362. *affrayed*] alarmed, disturbed (probably with a pun on 'afraid').
363 ff.] Fancy hints in this speech that he deserves some remuneration for his trouble.
365 *this night*] presumably 'this evening', for in 322 Magnificence spoke of joining Felicity 'this afternoon'.
372. *he that I came fro*] Conveyance, in fact, though Magnificence thinks Fancy means Circumspection.
376. *Say*] who say (see note on 504).
379. *With yea*] emphatically yes.
380.] Proverbial; Tilley M804 (see 188).
382. *merchant's hall*] For the possible significance of this, see Intro., p. 43.

But largesse becometh a state royal.
What should you pinch at a peck of groats?
Ye would soon pinch at a peck of oats!   385
Thus is the talking of one and of other,
As men dare speak it, hugger-mugger:
'A lord a niggard, it is a shame'.
But largesse may amend your name.

Magnificence. In faith, Largesse, welcome to me.   390
Fancy. I pray you, sir, I may so be,
And of my service you shall not miss.
Magnificence. Together we will talk more of this:
Let us depart from hence home to my place.
Fancy. I follow even after your noble grace.   395

> *Here let* MAGNIFICENCE *depart with* FANCY,
> *and enter* COUNTERFEIT COUNTENANCE.

Countenance. [*To* FANCY] What, I say! Hark, a word.
Fancy. Do away, I say, the devil's turd!
Countenance. Yea, but how long shall I here await?
Fancy. By God's body, I come straight!
I hate this blundering that thou dost make.   400

> [*Exit* FANCY.]

Countenance. Now to the devil I thee betake,
For in faith ye be well met.

383. royal] ryall *F*.   384. groats] grotes *Ramsay;* otes *F*.   385. oats] otes
Ramsay; grotes *F*.   386. *other*] oder *F*.   387. mugger] *So F*.
395.1–2.] Hic discedat magnificens cum fansy et intrat counterfet countenaunce. *F*.

383. *royal* F *ryall* (stress on second syllable).
384. *What*] why (*O.E.D.* 19).
groats] The English groat coined in 1351–52 was made equivalent to four
pence. Though of small value, a groat is worth more than an oat, hence Ramsay's
emendation.
387. *hugger-mugger*] secretly.
392. *of my service . . . miss*] fail to obtain my service (*O.E.D.* v.¹ 23a).
395.1.] Fancy must leave a little behind Magnificence, in order to hold the
whispering conversation with Countenance that follows.
397. *Do away*] leave off.
401–2.] These lines are probably intended for Fancy, but they might be
addressed to the audience.
betake] commit, assign.

[*To audience*] Fancy hath catched in a fly-net
This noble man Magnificence,
Of Largesse under the pretence.   405
They have made me here to put the stone,
But now will I, that they be gone,
In bastard rhyme, after the doggrel guise,
Tell you whereof my name doth rise.

For Counterfeit Countenance known am I;   410
This world is full of my folly.
I set not by him a fly
That cannot counterfeit a lie,
Swear and stare, and bide thereby,
And countenance it cleanly,   415
And defend it mannerly.

A knave will counterfeit now a knight,
A lurden like a lord to fight,

418. fight] fyght *F;* syght *Ramsay.*

---

403. *fly-net*] butterfly net (*O.E.D.*, 1737).

405.] 'By professing to be Largesse'.

406. *put the stone*] hurl the stone; a reference to an athletic exercise, here a metaphor similar to 'throw one's weight about'.

407.] 'But now that they are gone, I will'.

408. *bastard*] debased, inferior.

after the doggrel guise] in the burlesque manner; *doggrel* = any sort of bad or irregular verse. Cf. the Host's words to Chaucer: 'Now swich a rym the devel I biteche! / This may wel be rym dogerel' (*Canterbury Tales*, VII. 924–5), and Puttenham's description: 'a rymer that will be tyed to no rules at all . . . such maner of Poesie is called in our vulgar, ryme dogrell' (*op. cit.* (p. 59, note 2), p. 76).

412.] 'I don't give a fig for him'. Proverbial; Whiting F344. See also 1711, 1890.

414. *stare*] look amazed, or perhaps 'glare'; 'swear and stare' often occurs as a doublet, see the citation from Hall under *O.E.D.* stare v. 3a, and 'They fors not to swere and starre' (*Wisdom*, 739). See *O.E.D.* 'staring' vbl. sb., ppl. a. for further examples.

415] 'And put on an innocent expression'.

416. *mannerly*] politely.

418. *lurden*] rogue.

to fight] If we understand 'to counterfeit' from 417, there is no reason to emend to *sight*, as Ramsay does. That *fight* recurs as a rhyme-word in 421 does not matter, since this is 'doggrel'.

A minstrel like a man of might,
A tappister like a lady bright: 420
Thus make I them with thrift to fight;
Thus at the last I bring him right
To Tyburn, where they hang on height.

To counterfeit I can by pretty ways:
Of nights to occupy counterfeit keys;   425
Cleanly to counterfeit new arrays;
Counterfeit earnest by way of plays;
Thus I am occupied at all assays.
Whatsoever I do, all men me praise,
And mickle am I made of, nowadays.   430

Counterfeit matters in the law of the land:
With gold and groats they grease my hand,
Instead of right that wrong may stand,
And counterfeit freedom that is bound.

425. keys] kayes *F*.   434. bound] bounde *F*.

---

420. *tappister*] tapster.

422. *him*] This should be seen in contrast with *them*, 421: 'I make those people spendthrifts, [and] bring *this* one to Tyburn, where they all hang.' For the change from plural to singular, cf. 350 ff., 1239 ff. (Possibly, however, F. *hym* is a misprint for *hem*, cf. 1261, 1366).

423. *Tyburn*] The place of public execution for Middlesex until 1783, situated at the junction of the present Oxford Street, Bayswater Road and Edgware Road.

424. *can*] know how.
pretty] ingenious.

425. *Of nights*] at night-time.
occupy] use (*O.E.D.* v. 5), or perhaps 'seize' (v.¹).

426. *arrays*] arrangements, states of affairs (*O.E.D.* sb. 9). Perhaps also 'clothing' (sb. 11), Countenance being disguised.

427. *plays*] jests.

428. *occupied*] employed (*O.E.D.* v. 6b), also 'used' (as a quality, by others).
at all assays] on every occasion.

432.] Cf. the proverb 'To grease a man in the fist'; Tilley M397 ('grease me in the hand' occurs in *Tide Tarrieth*, 493, not cited by Tilley).

434.] 'And what is bound [may] counterfeit freedom.'

I counterfeit sugar that is but sand;   435
Counterfeit capitans by me are manned;
Of all lewdness I kindle the brand.

Counterfeit kindness, and think deceit;
Counterfeit letters by the way of sleight;
Subtly using counterfeit weight;   440
Counterfeit language: *fayty bone geyte*.
Counterfeiting is a proper bait:
A count to counterfeit in a receipt—
To counterfeit well is a good conceit.

Counterfeit maidenhood may well be borne,   445
But counterfeit coins is laughing to scorn;
It is evil patching of that is torn,
When the nap is rough, it would be shorn.
Counterfeit halting without a thorn,

435. sand] sande *Ramsay;* founde *F.*   446. coins] coynes *F.*

---

436. *capitans*] captains.
manned] provided with followers (*O.E.D.* v. 3).

437. *lewdness*] wickedness.

439.] An aspect of Countenance's skill that was helpful to Fancy.

441. fayty bone geyte] Perhaps a corruption of 'faits et bons gestes'; an example of 'counterfeit language'.

443.] 'To fabricate a total [less than the true one] when receiving money.' If *receipt* = a *written* acknowledgement here, it considerably antedates the first entry under *O.E.D.* sb. 4c (1602).

444. *conceit*] notion, device.

445 ff.] This stanza contains obscene jokes (following from *counterfeit maidenhood*) on lost virginity.

446. *coins*] F. *coynes* could be modern *coyness*. *O.E.D.* gives the earliest occurrence as 1579, though cf. *make it coy*, 1248. But Skelton seems to intend a contrast, rather than a parallel, with *counterfeit maidenhood* in 445, hence my decision to print *coins*.
laughing to scorn] mockery or nonsense. (For the use of the form in *-ing* here and in 447, see Visser, I, p. 395.)

447.] 'It is difficult patching what is torn' (*O.E.D.* evil a. 4b).

449. *halting*] limping.
thorn] i.e. in the foot, with innuendo (see Partridge, p. 200: *thorn*).

Yet counterfeit chaffer is but evil corn,   450
All thing is worse when it is worn.

What would ye wives counterfeit
The courtly guise of the new jet?
An old barn would be underset;
It is much worth that is far-fet.   455
'What, wanton, wanton, now well ymet!'
'What, Margery Milk-duck, marmoset!'
It would be masked in my net,

452. counterfeit] counterfet *F*.   458. would] wolde *Dyce;* wolbe *F*.

---

450. *chaffer*] 'merchandise', with a pun on 'chaff'.

451. *thing*] See *O.E.D.* thing sb.[1] 11c: 'Privy member'.

worn] 'impaired by use', also 'put on', as of clothes, which Countenance comments on next.

453. *new jet*] latest fashion.

454. *underset*] propped up by a pole placed beneath: probably another obscene pun; *old barn* here is an image for the kind of woman Skelton sees as going in for the latest fashion.

455. *far-fet*] brought from far; i.e. (the women would say) foreign fashions are preferable. Cf. the proverb 'Far fetched and dear bought (is good for ladies)'; Whiting F58.

456–61.] In these lines Countenance mimics an exchange between a man (perhaps himself) and his mistress. He imitates their mutual greetings (456–7), then reports (458–60) in his own voice (but mimicking the lovers) the woman's desire for new clothes which she states her husband must pay for. This rather complicated use of reported speech is similar to that in Chaucer's *Shipman's Tale*: 'The sely housbonde, algate he moot paye / He moot us clothe, and he moot us arraye' (*Canterbury Tales*, VII. 11–12, the Shipman speaking). The sentiments are also similar.

456.] The woman speaking.

ymet] met.

457.] The man replying.

Margery Milk-duck] A term of (mock) endearment; cf. *Rummyng*, 418.

458–60.] Countenance speaking, mimicking the lover's view of his mistress.

458.] Cf. 'women have many lets, / And they be masked in many nets: / As frontlets, fillets, partlets, and bracelets; / And then their bonnets and their poignets: / By these lets and nets the let is such, / That speed is small when haste is much' (*The Four PP*, Farmer, *Heywood*, p. 36).

It] i.e. 'she' (*O.E.D.* It pron. 1b: 'used in childish language', and cf. 'go to it grandam, child. / Give grandam kingdom, and it grandam will / Give it a plum' (*John*, II.i.160–2)). The pronoun is used frequently in affectionate exchanges, of course.

masked] enmeshed.

It would be nice, though I say nay,
By creed, it would have fresh array,   460
'And therefore shall my husband pay'.
To counterfeit she will assay
All the new guise fresh and gay,
And be as pretty as she may,
And jet it jolly as a jay.   465

Counterfeit preaching, and belief the contrary;
Counterfeit conscience, peevish pope-holy;
Counterfeit sadness with dealing full madly;
Counterfeit holiness is called hypocrisy;
Counterfeit reason is not worth a fly;   470
Counterfeit wisdom, and works of folly;
Counterfeit countenance every man doth occupy.

Counterfeit worship outward men may see:
Riches rideth out, at home is poverty;
Counterfeit pleasure is borne out by me;   475
Coll would go cleanly, and it will not be,

466. belief] byleue *F*.

---

459. *nice*] smart (*O.E.D.* a. 2d); Countenance also means 'wanton' (2a).

460. *By creed*] in faith.

461.] The woman speaking.

465. *jet it*] strut about (wearing the 'new jet').

jolly as a jay] Cf. the proverb 'As merry as a pie'; Tilley P281.

466. *belief*] F's *byleue* could represent the verb 'believe'. Here the noun seems intended, as it contrasts with *preaching*; cf. the contrast of *wisdom* and *works*, 471.

467. *peevish pope-holy*] malignant hypocrite.

468. *sadness*] seriousness.

470. *not worth a fly*] worthless. Proverbial; Tilley F396. Cf. 412.

472.] 'Everyone uses counterfeit countenance'; probably also 'Counterfeit Countenance employs everyone' (see note on 428 for meanings of *occupy*).

473. *outward*] (qualifies *worship*, rather than *men*).

475. *borne out*] backed up (*O.E.D.* v. 3a).

476–7.] A marvellous description of two lovers pretending to behave 'nicely' and indulge in a bit of 'good clean fun', whose vulgarity nevertheless emerges.

Coll] abbreviation for Colin.

go cleanly] (1) be neat or elegant (*O.E.D.* go v. 6; clean a. 9, etc.) (2) copulate (or ejaculate?) innocently (Partridge, p. 115, *go*; *O.E.D*, cleanly adv. 1).

And Annot would be nice and laughs 'tehe wehe';
Your counterfeit countenance is all of nicety,
A plumed partridge all ready to fly.

A knuckleboniard will counterfeit a clerk: 480
He would trot gentilly, but he is too stark;
At his cloaked counterfeiting dogs doth bark;
A carter a courtier (it is a worthy work!)
That with his whip his mares was wont to yark,
A custrel to drive the devil out of the dark,   485
A counterfeit courtier with a knaves mark.

To counterfeit this, friars have learned me,
483. work] warke *F*.

---

477. *nice*] (1) refined, 'dainty' (*O.E.D.* a. 7 (1551)); (2) coy, shy (a. 5).

and laughs 'tehe wehe'] i.e. tries to laugh elegantly, but produces the opposite of 'nice' behaviour: cf. the laughter of Alisoun in the *Miller's Tale*: '"Tehee," quod she, and clapte the wyndow to' (*Canterbury Tales* I.3740); that of the students' horse in the *Reeve's Tale*, which chased after the mares 'forth with "wehee", thurgh thikke and thurgh thenne' (I.4066); and 'as wilde bestis with wehe worthen vppe and worchen, / And bryngeth forth barnes that bastardes men calleth' (*Piers Plowman*, VII, 91–2).

478.] Cf. 'My countenaunce is nycete' (*The Book of the Duchess*, 613).

nicety] excessive refinement (*O.E.D.* 5), but also wantonness or lust (2).

480 ff.] This verse seems to be aimed at some particular individual. Cf. *Coystrowne*, especially 'For Jak wold be a jentylman, that late was a grome' (42); 'Thys docter Deuyas commensyd in a cart' (55). *Carter* probably refers to Wolsey, see Intro., pp. 34ff.

480. *knuckleboniard*] Apparently a coinage of Skelton's. It might mean: (1) a knobbly-fingered person (who would write clumsily, therefore 'counterfeit a clerk'); (2) a player of the game of knucklebones (in which the bones were tossed up and caught in the same way as 'fivestones' or 'jacks'), i.e. a common gamester; (3) a clumsy fellow (the sense given in *O.E.D.* under 'knuckyl-bonyard'; cf. 'boinard', fool).

481. *gentilly*] elegantly.

stark] stiff. (The rhythm of this line imitates the knucklebonyard's awkward riding.)

484. *yark*] lash.

485. *custrel*] rogue.

487. *this*] i.e. this thing or action. Countenance might make some illustrative gesture here, using a different one to accompany *this* in the next line.

learned me] learned for or from me, if *me* is ethic dative; otherwise 'taught me' (*O.E.D.* v. 4). The former seems preferable, Countenance being the source and sum of all counterfeiting.

This, nuns now and then, and it might be,
Would take in the way of counterfeit charity,
The grace of God under *benedicite*; 490
To counterfeit their counsel they give me a fee.
Canons cannot counterfeit, but upon three;
Monks may not, for dread that men should them see.

> *Here let* FANCY *come in hurriedly with* CRAFTY
> CONVEYANCE, *gabbling many things together; finally*
> *on seeing* COUNTERFEIT COUNTENANCE *let* CRAFTY
> CONVEYANCE *say:*

Conveyance. What, Counterfeit Countenance!
Countenance. What, Crafty Conveyance! 495
Fancy. What the devil, are ye two of acquaintance?
　　　God give you a very mischance!
Conveyance. Yes, yes, sir, he and I have met.
Countenance. We have been together both early and late.
　　　But Fancy, my friend, where have ye been so long? 500

493.1–3.] *this ed.*; Hic ingrediatur fansy properantur cum crafty conueyaunce cum famina multa adinuicem garrulantes tandem viso counterfet countenaunce dicat crafty conueyaunce. *F*; . . . *properanter cum* CRAFTY CONUEYAUNCE, *cum famine multo* . . . *Dyce*.

---

488. *This*] another thing or action, differing from that suggested in the previous line.
　　and] if.
　489.] There may be an obscene friar/nun joke intended here, the 'charity' the nuns receive not being pure, but 'counterfeit'.
　490.] 'Under the pretext of [giving] the blessing of God's grace' (*O.E.D.* under prep. 16b).
　491.] 'They pay me to fabricate their advice for them' (?).
　492. *but upon three*] except for about three [of them] (*O.E.D.* upon prep. 3b). Meaning obscure.
　493.1–2. hurriedly . . . together;] My translation is based on the following emendation and punctuation of F: *properantur cum Crafty Conveyaunce famina multa adinvicem garrulantes* (see Collation).
　496.] We later learn that Fancy and Conveyance have been thinking about a suitable alias for Countenance (see 670); Fancy should not therefore be surprised that the other two are acquainted, and probably this line and 498 are ironic.
　497. *a very mischance*] extremely bad luck.

Fancy. By God, I have been about a pretty prong—
Crafty Conveyance, I should say, and I.

Conveyance. By God, we have made Magnificence to
eat a fly.

Countenance. How could ye do that, and was away?

Fancy. By God, man, both his pageant and thine he
can play.   505

Countenance. Say truth?

Conveyance.   Yes, yes; by lakin, I shall thee warrant,
As long as I live thou hast an heir parent.

Fancy. Yet have we picked out a room for thee.

Countenance. Why, shall we dwell together all three?

Conveyance. Why, man, it were too great a wonder   510
That we three gallants should be long asunder.

Countenance. [*To* CONVEYANCE] For cock's heart,
give me thy hand.

Fancy. [*To* COUNTENANCE] By the mass, for ye are able
to destroy an whole land.

Conveyance. [*To* FANCY] By God, yet it must begin
much of thee.

Fancy. Who that is ruled by us, it shall be long or he thee.   515

Countenance. [*To* CONVEYANCE] But I say, keepest
thou the old name still that thou had?

504. and was away] *F;* and [I] was away *Dyce.*

---

501. *prong*] trick, prank. Not in *O.E.D.* Dyce compares Dutch *pronk.* Cf. also
'howe at a pronge / We tourne ryght into wronge' (*Cloute*, 1196–7).

503.] i.e. we have caught Magnificence (like a fish); cf. the proverb 'The blind
eat many a fly'; Tilley B451. See also 1194.

504. *and was away*] if [I] was away. 'Skelton's greatest departure from normal
English usage is in his omission of the subject, usually of subject pronouns'
(*Diodorus*, II, p.xxxi; cf. 376, 773, etc.).

505. *pageant*] part (or trick). (*O.E.D.* sb. 1b, c).

506a.] Really?

507. *parent*] apparent; with a pun on 'parent'.

508. *room*] opportunity or scope to do something (*O.E.D.* sb.¹ 4), but
Countenance understands 'accommodation' (sb.¹ 2).

510–11.] Cf. 'hit were grete wonder / That I and thou shuld go in sonder'
(*Mactacio Abel*, 154–5, in *The Wakefield Pageants in the Towneley Cycle*, ed. A.
C. Cawley (1958), p. 5).

512. *cock's*] corruption of 'God's'.

515. *or he thee*] before he prospers.

Conveyance. Why, weenest thou, whoreson, that I
    were so mad?
Fancy. Nay, nay, he hath changed his, and I have
    changed mine.
Countenance. Now what is his name, and what is thine?
Fancy. In faith, Largesse I hight,   520
    And I am made a knight.
Countenance. A rebellion against nature:
    So large a man, and so little of stature!
    [*To* CONVEYANCE] But sir, how counterfeited ye?
Conveyance. Sure Surveyance I named me.   525
Countenance. Surveyance! Where ye survey
    Thrift hath lost her coffer key.
Fancy. But is it not well? How thinkest thou?
Countenance. Yes sir, I give God avow,
    Myself could not counterfeit it better.   530
    But what became of the letter
    That I counterfeited you underneath a shroud?
Fancy. By the mass, oddly well allowed.
Conveyance. By God, had not I it conveyed,
    Yet Fancy had been descrived.   535

525. *Conveyance.*] *Dyce; not in* F.   526. *Countenance.*] *Dyce;* Crafty conuey.
F.   527. key] kay *F.*   534. conveyed] conuayed *F.*   535. descrived]
dyscryued *conj. Dyce;* dysceyued *F.*

519.] Countenance already knows Fancy's assumed name (see 405). Presumably Skelton wishes to remind the audience what it is.

523.] Countenance puns on *large*: 'generous' and 'big', and *stature*: 'position' and 'size'.

527.] Cf. the proverb 'Kit has lost her key'; Tilley K109 (1533).

529. *God avow*] promise to God.

531 ff.] It now becomes clear that the letter supposed to be from Circumspection was forged by Countenance. He had, of course, seen Magnificence reading the letter (see 324.1), and wonders what it has achieved.

532. *underneath a shroud*] under a disguise (*O.E.D.* sb.[1] 6 (1558)). Countenance had 'disguised' the letter by claiming it was written by Circumspection.

533. *oddly well allowed*] remarkably well received (*O.E.D.* oddly adv. 3; allow v. 3).

534–5.] Conveyance wishes to claim his share of the credit.

conveyed] If *it* = the letter, this means either 'carried' or, more probably 'stolen' (*O.E.D*, v. 4, 6b). But perhaps *it conveyed* = 'managed things' (v.12).

535. *descrived*] found out. For the rhyme (F *conuayed/dyscryved*) on an unstressed final syllable, cf. 675/6, 725/7/8, 1348/50, 1848/9.

Countenance. I wot thou art false enough, for one.
Fancy. By my troth, we had been gone,
           And yet in faith man, we lacked thee
           For to speak with Liberty.
Countenance. What, is Largesse without Liberty?   540
Conveyance. By Measure mastered yet is he.
Countenance. What, is your conveyance no better?
Fancy. In faith, Measure is like a tetter
           That overgroweth a man's face,
           So he ruleth over all our place.   545

            [COUNTENANCE *starts to walk away in disgust.*]

Conveyance. Now therefore, whilst we are together—
               Counterfeit Countenance, nay, come hither—
               I say whilst we are together in same—
Countenance. Tush, a straw! It is a shame
               That we can no better than so.   550
Fancy. We will remedy it, man, or we go;
           For like as mustard is sharp of taste,
           Right so a sharp fancy must be found
           Wherewith Measure to confound.
Conveyance. Can you a remedy for a tisic,   555

---

537. *gone*] ruined.

538–9.] Fancy realises it is best not to give all the credit to Conveyance, and tactfully suggests that the help of Countenance was also required. Countenance and Liberty were played by the same actor, so could not meet. See Intro., p. 48.

540.] Since *largesse* = 'freedom of expenditure', Countenance is surprised that 'Largesse' does *not* have Liberty.

541.] True 'largesse', however, is dealt in moderation; see Intro., pp. 26–7.

543. *tetter*] skin disease.

548. *in same*] together.

550. *can*] know.

552.] Cf. the proverb 'As strong as mustard'; Tilley, M1332 (1659). A line may be wanting to rhyme with this. 'In view of the number of single unrimed lines among the couplets . . . it seems unnecessary to suppose that a line has fallen out; the case is, however, different with the more strictly handled stanzas' (Ramsay, p. 18). See notes on 745, 1116, 1180, 2083, 2251, 2277; 1337, 2436, 2462 ff., 2496.

555. *Can you*] do you know.

tisic] lung or throat infection, such as a cough or asthma.

That showeth yourself thus sped in physic?
Countenance. It is a gentle reason of a rake!
Fancy. For all these japes yet that we make—
Conveyance. Your fancy maketh mine elbow to ache.
Fancy. Let see find you a better way.   560
Countenance. [*To* FANCY] Take no displeasure of that
    we say.
Conveyance. Nay, and you be angry and overwhart
    A man may beshrew your angry heart.
Fancy. Tush, a straw! I thought none ill.
Countenance. What, shall we jangle thus all the day still?   565
Conveyance. Nay, let us our heads together cast.
Fancy. Yea, and see how it may be compassed
    That Measure were cast out of the doors.
Countenance. Alas, where is my boots and my spurs?
Conveyance. In all this haste whither will ye ride?   570

558. we make] *F;* ye make *Dyce.*   569. spurs] spores *F.*

556.] 'Who show yourself so versed in medicine'. Conveyance is referring ironically to Fancy's image of mustard (a traditional remedy for colds, etc.), also to his small size and pallid complexion (see 259–60), which suggest that he is in need of 'physic' himself.

557.] 'It is a fine argument from a skinny man' (for *reason* see note on 99; *O.E.D.* rake sb.¹ 1c, (1582)). Cf. 'Lo, here a parfit resoun of a goos!' (*Parlement of Fowles*, 568) 'Her is a gentil reson of an Hors!' ('The Debate of the Horse, Goose and Sheep,' 477, Lydgate, *Minor Poems*, p. 559).

558.] Fancy probably intends to say that they should stop joking and get to work. (It does not seem necessary to follow Dyce by emending *we* to *ye*; Fancy wishes to associate himself with the joking, not to admit that he is the butt of it.)

559.] i.e. Fancy has given him another pain for which he can diagnose the remedy.

560.] i.e. than 'confounding' Measure with a 'sharp fancy' like mustard.
Let see find you] let's see you find.

562. *overwhart*] cross.

563. *beshrew*] curse.

565. *jangle*] squabble.

566.] Cf. the proverb 'They laid their heads together'; Tilley H280. See also 2200.
cast] put.

567. *compassed*] contrived.

568. *out of the doors*] out (*O.E.D.* door 5). Later, Measure is literally cast out of the 'doors'; see 1726.

569.] Countenance is anxious to get to work.

Countenance. I trow it shall not need to abide.
    Cock's wounds! See, sirs, see, see!

Here let CLOAKED COLLUSION *come in with a haughty
    expression, strolling up and down.*

Fancy. Cock's arms, what is he?
Conveyance. By cock's heart, he looketh high;
    He hawketh, me think, for a butterfly.   575
Countenance. [*To* COLLUSION] Now, by cock's heart,
    well abidden,
    For had you not come I had ridden.
Collusion. Thy words be but wind, never they have
    no weight;
    Thou hast made me play the John de Height.
Countenance. And if ye knew how I have mused   580
    I am sure ye would have me excused.

572.1–2.] Hic ingrediatur cloked colusyon cum elato aspectu deor-sum et
sursum ambulando. *F.*   578. weight] wayght *F.*   579. John de Height]
this ed.; Iurde hayte *F.*

571.] 'I don't believe there is any need to stay', a litotes for 'I think we ought to
get going'.

572.] Countenance draws their (and the audience's) attention to Collusion.
On the 'heralded' entry in *Magnificence*, see Southern, pp. 189–94.

572.1–2 with a haughty expression] Cf. 1693.2, and see Intro., p. 29.

574. *he looketh high* 'he looks haughty', also 'he's looking upwards' ('he has
his head in the air').

575.] Proverbial; Tilley H231.
hawketh] hunts.
butterfly] See Intro., p. 41, note 130.

576. *abidden*] awaited.

577.] Countenance was going to ride away (see 569), till he saw Collusion
coming (perhaps he intended to fetch him).

578. *Thy words be but wind*] your words mean nothing. Proverbial; Tilley,
W833; see notes on 984–5, 1819.

579. *John de Height*] John High, or Mr High, cf. 'he looketh high' (574).
Collusion is complaining that he had to act superior in order to attract attention.
F's obscure 'Iurde hayte' is emended (to *John de hayte* in the original spelling) by
analogy with John de Gay, 959 (*O.E.D.* John 4: 'Prefixed to another word so as
to form a name or nickname'; cf. *Sir John Double-Cloak*, 605, John a Bonam,
1206, and see note on 917). For *hayte*, 'high', see *O.E.D.* height a.; for the
rhyme (F *wayght/hayte*), cf. 960–1.

580. *mused*] meditated (perhaps on some plan they had concocted).

Collusion. [*Aside to* COUNTENANCE] I say, come
     hither; what are these twain?
Countenance. By God, sir, this is Fancy small-brain,
     And Crafty Conveyance, know you not him?
Collusion. 'Know him, sir?' quod he! Yes, by Saint Sim!   585
     Here is a leash of ratches to run an hare.
     Woe is that purse that ye shall share.
Fancy. What call ye him, this?
Conveyance. I trow that he is—
Countenance. Tush, hold your peace!   590
     [*To* COLLUSION]. See you not how they press
     For to know your name?
Collusion. Know they not me? They are to blame.
     [*To* FANCY *and* CONVEYANCE] Know you not
       me, sirs?
Fancy.   No indeed.
Conveyance. Abide . . . let me see.
     [*Peers at* COLLUSION] Take better heed—   595
     Cock's heart, it is Cloaked Collusion!
Collusion. Ah sir, I pray God give you confusion.
Fancy. Cock's arms, is that your name?
Countenance. Yea, by the mass, this is even the same
     That all this matter must undergrope.   600
     [*Examining* COLLUSION's *clothes*] What is this?
     He weareth a cope!

597. confusion] confusyon *Dyce;* coufusyon *F*.   601. this? . . . cope!] *this
ed.;* this he wereth, a cope? *Dyce.*

---

585. *Sim*] Simon.
586. *ratches*] hunting dogs.
run] pursue, follow the scent of (*O.E.D.* v. 34b (1607)).
600. *undergrope*] investigate.
601.] Collusion is probably wearing two layers (see 603, and *Double-Cloak,*
605). A *cope* may be any long cloak or cape (*O.E.D.* sb. 1), but Fancy's question
in 604 suggests that Collusion's *cope* is of the ecclesiastical variety (sb. 2). This
line could be punctuated *What is this he weareth? A cope!* (see Collation for
Dyce's version). But the pause or caesura normally falls in the middle of a line.

Collusion. Cap, sir, I say; you be too bold.
Fancy. See how he is wrapped for the cold:
    Is it not a vestment?
Collusion.   Ah, ye want a rope.
Countenance. [*To* FANCY] Tush, it is Sir John Double-
    Cloak.   605
Fancy. Sir, and if ye would not be wroth—
Collusion. What sayst?
Fancy.   Here was too little cloth.
Collusion. Ah, Fancy, Fancy, God send thee brain.
Fancy. Yea, for your wit is cloaked for the rain.
Conveyance. Nay, let us not clatter thus still.   610
Collusion. Tell me, sirs, what is your will?
Countenance. Sir, it is so that these twain
    With Magnificence in household do remain,
    And there they would have me to dwell;
    But I will be ruled after your counsel.   615
Fancy. Marry, so will we also.
Collusion. But tell me whereabout ye go.

602. Cap, . . . you] *this ed.;* Cappe, syr; I say you *Dyce;* Cappe, Syr? I say you
Ramsay.   605. Double-Cloak] double cloke *F;* Double-Cope *Ramsay.*   614. have] haue *Dyce;* hane *F.*

---

602. *Cap*] If this = 'a cloak with a hood' (*O.E.D.* sb.[1] 2), Collusion's reply
means 'I'm *not* wearing an ecclesiastical cope; it's only a cloak'. But *cap* may
mean any sort of headgear, including the ensign of the cardinalate, the cardinal's
biretta (sb.[1] 3d (1591)), so Collusion may be implying 'Not *merely* a cope, but a
[cardinal's] cap', i.e. 'you'd better treat me with respect'. If this is so there is
pointed reference to Wolsey. A *biretta* of some variety is probably indicated by a
later stage direction; see note on 748.1. Views differ as to how this line should be
punctuated (see Collation). I place the semicolon after *say*, as that is where the
caesura falls; see note on 601.

604 b.] i.e. to hang yourself with.

605. *Sir John Double-Cloak*] refers to Collusion's layers of clothing, and also to
his *double-dealing*, cf. 696. For the use of *John*, see notes on 579, 917, 1188. (F
rope/cloke have rhyme on the vowel; there seems insufficient reason to
emend *cloke* to *cope* as does Ramsay; cf. 1048/9, 1189/90, 1264/5. There are
several examples in the play of rhyme on internal vowels but not on final
consonants; cf. 1048/9, 1351/2, 1652/3, 2021/2, 2380/1.)

607 b.] 'You didn't use enough material' (ironic).

609. *cloaked for the rain*] pretended or mocking. Proverbial; Tilley C417.

610. *clatter*] talk idly.

617.] 'But tell me your plans'.

Countenance. By God, we would get us all thither.
    Spell the remenant, and do together.
Collusion. Hath Magnificence any treasure? 620
Conveyance. Yea, but he spendeth it all in measure.
Collusion. Why, dwelleth Measure where ye two dwell?
    In faith, he were better to dwell in hell.
Fancy. Yet where we wone now, there woneth he.
Collusion. And have you not among you Liberty? 625
Countenance. Yea, but he is a captivity.
Collusion. What the devil, how may that be?
Countenance. I cannot tell you; why ask you me?
    Ask these two that there doth dwell.
Collusion. [*To* CONVEYANCE] Sir, the plainness you
    me tell. 630
Conveyance. There dwelleth a master men calleth
    Measure—
Fancy. Yea, and he hath rule of all his treasure—
Conveyance. [*To* FANCY] Nay, either let me tell, or
    else tell ye.
Fancy. I care not, I; tell on for me.
Countenance. I pray God let you never to thee. 635
Collusion. What the devil aileth you? Can you not
    agree?
Conveyance. I will pass over the circumstance
    And shortly show you the whole substance:

630. *Collusion.*] *Dyce;* Crafty conuey *F.*   you me tell] *conj. Dyce;* you tell me
F.   631. *Conveyance.*] *Dyce; not in F.*
633. *Conveyance*] Crafty conuey. *F(BL);* Crafty onucey. *F(CUL).*

619.] 'Tell the rest of it, and [let us] do something together.' (*O.E.D.* spell v.[1]
2). Countenance has been anxious to get going since 569. Ramsay, however,
glosses *spell* as 'expel' and would render 'expel the remainder' (i.e. of those at
court).
    626. *a captivity*] in captivity (*O.E.D.* A prep.[1] 4).
    627.] Liberty should not be in captivity by definition (and is not), but, being
ruled by Measure, seems so to the Vices.
    630. *plainness*] the plain truth.
    632. *his*] i.e. Magnificence's.
    634. *for me*] as far as I am concerned (*O.E.D.* for 26b).
    637. *circumstance*] circumlocution (*O.E.D.* sb. 6).

Fancy and I, we twain,
With Magnificence in household do remain,   640
And counterfeited our names we have
Craftily all things upright to save;
His name Largesse, Surveyance mine;
Magnificence to us beginneth to incline
Counterfeit Countenance to have also,   645
And would that we should for him go—
Countenance. But shall I have mine old name still?
Conveyance. Peace, I have not yet said what I will.
Fancy. Here is a 'pistle of a postic!
Collusion. Tush, fonnish Fancy, thou art frantic.   650
    [*To* CONVEYANCE] Tell on, sir; how then?
Conveyance. Marry, sir, he told us when
    We had him found we should him bring,
    And that we failed not for nothing.
Collusion. All this ye may easily bring about.   655
Fancy. Marry, the better and Measure were out.
Collusion. Why, can ye not put out that foul freke?
Conveyance. No; in every corner he will peek
    So that we have no liberty,
    Nor no man in court but he,   660
    For Liberty he hath in guiding.
Countenance. In faith, and without Liberty there is no
        biding.
Fancy. In faith, and Liberty's room is there but small.

---

642. *all things upright to save*] to keep everything correct (*O.E.D.* upright a.
9b).

649.] 'Here's a tale from a tail'.

'pistle] epistle.

postic] back, behind (from Lat. *posticus*). *O.E.D.* gives only the adjective,
(1638), F *postyke* is considered there a variant of *potstick*: 'a stick for stirring
porridge or anything cooked in a pot'.

650. *fonnish*] foolish.

652–4.] Fancy and Conveyance 'found' Countenance at 493, and he has been
ready to leave since 569, so they have been wasting a considerable amount of
time.

657. *freke*] fellow.

662. *biding*] staying, or perhaps 'tolerating' (the situation) (*O.E.D.* v. 9).

663. *room*] position, authority (*O.E.D.* sb.[1] 12b).

Collusion. Hem; that like I nothing at all.

Conveyance. But Counterfeit Countenance, go we
     together   665
  All three, I say.

Countenance.   Shall I go? Whither?

Conveyance. To Magnificence with us twain,
  And in his service thee to retain.

Countenance. But then, sir, what shall I hight?

Conveyance. [*To* FANCY] Ye and I talked thereof
     tonight.   670

Fancy. Yea, my fancy was out of owl-flight,
  For it is out of my mind quite.

Conveyance. And now it cometh to my remembrance:
  Sir, ye shall hight Good Demeanance.

Countenance. By the arms of Calais, well conceived.   675

Conveyance. [*To* COLLUSION] When we have him
    thither conveyed,
  What and I frame such a sleight
  That Fancy, with his fond conceit,
  Put Magnificence in such a madness
  That he shall have you in the stead of sadness,   680
  And Sober Sadness shall be your name?

---

665. *Conveyance.*] *Dyce; not in F.*   667. *Conveyance.*] *Dyce;* Cloked colusyon
F.   675. conceived] conceyued *F.*   676. conveyed] conuayed *F.*

666b. *Shall I go?*] Probably 'am I to go at *last*?', but perhaps Countenance is
perversely reluctant, now that the time has come.

670. *tonight*] this evening.

671. *of owl-flight*] during the twilight. For *owl-flight*: 'dusk' or 'dark', cf. 'in
the howll-flyght let hym passe' (*Mankind*, 571); 'He ran away by nyght / In the
owle flyght' (*Albany*, 311–12); *O.E.D.* owl-light. Fancy may be thinking,
though, of his own 'owl', the hawk he brings on when he returns (see note on
921). 'To walk by owl-light' is proverbial; Tilley O98 (1659).

675. *By the arms of Calais*] Possibly the people of Calais were not notorious for
'good demeanance' (cf. 346 ff.).

675–6.] For the rhyme (F *conceyued/conuayed*), cf. 534–5.

677. *frame*] contrive.

678. *fond conceit*] foolish thought or disposition (*O.E.D.* conceit sb. 1, 2c), or
even 'foolish fancy' (sb. 7).

681. *Sadness*] seriousness.

Collusion. By cock's body, here beginneth the game!
　　For then shall we so craftily carry
　　That Measure shall not there long tarry.
Fancy. For cock's heart, tarry whilst that I come again.　685
Conveyance. We will see you shortly, one of us twain.
Countenance. Now let us go and we shall, then.

　　　[*Exit* FANCY, CONVEYANCE, *and* COUNTENANCE.]

Collusion. Now let see quit you like pretty men.

　　　　　Here he walks about.

　　To pass the time another while, a man may talk
　　Of one thing and other to occupy the place;　　　690
　　Then for the season that I here shall walk,
　　As good to be occupied, as up and down to trace
　　And do nothing; howbeit full little grace
　　There cometh and groweth of my coming,
　　For cloaked collusion is a perilous thing.　　　695

　　Double-dealing and I be all one;
　　Crafting and hafting contrived is by me:
　　I can dissemble, I can both laugh and groan;
　　Plain-dealing and I can never agree;

687.1.] *Ramsay.*　　688.1.] Hic deambulat. *F.*　　689. another] *this ed.; and*
order *F.*

---

　683. *carry*] manage.
　688. *let see quit you*] let's see you acquit yourselves.
　688.1.] Collusion 'walks about' the *place* (690). See note on 239.1.
　689. *another*] Based on emendation of F to *an oder* (see Collation).
　690. *occupy*] make use of.
　691. *season*] time.
　692. *occupied*] employed, busy.
　trace] tread.
　696.] Collusion's 'double-dealing' is expressed in this speech by a frequent use
of doublets: *crafting and hafting, hurt and hinder, to spy and to point, I gape and I
gasp, to flatter and to flery*, as well as by antithesis.
　697. *Crafting*] trickery.
　hafting] trickery.

But division, dissension, derision: these three 700
And I am counterfeit, of one mind and thought,
By the means of mischief to bring all things to
   nought.

And though I be so odious a guest
And every man gladly my company would refuse,
In faith, yet am I occupied with the best, 705
Full few that can themself of me excuse;
When other men laugh then study I and muse,
Devising the means and ways that I can
How I may hurt and hinder every man.

Two faces in a hood covertly I bear; 710
Water in the one hand, and fire in the other;
I can feed forth a fool and lead him by the ear;
Falsehood-in-Fellowship is my sworn brother;
By cloaked collusion, I say, and none other
Cumberance and trouble in England first I began, 715
From that lord to that lord I rode and I ran,

700–2. *these three . . . nought*] these three and I are dissembling, [and] all of the same intention, [which is] to use evil to reduce everything to nothing.

701. *am*] Singular following *I*, though *these three* (700) are also part of its subject. Cf. 24.

703. *guest*] fellow (*O.E.D.* sb. 4).

705. *occupied with*] used or employed by.

707. *study*] ponder.

709. *hinder*] harm.

710.] Proverbial; Tilley F20. But cf. particularly Skelton's description of the character Dissimulation in *Bowge*: 'Than in his hode I sawe there faces tweyne' (428). He has a knife with mischief written on it in one sleeve, and a spoon of honey in the other 'to fede a fole', cf. 712 here. He also wears a *cope*, like Collusion. Another use of the proverb relevant to this play's theme is 'And he that euer of mesure takith counsaile, / Can nat shewe in one hoode two visages' (Lydgate, 'Song', 75–6). See also *Rede me*, p. 76.

711.] Cf. the proverb 'Water and fire are contrarious'; Whiting W83.

712. *feed forth*] beguile (*O.E.D.* v. 2b).

lead . . . by the ear] 'keep in abject dependence' (*O.E.D.* ear sb.[1] 1c), cf. 'a man of your behaving / Should have alway sufficient cunning / . . . To guide himself everywhere; / And not to be led by the ear' (*Nature*, Farmer, *Tudor Plays*, p. 74). Cited as proverbial by Whiting (E9), but with only these two examples.

715. *Cumberance*] annoyance.

And flattered them with fables fair before their face,
And told all the mischief I could behind their back,
And made as I had known nothing of the case.
(I would begin all mischief, but I would bear no lack).   720
Thus can I learn you, sirs, to bear the devil's sack,
And yet I trow some of you be better sped than I
Friendship to feign and think full litherly.

Paint to a purpose good countenance I can,
And craftily can I grope how every man is minded;   725
My purpose is to spy and to point every man;
My tongue is with favel forked and tined;
By Cloaked Collusion thus many one is beguiled.
Each man to hinder I gape and I gasp;
My speech is all pleasure, but I sting like a wasp.   730

I am never glad but when I may do ill,
And never am I sorry but when that I see
I cannot mine appetite accomplish and fulfil
In hinderance of wealth and prosperity;
I laugh at all shrewdness and lie at liberty;   735

725. minded] mynded *F*.   727. tined] tyned *F*.   728. beguiled] begyled
F.

---

717. *fables*] lies.
720. *lack*] blame (*O.E.D.* sb.¹ 2b).
721. *learn*] teach (*O.E.D.* v. 4).
to bear the devil's sack] i.e. to assist the devil in his work. Proverbial; Tilley
D318.
722. *better sped*] more accomplished (*O.E.D.* v. 8).
723. *litherly*] wickedly.
724. *Paint to a purpose*] feign for a certain effect.
725–8. *minded . . . tined . . . beguiled*] For the rhyme (F *mynded* / *tyned* /
begyled) cf. 534–5.
725. *grope*] probe.
726. *point*] point out, indicate ('inform on') (*O.E.D.* v.¹ 10).
727. *favel*] flattery.
tined] pronged.
729. *gape*] desire eagerly (*O.E.D.* v. 4).
gasp] long for (*O.E.D.* v. 2).
735. *shrewdness*] wickedness.
at liberty] freely.

I muster, I meddle among these great estates;
I sow seditious seeds of discord and debates.

To flatter and to flery is all my pretence,
Among all such persons as I well understand
Be light of belief and hasty of credence;   740
I make them to startle and sparkle like a brand;
I move them, I maze them, I make them so fond
That they will hear no man but the first tale;
And so by these means I brew much bale.

Here let COURTLY ABUSION *come in singing.*

Abusion. Huffa huffa, taunderum taunderum tayne, huffa   745
       huffa!

739. understand] vnderstonde *F*.   741. brand] bronde *F*.   744.1] Hic
ingrediatur courtly abusyon cantando. *F*.

---

736. *muster*] display myself.
738. *flery*] smile obsequiously (= 'fleer').
pretence] hypocritical purpose (see note on 405).
740. *Be*] to be.
light] easy.
741. *startle*] start.
742. *move*] disturb.
maze] bewilder.
743.] 'That they will hear no man speak except the first' (*O.E.D.* tale v. 5), i.e.
'they will not believe the truth, once they have been told a lie'. Or perhaps *tale* is
a noun: 'they will hear no man, only the first story'. Cf. the proverb 'One tale is
good till another be told'; Tilley T42 (1593) and contrast 'A man should hear all
parts ere he judge any'; Tilley M299 (1546).
744.1. singing] Courtly Abusion's opening words consist of a jumble of
snatches from popular lyrics of the time; see notes on 745, 747.
745.] This might be a continuation of the stage direction (cf. 778.1, 910.1),
especially as it is extra to the rhyme scheme. But see note on 552.
Huffa, huffa] From a lost lyric *huffa gallant*, phrases of which are frequently
sung by Vices in the interludes. Cf. 'Hof, hof, hof, a frysch new galavnt'
(Curiosity in *Mary Magdalen*, 491); 'Make room, sirs, and let us be merry, /
With huffa gallant, sing tirl on the berry' (Sensuality in *The Four Elements*,
Dodsley, I, p. 20); '"There goeth a rutter," men will say; / "A rutter, huffa
gallant!"' (Pride in *Nature*, Farmer, *Tudor Plays*, p. 77); 'Huff, huff, huff! who
sent after me?' (Imagination in *Hickscorner*, Dodsley, I, p. 188); 'Huffa! huffa!
who calleth after me?' (Riot in *Youth*, Dodsley, II, p. 13). In the *Macro* MS a
sixteenth-century hand has written, 'Wythe hufa / Wythe huffa w^t huffa w^t huffa
onys agen / A gallant glorius' in the margin of fol. 117r. (see *Macro*, p. xxix). It

Collusion. [*To audience*] This was properly prated, sirs;
    what said a?
Abusion. Rutty bully, jolly rutterkin, heyda!
Collusion. De que pays este vous?

   And let him make as if he doffs his cap ironically.

Abusion. Deck your hofte and cover a louse.
Collusion. Say vous chaunter 'Venter tre dawse?'   750
Abusion. Wyda, wyda.
    How sayst thou, man; am not I a jolly rutter?

748.1.] *this ed.;* Et faciat tanquam exiat beretrum cronice. *F; exuat barretum ironice. conj. Dyce; exuat beretum ironice. Ramsay.*

---

was perhaps the same as the popular dance *Lusty Gallant* (see *O.E.D.*, which cites no reference earlier than 1569, however). Evidently used as a formula of introduction for 'gallants'; also, by Skelton, as a term of abuse: 'Huf a galante Garnesche' (*Garnesche* II, 16).

taunderum taunderum tayne] Probably a garbled version of *Taunder naken*, a popular Flemish tune, of which there is an arrangement by Henry VIII (Stevens, Index no. 292).

746. *properly prated*] splendidly uttered.

a] he.

747. Rutty bully] *Roti bouilli joyeulx* was a fifteenth-century *basse-dance*, which Skelton also refers to in *Coystrowne*: 'He lumbryth on a lewde lewte, Roty bully joyse' (29). It is also mentioned in the fifteenth-century Scots poem *Colkelbie Sow*; 'Sum ourfute sum orliance / Sum rusty bully w^t a bek' (*The Bannatyne Manuscript* ed. W. Tod Ritchie (1930), IV, p. 291). See Nan C. Carpenter, 'Skelton and Music: *Roti bully joys*', *R.E.S.*, VI (1955), pp. 279–284.

jolly rutterkin, heyda] *Hoyda, hoyda, joly rutterkin* appears in the Fairfax MS of *c.* 1500, with music by William Cornish. Dyce attributed the words of this lyric to Skelton. See Stevens, Index no. 115.

748.1 he doffs his cap ironically] Based on emendation of F to *exuat berettum ironice*. I follow Ramsay here (see Collation); *beret[t]um* is clearly correct in view of 'deck your hofte' (749): Collusion takes off his cap and Abusion asks him to put it on again. This may be ordinary headgear, but is probably a *biretta*: 'The square cap worn by clerics of the Roman Catholic church' (*O.E.D.*), since Collusion seems to be in ecclesiastical garb (see note on 601).

749. *Deck your hofte*] cover your head.

750.] i.e. 'savez vous chanter *Votre trey dowce*', another contemporary popular lyric, *Votre trey dowce regaunt plesaunt* (Stevens, Index no. 340). Either Collusion does not know the correct words, or he is punning on *ventre*, 'belly', and its associations with *roti boulli joyeulx*.

751.] Abusion's version of *oui oui*. No doubt Collusion and the audience are here treated to his rendering of *Votre trey dowce*.

752. *jolly rutter*] dashing gallant (with an allusion to the lyric *Rutterkin*).

Collusion. [*To audience*] Give this gentleman room,
    sirs; stand utter!
    By God, sir, what need all this waste?
    What is this, a beetle, or a botowe, or a buskin laced?   755
Abusion. What, weenest thou that I know thee not,
    Cloaked Collusion?
Collusion. And weenest thou that I know not thee,
    cankard Abusion?
Abusion. Cankard! Jack Hare, look *thou* be not rusty,
    For thou shalt well know I am nother dirty nor dusty.
Collusion. Dusty; nay, sir, ye be all of the lusty;   760
    Howbeit of scapethrift your cloaks smelleth
    musty.
    But whither art thou walking, in faith unfeigned?
Abusion. Marry, with Magnificence I would be retained.
Collusion. By the mass, for the court thou art a meet
    man:
    Thy slippers they swap it, yet thou foots it like a
    swan.   765

755. botowe] *conj. Dyce;* batowe *F.*

---

753. *utter*] further away.
754. *waste*] (referring to Abusion's dress) 'expenditure', with a pun on 'waist'; Abusion is very tightly laced, see 843 ff.
755. *beetle*] Dyce thought this meant 'cudgel', but Collusion is probably referring, as in the rest of this line, to one of Abusion's boots, which, intricately laced and shiny black, would resemble a beetle.
botowe] short boot (*O.E.D.* botew).
buskin] boot (usually knee-length).
757. *cankard*] tarnished (or 'rusty') fellow. *O.E.D.* cites this as a variant of cankered ppl. a, but the suffix -ard is a formative of common nouns (see *O.E.D.*), cf. *knucklebonyard* (480), *niggard* (388, 2489).
758. *Jack Hare*] proverbial name for a foolish, lazy fellow. See 'A Ballade of Jak Hare' (Lydgate, *Minor Poems*, pp. 445–8); *Hauke*, 270.
rusty] (1) morally foul or corrupt; (2) rough in appearance.
760. *all of the lusty*] very gaily dressed.
761.] 'Though your clothes—those of a spendthrift—smell stale'.
765. *slippers*] 'light covering for the feet', here an ironic reference to Abusion's boots.
swap it] flap about.
like a swan] ironic: swans do not *walk* gracefully. Cf. 'Fat as a whale, and walkynge as a swan', *Canterbury Tales*, III.1930. Cited as a proverb by Whiting, S936, but with only these two examples.

Abusion. Yea, so I can devise my gear after the courtly
    manner.

Collusion. So thou art personable to bear a prince's
    banner.

Abusion. By God's foot, and I dare well fight, for I will
    not start.

Collusion. Nay, thou art a man good enough, but for thy
    false heart.

Abusion. Well, and I be a coward, there is mo than I.   770

Collusion. Yea, in faith, a bold man and a hardy:
    A bold man in a bowl of new ale in corns.

Abusion. [*To audience*] Will ye see this gentleman is
    all in his scorns!

Collusion. But are ye not advised to dwell where ye spake?

Abusion. I am of few words, I love not to bark: 775
    Bear'st thou any room, or canst thou do aught?
    Canst thou help in favour that I might be brought?

Collusion. I may do somewhat, and more I think shall.

> *Here cometh in* CRAFTY CONVEYANCE *pointing with his
> finger, and saith: 'Hem, Collusion'.*

768. *Abusion.*] *Dyce; not in* F.   769. *Collusion.*] *Dyce;* Courtly abusyon
F.   770. *Abusion.*] *conj. Dyce;* Cloked colusyon F.   771. *Collusion.*] *conj.
Dyce;* Courtly abusyon F.   772. A bold] *conj. Dyce;* Cloked colusyon A bolde
F.   774. spake] *So* F.   775. bark] barke F; crake *Ramsay.*

---

768. *start*] flinch.

770. *there is mo than I*] i.e. 'you're one too'.

771. *hardy*] daring, bold.

772. *bold*] presumably with a pun on 'bowl[ed]'.

new ale in corns] ale as drawn off the malt? (*O.E.D.* corn sb.[1] 7). Chaucer's
Pardoner speaks boldly after drinking 'a draughte of corny ale' (*Canterbury
Tales*, VI.456).

773. *is*] who is. (See note on 504.)

scorns] insults.

774. *advised*] determined (*O.E.D.* ppl. a. 5).

775. *bark*] i.e. insistently, like a demanding dog. Ramsay emends to *crake*, for
the rhyme, but F. *spake / bark* has near rhyme, on its consonants, cf. 1310/11.

776. *Bear'st thou any room*] have you any authority (see note on 663).

778.1.] Conveyance remains 'yond' (779), at some distance from the others;
see Intro., pp. 44–5.

Abusion. Cock's heart, who is yond that for thee doth call?

Conveyance. [*Calling*] Nay, come at once, for the arms
    of the dice! 780

Abusion. Cocks arms, he hath called for thee twice.

Collusion. By cock's heart, and call shall again;
    To come to me I trow he shall be fain.

Abusion. What is thy heart pricked with such a proud
    pin?

Collusion. Tush, he that hath need, man, let him run. 785

Conveyance. Nay, come away man, thou play'st the
    caiser.

Abusion. [*Imitates* COLLUSION] 'By the mass; thou shalt
    bide my leisure.'

Conveyance. 'Abide, sir' quod he! Marry, so I do.

Abusion. He will come, man, when he may tend to.

Conveyance. What the devil, who sent for thee? 790

Collusion. Here he is now, man, mayst thou not see?

Conveyance. What the devil, man, what thou meanest?
    Art thou so angry as thou seemest?

Abusion. What the devil, can ye agree no better?

---

780. Conveyance] *Dyce;* Clokyd colusyon *F.*   785. run] rynne *F.*   787.
Abusion.] Courtly abusion *F; Cl. Col. Dyce.*

---

780. *for the arms of the dice*] 'Some cant exclamation' (Dyce, II, p. 247). Cf. 'by
the arms of Calais', 675, etc. But dice do not usually have 'arms', only numbers
of spots. Perhaps *arms* is printed in error, as it occurs in the next line, though this
sort of repetition is extremely common in the play; see 757–60 for the most
recent example.

783. *fain*] obliged.

784.] 'Why are you in such a proud frame of mind?' (Cf. *O.E.D.* pin sb.[1] 15:
'*to set the heart on a merry pin*', origin obscure.)

785.] Cf. the proverb 'Need makes the naked man run'; Tilley N77.

786. *thou play'st the caiser*] i.e. 'you're acting too superior' (*caiser* = emperor).
Cf. 'His countynaunce like a kayser. / My lorde is nat at layser' (*Why come*,
621–2).

787.] Abusion answers for Collusion, using his tone. (Dyce gives this line to
Collusion, however.)

788. *Abide*] wait.

789. *tend to*] give his mind to [it].

792. *thou meanest*] meanest thou.

Conveyance. What the devil, where had we *this* jolly
                  jetter?   795
Collusion. [*To* ABUSION] What sayst thou, man?
          Why dost thou not supplie,
     And desire me thy good master to be?
Abusion. Speakest thou to me?
Collusion. Yea, so I tell thee.
Abusion. Cock's bones, I ne tell can   800
          Which of you is the better man,
          Or which of you can do most.
Conveyance. In faith, I rule much of the roast.
Collusion. Rule the roast; thou wouldest, ye,
          As scant thou had no need of me.   805
Conveyance. Need; yes, marry, I say not nay.
Abusion. Cock's heart, I trow thou wilt make a fray.
Conveyance. Nay, in good faith, it is but the guise.
Collusion. No, for or we strike we will be advised twice.
Abusion. What the devil, use ye not to draw no swords?   810
Conveyance. No, by my troth; but crake great words.
Abusion. Why, is this the guise nowadays?
Collusion. Yea, for surety oft peace is taken for frays.
          [*Indicates* ABUSION] But sir, I will have this man
               with me.

804. thou wouldest, ye] thou woldest, ye *conj. Dyce;* ye thou woldest *F*.   807.
heart] ha[r]te *Dyce;* hate *F*.   809. twice] twyse *F*.

---

795. *jetter*] braggart (one who 'jets it', see note on 465).

796. *supplie*] supplicate.

800. *ne tell can*] cannot tell.

803. *rule . . . the roast*] have the authority (*O.E.D.* sb. 1b: 'none of the early
examples throw any light on the precise origin of the expression'). Proverbial;
Tilley R144.

805.] 'As if you had hardly any need of me'. (For *scant* = 'hardly', see *O.E.D.*
adv. B.1.)

807. *fray*] brawl.

808. *but the guise*] only the fashion.

809. *be advised*] think (*O.E.D.* ppl. a. 1).

811. *crake*] brag, boast. This 'guise' resembles the 'game of vapours' of
Bartholomew Fair: *every man to oppose the last man that spoke, whether it concern'd
him, or no* (IV.iv.28.1–2).

813.] A reference to taking surety of the peace. (See *Macro*, p. 214.)

Conveyance. Convey yourself first let see. 815

Collusion. [*To* ABUSION] Well, tarry here till I for you
    send.

Conveyance. Why, shall he be of your band?

Collusion. [*To* ABUSION] Tarry here; wot ye what I say?

Abusion. I warrant you I will not go away.

Conveyance. By Saint Mary, he is a tall man. 820

Collusion. Yea, and do right good service he can;
    I know in him no default
    But that the whoreson is proud and haut.

And so they go out of the place.

Abusion. [*Shouts after them*] Nay, purchase ye a pardon
    for the pose,
    For pride hath plucked thee by the nose 825
    As well as me. I would and I durst—
    But now I will not say the worst.

COURTLY ABUSION *alone in the place.*

    What now? Let see
    Who looketh on me
    Well round about, 830
    How gay and how stout
    That I can wear
    Courtly my gear.

---

817. band] bende *F*.

---

815. *let see*] let's see [you] (*O.E.D.* see v. 15a).

820. *tall*] fine, splendid (here used ironically).

823. *haut*] haughty.

824. *pose*] catarrh.

828. *Let see*] show ('often with ellipsis of personal object', *O.E.D.* v. 15a).

829. *Who*] (anyone) who.

831–2.] 'How brightly and splendidly I can wear' (adjectives used adverbially; for *stout*, 'splendid', see *O.E.D.* a. 1b).

833.] Either 'my outfit in a courtly manner' (if *courtly* is used adverbially, like *gay* and *stout*, 831) or 'my courtly outfit' (with inversion of adjective and possessive).

My hair busheth
So pleasantly,   835
My robe rusheth
So ruttingly;
Meseem I fly,
I am so light;
To dance delight.   840

Properly dressed
All point-device,
My person prest
Beyond all size
Of the new guise,   845

---

842. device] deuyse *F*.

---

834 ff.] The following verses have much in common with Barclay's account of 'newe fassions and disgised garmentes' in his translation of Brandt's *Ship of Fools* (1509), as Dyce observed. The word *abusion* is frequently used in his satire of court gallants. See *Ship*, esp. I, pp. 36–7. But satire of 'newfangledness' is very common in the interludes, from *Mankind's* Vices Newguise, Nowadays and Nought onwards.

834. *busheth*] grows thick like a bush, perhaps because he is wearing a wig. Cf. 'Another by pryde hys wit hath so obscure / To hyre the busshe of one that late is dede / Therwith to disgyse his folys dotynge hede' (*Ship*, II, p. 268); also the reference to gallants 'wyth your set Busshes Curlynge as men of Inde' (*Ship*, I, p. 37); 'My hair is royal and bushed thick' (*Youth*, Dodsley, II, p. 6).

836. *rusheth*] Probably 'flows quickly' (see *O.E.D.* v.^{2} 7), but perhaps 'rushes it' i.e. 'moves with spirit', see note on 846. Onomatopoeic; reflecting the swishing sound of Abusion's garments.

837. *ruttingly*] dashingly (in the manner of a 'rutter', see 752).

838–9.] Cf. 'I am so lyght me thinke I flee' (*Impatient Poverty*, Dir).

840.] Probably 'to dance I delight' (with pronoun omitted as frequently by Skelton, see note on 504), though perhaps we should see the phrase as analogous to 'to dance attendance' (cf. 'And, syr, ye must daunce attendaunce, / And take pacient sufferaunce', *Why come*, 625–6), *to dance delight* thus meaning something like 'to engage in pleasurable activity'. See also *she danceth variance* (2027).

842.] 'All quite correct'.

843. *prest*] brisk, sprightly (with a pun on 'pressed' = 'squeezed in').

844. *size*] (1) limit; (2) dimensions (*O.E.D.* sb.^{1} 6, 10).

To rush it out
In every rout.

Beyond measure
My sleeve is wide,
All of pleasure   850
My hose straight tied,
My buskin wide,
Rich to behold,
Glittering in gold.

Abusion   855
Forsooth, I hight.
Confusion
Shall on him light
By day or by night
That useth me;   860
He cannot thee.

A very fon,
A very ass,
Will take upon
To compass   865

---

846. *rush it out*] move or act with spirit? (*O.E.D.* v.² 6f; cf. *rusheth*, 836).
Rushing would be analogous to 'dashing': (1) 'rushing with impetuosity'
(*O.E.D* dash v.¹ 13); (2) 'stylish or swell' (*O.E.D.* dashing ppl. a. 3b). See also
1319.

847. *rout*] company.

848–9.] Cf. 'Theyr sleues blasinge lyke to a Cranys wynges'; (*Ship*, I, p. 36);
'have I such a short gown, / With wide sleeves that hang a-down— / They would
make some lad in this town / A doublet and a coat' (*Nature*, Farmer, *Tudor
Plays*, p. 67); 'All that doth that fashion wear / They have wings behind ready to
fly, / And a sleeve that would cover all the body' (*Fulgens*, I, 746–8).

848.] A reminder that Abusion is one of Measure's enemies.

850. *pleasure*] 'Lusty Pleasure' will be Abusion's assumed name, see 963.

854.] It is not clear whether this refers merely to Abusion's *buskin* (which
might have gold tassels or laces, for instance), or to his whole outfit.

859–60.] 'Who employs me by day or night'.

862. *fon*] fool.

864. *take upon*] undertake (*O.E.D.* v. 18b); the object seems omitted here by
analogy with 'take on'.

865. *compass*] attain to (*O.E.D.* v.¹ 11 (1549)).

That never was
Abused before.
A very poor

That so will do,
He doth abuse   870
Himself too too;
He doth misuse
Each man, t'accuse,
To crake and prate;
I befool his pate.   875

This new fon jet
From out of France
First I did fet;
Made purveyance
And such ordinance   880
That all men it found
Throughout England.

---

873. t'accuse] *this ed.;* take a fe *F;* to akuse *Ramsay.*   875. befool] befoule
F.   878. fet] *this ed.;* set *F.*   881. found] founde *F.*   882. England]
Englonde *F.*

---

866. *That*] what.

868. *poor*] insignificant person (adjective used substantively, see *O.E.D.* a.
(sb.) 7b, and cf. *lither,* 1268, *hunger,* 1345).

871. *too too*] excessively (*O.E.D.* too adv. 4).

873. *t'accuse*] i.e. to accuse, meaning 'making accusations' (*O.E.D.* v. 5). (F
take a fe is clearly corrupt both on grounds of sense and rhyme). The infinitive is
used here and in the next line where modern English would have a gerund; this is
quite common in Tudor English, see Visser, I, p. 333.

874.] 'Bragging and boasting (or talking idly)'.

875.] 'I call him a fool' (*pate:* a synecdoche for the whole person). Cf. *I befool
thy face* (1044), *I befool thy brain-pan* (1806), where the F spelling *befole* indicates
that *befool* rather than *befoul* is meant here by F *befoule.*

876. *fon jet*] foolish fashion.

877.] Cf. 'As I remember it was brought out of France' (*Ship,* I, p. 39).

879. *purveyance*] provision.

All this nation
I set on fire
In my fashion;   885
This their desire,
This new attire,
This ladies have;
I it them gave.

Spare for no cost—   890
And yet, indeed,
It is cost lost
Much more than need
For to exceed
In such array.   895
Howbeit, I say

A carl's son
Brought up of nought,
With me will wone
Whilst he hath aught;   900
He will have wrought
His gown so wide
That he may hide

His dame and his sire
Within his sleeve;   905

---

884. fire] fyre *Dyce;* fyre; *Ramsay.*   905. sleeve] slyue *F.*

---

885. *in my fashion*] 'in my way'; but *fashion*, in view of the context, must also
have the sense 'vogue or style' as it does in the quotation from *Fulgens* cited in
the note on 848–9. The earliest citation given in *O.E.D.* sb. 9 and 10 is 1568; cf.,
though, 3b: '"cut" or style' (1529).
   890.] Cf. *Enough*, 288.
   901–2. *have wrought* / *His gown*] have his gown made.
   904. *dame*] dam.
   905.] Cf. the proverb 'To have in one's sleeve'; Whiting S381. Skelton also
uses it in *Parrot* (speaking of Wolsey): 'He caryeth a kyng in hys sleve, yf all the
worlde fayle' (423). On Abusion's sleeves, see 848–9.

Spend all his hire
That men him give;
Wherefore I preve
A Tyburn check
Shall break his neck.   910

Here cometh in FANCY *crying 'Stow, stow'* [*to his hawk*].

All is out of har
And out of trace,
Ay war and war
In every place—
[*To* FANCY] But what the devil art thou   915
That criest 'Stow, stow'?

Fancy. What, whom have we here, Jenkin Jolly?
       Now welcome, by the God holy!
Abusion. What, Fancy, my friend, how dost thou fare?

---

908. *preve*] known by experience (*O.E.D.* prove v. 3). See note on 33.

909. *Tyburn check*] i.e. hanging; see note on 423 (*check* = 'A sudden arrest given to the career or onward course of anything by some obstruction or opposition' (*O.E.D.* sb. 5)).

910.1 *stow*] 'stop'; a falconer's cry to his hawk. Cf. 'The fauconer then was prest, / Came runnyng with a dow, / And cryed, Stow, stow, stow!' (*Hauke*, 71–3). Fancy is about to start on his soliloquy but is interrupted. He begins again with *Stow* at 966.

hawk] See note on 921.

911. *out of har*] out of joint. Proverbial; Whiting H144. See also 2096.

912. *trace*] step.

913. *war*] worse.

915.] Fancy is now dressed in fool's costume (see 1045), though Abusion is so concerned with his own array he makes no reference to this.

917. *Jenkin Jolly*] A contemptuous nickname, like *Sir John Double-Cloak*, 605, *Simkin Titivel and Piers Pickthank*, 1269, and *Colin Coward*, 2193, formed by adding a surname representative of vice to a familiar Christian name (see 579 for use of *John* in this manner). Such names were often used for characters in the interludes, see esp. *Ralph Royster Doyster*, which (besides the eponymous hero) contains a gallery of such figures as Matthew Merrygreek, Madge Mumblecrust, and Tib Talkapace. In *Jenkin Jolly* Skelton might have had in mind the lyric *Jolly Jankin* (*Secular Lyrics of the XIVth and XVth Centuries*, ed. R. H. Robbins (1952), pp. 21–2), which describes the sweetness, especially in singing (unlike that of Abusion), of a gay parish clerk.

Fancy. By Christ, as merry as a March hare.	920
Abusion. What the devil hast thou on thy fist, an owl?	
Fancy. Nay, it is a farly fowl.	
Abusion. Methink she frowneth and looks sour.	
Fancy. Turd, man, it is an hawk of the tower;	
She is made for the mallard fat.	925
Abusion. Methink she is well beaked to catch a rat.	
But now what tidings can you tell let see.	
Fancy. Marry, I am come for thee.	
Abusion. For me?	
Fancy. Yea, for thee, so I say.	
Abusion. How so? Tell me, I thee pray.	930
Fancy. Why, heard thou not of the fray	
That fell among us this same day?	
Abusion. No, marry, not yet.	
Fancy. What the devil! Never a whit?	
Abusion. No, by the mass. What, should I swear?	935
Fancy. In faith, Liberty is now a lusty spear.	

926. beaked] becked *F*.   935. What, should I] *this ed.;* what sholde I *Dyce;* what! sholde I *Ramsay*.

920.] Cf. the proverb 'As mad as a march hare'; Tilley H148. 'Masid as a marche hare, he ran lyke a scut' (*Garlande*, 632) is not cited.

921. *an owl*] It is not clear whether Fancy's bird is a hawk which resembles an owl, or an owl which resembles a hawk. He insists here that it is a a hawk (924), calls it a hawk at the beginning of his soliloquy (967), in 1113 and 1808; on the other hand he addresses it as an owl at 969 and Folly asks if it is an owl at 1046. I think that in 969 he has in mind Abusion's question here, and, assuming that the bird is 'really' a hawk, have placed *owl* (969) in inverted commas. But Fancy's different names for the bird reflect his own instability (*Now I will this and now I will that*, 1026), and the bird partly symbolises his own inconstant 'fancy' (see 970–1, also *my fancy was out of owl-flight*, 671). For possible associations of the hawk/owl with Wolsey, see Intro., p. 41.

922. *farly*] strange, wonderful.

924. *hawk of the tower*] high-flying hawk (see *O.E.D.* sb.¹ 8a: 'Lofty flight; soaring'); cf. 'Ientyll as fawcoun / Or hawke of the towre (*Garlande*, 1021–2).

925. *mallard*] wild drake.

927. *let see*] See note on 297.

935. *What, should I swear?*] What, do you want me to swear [I did not]. Alternatively, *What should I swear?* would mean '[By] what do you want me to swear'.

936. *spear*] soldier armed with a spear (*O.E.D.* sb.¹ 4).

Abusion. Why, under whom was he abiding?

Fancy. Marry, Measure had him awhile in guiding,

    Till, as the devil would, they fell a-chiding

    With Crafty Conveyance.

Abusion.   Yea, did they so?   940

Fancy. Yea, by God's sacrament, and with other mo.

Abusion. What, needed that, in the devil's date?

Fancy. Yes, yes; he fell with me also at debate.

Abusion. With thee also! What, he playeth the state?

Fancy. Yea, but I bade him pike out of the gate;   945

    By God's body, so did I.

Abusion. [*Ironically*] By the mass, well done and boldly.

Fancy. Hold thy peace! Measure shall from us walk.

Abusion. Why, is he crossed then with a chalk?

Fancy. Crossed? Yea, checked out of conceit.   950

Abusion. How so?

Fancy.   By God, by a pretty sleight,

    As hereafter thou shalt know more.

    But I must tarry here; go thou before.

Abusion. With whom shall I there meet?

937.] 'Why, at whose disposal was he?' (*O.E.D.* abide v. 15: 'To await submissively, await the disposal of, submit to'). Like Collusion in 627, Abusion is surprised that Liberty should ever have had to submit to any authority. An 'in' joke, since the same actor plays Abusion and Liberty; see Intro., p. 48.

939. *a-chiding*] quarrelling.

942. *needed that*] was that necessary.

in the devil's date] an imprecation = 'in the devil's time', used also in *Bowge*, 375, 455; cf. also 'Ryn God, rynne Devyll! yet the date of ower Lord / And the date of the Devyll dothe shrewlye accord' (*Parrot*, 438–9). Proverbial; Whiting, D200. See also 2173.

943. *at debate*] in contention.

944. *state*] lord, great man (*O.E.D.* sb. 24).

945. *pike out of the gate*] be off (*O.E.D.* pike v.³; gate sb.² 1b).

948. *walk*] go away (*O.E.D.* v.¹ 8).

949. *crossed*] cancelled, crossed out like a score in a game (*O.E.D.* v. 4), probably also 'thwarted' (v. 14 (*c.* 1555)).

950. *checked*] (1) 'marked with a pattern of crossing lines' (*O.E.D.* v.² 1), continuing the image in 'crossed with a chalk'; (2) 'put in check', continuing the game imagery; (3) restrained, curbed.

conceit] favour (*O.E.D.* sb. 5).

Fancy. Crafty Conveyance standeth in the street   955
    Even of purpose for the same.

Abusion. Yea, but what shall I call my name?

Fancy. Cock's heart! Turn thee, let me see thine array—
    Cock's bones, this is all of John de Gay!

Abusion. So I am pointed after my conceit.   960

Fancy. Marry, thou jettest it of height.

Abusion. Yea, but of my name let us be wise.

Fancy. Marry, Lusty Pleasure, by mine advice,
    To name thyself. Come off, it were done.

Abusion. Farewell, my friend.

                    [*Exit* ABUSION.]

Fancy.   Adieu till soon.   965
    Stow, bird, stow, stow.
    It is best I feed my hawk now.
    [*To the hawk*] There is many evil-favoured and
        thou be foul;
    Each thing is fair when it is young. All hail, 'owl'!

---

960. conceit] consayte *F.*   961. jettest] *this ed.;* Iettes *F.*   height] hyght
F.   963. advice] aduyse *F.*   964.1.] *Ramsay.*

---

955. *in the street*] outside (*O.E.D.* sb. 3). Conveyance might poke his head
through one of the doors here.

959. *John de Gay*] See note on 579.

960. *pointed*] (1) accoutred ('appointed', see *O.E.D.* appoint v. 15); (2) laced
(*O.E.D.* pointed ppl. a. 3), see 755; cf. *point-device*, 842.

conceit] fancy (see note on 678).

961. *jettest it*] See note on 465.

of height] loftily or haughtily; perhaps also literally 'highly', in view of
Abusion's boots.

963.] For the appropriateness of Abusion's counterfeit name, cf. 'In this
counterfeit kind of pleasure they put them that I spake of before, which, the
better gowns they have on, the better men they think themselves' (*Utopia*, p.
87).

964. *it were done*] it is done: 'A special kind of modality is found in those
sentences in which the preterite is used instead of the present tense in order to
render the statements less . . . blunt and more modest' (Visser, I, p. 295).

966.] See note on 910.1.

968. *evil-favoured*] ill-favoured.

foul] with a pun on 'fowl'.

969. *'owl'*] See note on 921.

[*To the audience*] Lo, this is   970
My fancy, ywis;
Now Christ it bless!
It is, by Jess,

A bird full sweet,
For me full meet;   975
She is furred for the heat
All to the feet;

Her brows bent
Her eyen glent;
From Tyne to Trent,   980
From Stroud to Kent,

A man shall find
Many of her kind.
How standeth the wind,
Before or behind?   985

Barbed like a nun
For burning of the sun;
Her feathers dun;
Well-favoured bonne.

---

972. bless] blysse *F*.   973. Jess] Iesse *F*.   986. nun] nonne *F*.   987.
sun] sonne *F*.   988. dun] don ne *F*.

970–1. *this is / My fancy*] (1) this is my delight or love (*O.E.D.* sb. 8b and 10
(1559), but cf. 1296, 1551, 2077); (2) this is my caprice (this is the quality I
represent in my name). See notes on 921, 984–5.

973. *By Jess*] 'by Jesus', with a pun on 'jess': 'strap fastened round the legs of a
hawk'.

979. *glent*] glowing.

980–1.] i.e. from north to south, from west to east (the river Tyne, between
Northumberland and Durham; Trent in Somerset, Stroud in Gloucestershire).

984–5.] Here Fancy holds out the bird, as if to test the direction of the wind by
its feathers, so making another connection between the bird and his fancy, for
'feathers in the wind' is a proverbial expression for nonsense; see note on 1819;
cf. also 578.

986. *Barbed*] wearing a 'barb', a white linen headdress often worn by nuns.
987. *For*] against.
989. *bonne*] good girl.

Now let me see about   990
In all this rout
If I can find out
So seemly a snout

Among this press,
Even a whole mess!   995
[*To someone in audience*] Peace, man, peace.
[*Aside*] I rede we cease.

So farly fair as it looks,
And her beak so comely crooks;
Her nails sharp as tenterhooks;   1000
I have not kept her yet three weeks.

And how still she doth sit!
Tuwhit, tuwhit.
Where is my wit?
The devil speed whit.   1005

998. looks] lokys *F*.   999. beak] becke *F*.   crooks] crokys *F*.   1000.
tenterhooks] tenter hokys *F*.   1001. weeks] wokys *F*.

---

990 ff.] Here Fancy makes a careful scrutiny of the audience. Cf. 'How look
their faces here round about? / All fair and clear they, everyone' (*Wit and
Science*, 822–3), where Wit tests his mirror by trying it on the audience. In *Like
Will to Like* the Vice Newfangle asks a member of the audience, 'What sayst thou
to it, Jone with the long snout?' (Dodsley, III, p. 317); cf. 993. See Craik, pp.
23–6.

994–5.] Cf. 'after this merry drinking / . . . There are no words among this
press' (*Fulgens*, I, 15, 17).

press] throng.

995. *mess*] 'company of persons eating together' (*O.E.D.* sb. 4).

996.] The audience would be expressing annoyance at having their 'snouts'
examined, but possibly Fancy addresses this line, like the next, to himself.

997. *rede*] advise.

999. *comely*] attractively ('in a comely fashion'; adjective used adverbially).

1005.] An imprecation, which could mean either 'The devil a jot of success' or
'May the devil prosper not a jot', depending on whether *speed* is noun or verb
(see *O.E.D.* sb. 3, v. 1; whit sb.[1] 1b: 'with negative expressed or implied'). Cf.
'For as for wytte, / The deuyll spede whitte!' (*Why come*, 1013–14); 'Think ye
that she will amend yet? / Nay, by our lady, the devil speed whit!' (*Johan Johan*,
Farmer, *Heywood*, pp. 67–8).

That was before I set behind;
Now too curteys, forthwith unkind;
Sometime too sober, sometime too sad,
Sometime too merry, sometime too mad;
Sometime I sit as I were solemn proud,   1010
Sometime I laugh over-loud;
Sometime I weep for a gewgaw,
Sometime I laugh at wagging of a straw;
With a pear my love you may win,
And ye may lese it for a pin.   1015
I have a thing for to say,
(And I may tend thereto), for play,
But in faith I am so occupied
On this half and on every side,
That I wot not where I may rest.   1020
First to tell you what were best?—
Frantic Fancy Service I hight;
My wits be weak, my brains are light;
For it is I that other while
Pluck down lead and theke with tile;   1025
Now I will this, and now I will that;

1006. *That*] what.

1007. *curteys*] polite.

1008. *Sometime . . . sometime*] on one occasion . . . on another occasion.

1010. *as*] as if.

solemn proud] grandly majestic (*O.E.D.* a. 10 gives this example as a combined adjective *solemn-proud*, but probably *solemn* is used adverbially, as commonly with many adjectives at this time, cf. 831–3, 999).

1012. *gewgaw*] a trifling thing.

1013.] Proverbial; Tilley W5.

wagging] swaying.

1015. *lese*] lose.

1017. *And I may tend thereto*] if I can apply myself to it (*O.E.D.* v.¹ 2).

1019. *On this half*] on this side.

1024. *other while*] another time.

1025. *Pluck down lead*] Cf. 'And plucke awaye the leedes / Evyn ouer theyr heedes' (*Cloute*, 410–11), part of a passage referring to the dissolution of the nunneries of Lillechurch and Bromehall, arranged by Wolsey, 1521–22 (see Kinsman, *Poems*, p. 187); 'He pluckedth downe the costly leades / That it maye rayne on saynctis heades' (*Rede me*, p. 113). If this line refers to Wolsey's activities it would date the play later than 1521. But it may not.

theke] cover (a roof).

Make a windmill of a mat;
Now I would and I wist what—
Where is my cap? I have lost my hat.
And within an hour after, 1030
Pluck down an house and set up a rafter;
Hither and thither, I wot not whither,
Do and undo both together;
Of a spindle I will make a spar;
All that I make forthwith I mar; 1035
I blunder, I bluster, I blow and I blother;
I make on the one day and I mar on the other;
Busy, busy, and ever busy,
I dance up and down till I am dizzy;
I can find fantasies where none is; 1040
I will not have it so, I will have it this.

Here let FOLLY *enter [leading a dog], shaking a bauble and
making a commotion, beating on tables and suchlike.*

1041.1–2.] *this ed.;* Hic ingrediatur Foly quesiendo crema et faciendo multum
feriendo tabulas et similia. *F; . . .* FOLY *quatiendo crema . . . Dyce.*

1027.] Cf. 'For ye said, that he said, that I said, wote ye what? / I made, he
said, a windmil of an olde mat' (*Tongues,* 12–13). The expression sounds
proverbial, but I have not found any other examples (*mat* = 'A piece of coarse
fabric formed by plaiting rushes . . . etc.' *O.E.D.* sb.[1] 1).

1028. *and I wist what*] if I knew what.

1032.] Cf. *John John,* 7–8 (Farmer, *Heywood,* p. 67).

1034.] Proverbial; Tilley S756.

spar] either a rafter (see 1031) or a pole (*O.E.D.* sb.[1] 1, 2).

1035.] Cf. the proverb 'Make or mar'; Tilley M48, and see 1037.

1036. *blunder*] stumble.

blother] babble nonsensically.

1038.] Cf. *Parrot,* 59; *Cloute,* 990–1.

1041.1. [leading a dog]] See 1053.

bauble] The reviewer of Dyce's edition of Skelton's poems in the *Gentleman's
Magazine* suggested that F *crema* was a Latinised version of Greek χρημα,
meaning 'his thing or *bauble*' (Dyce, II, p. 487). Dyce conjectured *cremia:* 'dried
sticks'.

1041.2. making a commotion] The convincing emendation *faciendo tumultum*
(F *faciendo multum*) was suggested to me by George Foster. Kinsman translates
F *doing much stage business* (*Poems,* p. 73).

beating on tables] i.e. the tables at which the audience are sitting in the hall.
Tabula, however, may mean any sort of 'board', and perhaps some kind of

Folly. [*To audience*] Masters, Christ save everychone!
    What, Fancy, art thou here alone?

Fancy. What, fonnish Folly, I befool thy face!

Folly. What, frantic Fancy, in a fool's case!   1045
    What is this, an owl, or a glede?
    By my troth, she hath a great head!

Fancy. Tush, thy lips hang in thine eyen;
    It is a French butterfly.

Folly. By my troth, I trow well;   1050
    But she is less a great deal
    Than a butterfly of our land.

Fancy. What pilled cur leadest thou in thy hand?

Folly. A pilled cur?

Fancy. Yea, so I tell thee, a pilled cur.   1055

Folly. Yet I sold his skin to Mackmurre
    In the stead of a budge fur.

Fancy. What, flayest thou his skin every year?

1044. befool] befole *F*.   1048. eyen] *F;* eye *Dyce*.

---

percussion instrument, such as cymbals or castanets, is meant (see Du Cange, *tabula*, 4, 7), in which case *feriendo tabulas* would mean 'beating on percussion instruments'. (Kinsman renders 'striking clappers', *Poems*, p. 73). Southern suggests *taburas*: 'drums' (pp. 184, 188). Alternatively, *feriendo* might be emended to *ferendo*, and the phrase translated 'bringing writings (documents, or a book)'. This reading might be defended in view of 1222 (see note) and 1295.

  1042. *everychone*] everyone.

  1044. *I befool thy face*] See note on 875.

  1045. *case*] clothing (*O.E.D.* sb.² 2).

  1046. *glede*] kite.

  1048.] i.e. 'You're talking too much to see properly.' Proverbial; Tilley L330. Dyce and Ramsay print *eye*, for the rhyme, but there is near-rhyme here, cf. 604/5.

  1051–2.] For the possible significance of this remark, see Intro., note 130.

  1053. *pilled*] threadbare, bald.

  cur] A frequent epithet for Wolsey, see Intro., p. 40.

  1056. *Mackmurre*] i.e. an Irishman. One of the Irish princes who opposed Perkin Warbeck in 1495 was named Macmurrough (see J. D. Mackie, *The Earlier Tudors* (1952), p. 125, also the extract from Hardyng's *Chronicle*, quoted in Dyce, II, p. 253). The point of Folly's remark seems to be a jibe at the poverty of the Irish, cf. Kinsman, *Poems*, p. 159.

  1057. *budge fur*] 'A kind of fur, consisting of lambskin with the wool dressed outwards' (*O.E.D.* budge sb.¹ 1).

Folly. Yes, in faith, I thank God I may hear.
Fancy. What, thou wilt cough me a daw for forty pence? 1060
Folly. Marry, sir, Cockermouth is a good way hence.
Fancy. What? Of Cockermouth spake I no word.
Folly. By my faith, sir, the furbisher hath my sword.
Fancy. Ah, I trow ye shall cough me a fool.
Folly. In faith, truth ye say, we went together to school. 1065
Fancy. Yea, but I can somewhat more of the letter.
Folly. I will not give an halfpenny for to choose the
　　better.
Fancy. But, brother Folly, I wonder much of one thing:
　　That thou so high fro me doth spring,
　　And I so little alway still. 1070
Folly. By God, I can tell thee and I will:
　　Thou art so feeble fantastical,
　　And so brainsick therewithal,
　　And thy wit wandering here and there,
　　That thou canst not grow out of thy boy's gear; 1075
　　And as for me, I take but one foolish way,
　　And therefore I grow more on one day
　　Than thou can in years seven.
Fancy. In faith, truth thou sayst now, by God of
　　Heaven,
　　For so with fantasies my wit doth flete 1080

1063. furbisher] frubyssher *F*.

1059.] Folly proceeds to tease Fancy by pretending to be deaf.
　1060. *cough me a daw*] call me a fool. Proverbial; Tilley F508. Cf 1064, and
'You shall cough me a foole I make God auowe' (*The Longer*, Civr; not cited in
Tilley).
　1061. *Cockermouth*] in Cumberland; Folly's pretended misunderstanding of
cough me in the previous line.
　1063. *furbisher*] renovator.
　1064. *cough me a fool*] See note on 1060.
　1066.] 'Yes, but I am rather better educated.'
　1069-70.] Another reference to Fancy's small size.
　1071. *and I will*] if I wish.
　1072. *feeble fantastical*] weakly fanciful.
　1075. *gear*] (1) habits; (2) clothing.
　1076. *I . . . way*] I am consistently foolish.
　1080. *flete*] overflow.

That wisdom and I shall seldom meet.

Now of good fellowship, let me buy thy dog.

Folly. Cock's heart, thou liest; I am no hog.

Fancy. Here is no man that called thee hog nor swine.

Folly. In faith, man, my brain is as good as thine.   1085

Fancy. The devil's turd for thy brain!

Folly. By my sire's soul, I feel no rain.

Fancy. By the mass, I hold thee mad.

Folly. Marry, I knew thee when thou wast a lad.

Fancy. [*To audience*] Cock's bones, heard ye ever

sic another?   1090

Folly. Yea, a fool the tone and a fool the tother.

Fancy. Nay, but wottest thou what I do say?

Folly. Why sayst thou that I was here yesterday?

Fancy. Cock's arms, this is a work, I trow!

Folly. What, callest thou me a dunnish crow?   1095

Fancy. Now in good faith, thou art a fond guest.

Folly. Yea, bear me this straw to a daw's nest.

Fancy. What, weenest thou that I were so foolish and so

fond?

Folly. In faith, else is there none in all England.

Fancy. Yet, for my fancy sake, I say   1100

Let me have thy dog, whatsoever I pay.

Folly. Thou shalt have my purse and I will have thine.

Fancy. By my troth, there is mine.

1082. buy] by *F.*   dog] dogge *Dyce;* hogge *F.*   1083. hog] hogge *Dyce;*
dogge *F.*   1099. England] Englonde *F.*

1082. *of*] for.
1083 ff.] Folly is still pretending to be hard of hearing.
1090. *sic*] such.
1091. *the tone . . . the tother*] the one . . . the other.
1094. *work*] labour.
1095. *dunnish*] dusky.
1097. *daw's*] jackdaw's; also 'fool's' (*O.E.D.* sb. 2).
1100. *for my fancy sake*] for my fancy's sake (see note on 86).
1102.] A purse was a conventional part of the fool's costume, see Intro., p.
46.

Folly. Now by *my* troth, man, take there my purse,
    And I beshrew him that hath the worse.   1105
Fancy. Turd, I say, what have I do!
    Here is nothing but the buckle of a shoe,
    And in my purse was twenty mark.
Folly. Ha, ha, ha! [*To audience*] Hark, sirs, hark!
    [*To* FANCY] For all that my name hight Folly,   1110
    By the mass, yet art thou more fool than I.
Fancy. Yet give me thy dog and I am content;
    And thou shalt have my hawk to a botchment.
Folly. That ever thou thrive God it forfend,
    For God's cope thou will spend.   1115
    Now take thou my dog and give me thy fowl.
Fancy. [*Calling the dog*] Hey, chish, come hither.
Folly.   Nay, turd take him betime!
Fancy. What callest thou thy dog?
Folly.   Tush, his name is Grime.
Fancy. Come Grime, come Grime, it is my pretty dogs.
Folly. In faith, there is not a better dog for hogs,   1120

1104. take . . . purse] *this ed.;* take there is myne *F;* take, there is my purse
Ramsay.   1117. chish] chysshe *F*.

1104. *my purse*] Needed for the rhyme; F's *is myne* being repeated in error
from the previous line.
    1106. *do*] done.
    1107.] Cf. the proverb 'Not worth shoe buckles'; Tilley S382 (1670). In
Hickscorner, Imagination complains, 'nought have I but a buckle' (Dodsley, I, p.
156), when his purse has been stolen.
    1108. *twenty mark*] A mark was two-thirds of a pound, so this was a consider-
able sum. Fancy is probably lying.
    1113. *to a botchment*] as an extra.
    1114. *forfend*] forbid.
    1115.] Proverbial; Tilley G271: 'He would spend God's cope if he had it'
(*God's cope:* 'a proverbial expression for a very large sum', *O.E.D.* cope sb.³ 2).
    1116.] A line wanting to rhyme with this (ending in *owl*)? But see note on 552.
    1117. *chish*] A noise made to summon the dog.
    betime] in good time.
    1119. *it is my pretty dogs*] Affectionately childish language (see note on *it*, 458).
    1120.] See Intro., note 129, for parallels to this line in *Parrot* and *Why come*.

Folly trades his dog for Fancy's owl
From the production of *Magnificence* by the *Poculi Ludique Societas*,
University of Toronto, 1975.

   Not from Alnwick unto Angey.
Fancy. Yea, but trowest thou that he be not mangy?
Folly. No, by my troth, it is but the scurf and the scab.
Fancy. What, he hath been hurt with a stab?
Folly. Nay, in faith, it was but a stripe   1125
   That the whoreson had for eating of a tripe.
Fancy. Where the devil gat he all these hurts?
Folly. By God, for snatching of puddings and worts.
Fancy. What, then he is some good poor man's cur?
Folly. Yea, but he will in at every man's door.   1130
Fancy. Now thou hast done me a pleasure great.
Folly. In faith, I would thou had a marmoset.
Fancy. Cock's heart, I love such japes!
Folly. Yea, for all thy mind is on owls and apes.
   But I have thy poultry, and thou hast my cattle.   1135
Fancy. Yea, but thrift and we have made a battle.
Folly. Rememb'rest thou not the japes and the toys—
Fancy. What, that we used when we were boys?
Folly. Yea, by the rood, even the same.
Fancy. Yes, yes, I am yet as full of game   1140

1121. Alnwick] Anwyke *F*.

   1121. *Alnwick*] in Northumberland (pronounced 'Annick'). Or possibly
Anwick in Lincolnshire? This is Kinsman's view; see *Poems*, p. 159.

   Angey] Anjou, or perhaps Angers, in Anjou (suggested by Whiting, who cites
this as a proverb (A135), but as the only example).

   1122.] See Intro., note 129 for other mangy curs in Skelton.

   1123. *scab*] Folly means 'a crust which forms over a healing wound' (*O.E.D.*
sb. 3); it can also mean 'mange', however (sb. 2).

   1125. *stripe*] A *stab* (1124) was a more honourable wound than a *stripe*, which
results from a whipping.

   1128.] Cf. the proverb 'Hungry dogs will eat dirty puddings'; Tilley D538
(1546), and see Folly's 'rhyme', 1156–7.

   worts] vegetables.

   1129. *poor man's cur*] Like Wolsey, see Intro., p. 40.

   1134.] Cf. 'Men dreme alday of owles and of apes' (*Canterbury Tales*,
VII.3092). C. L. Shaver, 'Chaucer's "Owles and Apes"', *M.L.N.*, LVIII
(1943), pp. 105–7, gives some other examples of owls and apes in combination.

   1135. *cattle*] livestock.

   1136. *thrift and we*] 'thrift and I', really, for only Fancy has lost, or implies he
has, by the exchange of purses.

   1137. *toys*] antics (*O.E.D.* sb. 2).

As ever I was, and as full of trifles:
Nil, nichelum, nihil; anglice: nifles.

Folly. What, canst thou all this Lutin yet,
And hath so mazed a wand'ring wit?

Fancy. Tush, man, I keep some Latin in store.   1145

Folly. By cock's heart, I ween thou hast no more.

Fancy. No—yes, in faith, I can versify.

Folly. Then I pray thee heartily,
Make a verse of my butterfly.

It forseth not of the reason, so it keep rhyme.   1150

Fancy. But wilt thou make another on Grime?

Folly. Nay, in faith, first let me hear thine.

Fancy. Marry, as for that, thou shalt soon hear mine:

> *Verses:*

Est suavis vago

1142. *nichelum*] nichelum *F; nihilum Dyce.*   1153.1.] *this ed.;* VERSUS.
Ramsay; Versus. *F (after 1155).*   1154. *Est suavis vago*] *this ed.;* Est snaui
snago *F.*

1142.] 'Nothing, nothing, nothing; in English "nothingness"' (*O.E.D.* nifle
sb. 1).

1143. *canst thou*] do you know.

Lutin] Perhaps merely a misprint for *Latin*, but Folly may be mispronouncing
the word deliberately, to mock Fancy's 'scholarship'; in view of this possibility
F spelling is retained.

1144.] 'When you have such a confused, unstable mind'.

1149. *my butterfly*] i.e. the hawk; see 1049.

1150.] 'It doesn't matter whether it makes sense, as long as it rhymes.' Cf. the
proverbs 'Neither rhyme nor reason' and 'It may rhyme but it accords not';
Tilley R98 and 99.

1153.1] The following *Verses* are macaronic hexameters; printed as two lines
here because of their (internal) rhyme. Fancy produces a perfect hexameter;
Folly's *would* be perfect if the words *pudding* and *roast* were reversed. (As it
stands, the fourth foot has an extra short syllable, and the fifth is lacking one.)

1154. Est suavis vago] 'It is a sweet wag.' Following Folly's instructions in
1150, Fancy has coined a dog-latin word by analogy with the English 'wag':
'term of endearment . . . "fellow", "chap"' (*O.E.D.* sb.² 1). The expression
'sweet wag' is quite common in Elizabethan English, cf. 'What ist sweet wagge I
should deny thy youth' (*Dido, Queen of Carthage*, I.i.23); 'I prithee, sweet wag,
shall there be gallows standing in England when thou art king?' (*1H4*, I.ii.57–9;
see also I.ii.5, I.ii.23). *O.E.D.* does not record an instance of *wag* in this sense
before 1553, however.

With a shrewd face, *vilis imago*.   1155
Folly. *Grimbaldus* greedy
   Snatch a pudding till the roast be ready.
Fancy. By the heart of God, well done!
Folly. Yea, so readily and so soon!

    Here cometh in CRAFTY CONVEYANCE.

Conveyance. What, Fancy! Let me see who is the
   tother.   1160
Fancy. By God, sir, Folly, mine own sworn brother.
Conveyance. Cock's bones, it is a farly freke!
   Can he play well at the hoddypeak?
Fancy. [*To* FOLLY] Tell, by thy troth, what sport can
   thou make?
Folly. Ah, hold thy peace, I have the toothache.   1165
Conveyance. The toothache! Lo, a turd ye have!
Folly. Yea, thou hast the four quarters of a knave.

1162. farly] farle *F*.

1155. *shrewd*] vile.
vilis imago] of vile appearance.
1156. Grimbaldus] Latinisation of Grime.
1157.] See note on 1128.
1163. *hoddypeak*] 'A fool, simpleton, noodle, blockhead' (*O.E.D.*); but for most of the examples any term of abuse would fit. In Dunbar's *Dance of the Sevin Deidly Synnis*, 59 (not cited in *O.E.D.*), *hud-pykis*, who accompany Covetousness along with *hurdaris and gadderis* ('hoarders and gatherers'), seem to be 'misers' (glossed so by W. Mackay Mackenzie, *The Poems of William Dunbar* (1932), p. 255). The sense 'miser' would fit here, for Folly is clutching the purse containing Fancy's money. Perhaps *hoddypeak* is simply a general term of abuse: Ignorance in *The Four Elements* is called 'Master Huddypeke' (Dodsley, I, p. 42).
1165. *I have the toothache*] Probably just a general expression of discontent or anger, cf. the proverb 'To have an aching tooth at one'; Tilley T421. The earliest citation there is 1667, but cf. Benedick's complaint 'I have the toothache' (*Ado*, III.ii.19). *The toothache* is later 'bequeathed' to Magnificence by Countenance; see 2254.
1167. *quarters*] 'The four parts, each containing a limb, of a human body, . . . divided, as was commonly done in the case of those executed for treason' (*O.E.D.* sb. 2b). Folly means 'You are a knave who is due to be hanged, drawn and quartered'. *The four quarters of a knave* is also 'bequeathed' to Magnificence, by Conveyance, see 2253. Cited as proverbial by Whiting (Q13), but with only

Conveyance. Wottest thou, I say, to whom thou speaks?
Fancy. Nay, by cock's heart, he ne recks,
     For he will speak to Magnificence thus.   1170
Conveyance. Cock's arms, a meet man for us!
Folly. What, would ye have mo fools, and are so many?
Fancy. [*To* CONVEYANCE] Nay, offer him a counter
     instead of a penny.
Conveyance. Why, thinks thou he can no better skill?
Folly. In faith, I can make you both fools and I will.   1175
Conveyance. What hast thou on thy fist, a kesterel?
Folly. Nay, ywis, fool, it is a dotterel.
Conveyance. In a coat thou can play well the dicer.
Folly. Yea, but thou can play the fool without a visor.
Fancy. [*To* CONVEYANCE] How rode he by you? How
     put he to you?   1180
Conveyance. [*To* FANCY] Marry, as thou sayst, he gave
     me a blur;

1176. kesterel] kesteryll *Dyce;* besteryll *F.*

---

these two examples. Cf. 'Thou shalt beare iiii quarters of a foole' (*The Longer,*
Diir), 'What shall I haue? / Foure quarters of a knaue / Rosted vpon a spytte'
(*Impatient Poverty,* Div).

   1170.] It is in fact Conveyance himself who speaks so to Magnificence; see
note on 1167.

   1173.] i.e. 'Don't be so keen to get him' (*counter* = 'an imitation coin of brass,
or inferior metal' (*O.E.D.* sb.³ 2)).

   1174. *can no better skill*] has no better discrimination (*O.E.D.* sb.¹ 5).

   1175. *and I will*] See note on 1071.

   1176.] Cf. 922.

   kesterel] kestrel.

   1177. *dotterel*] (1) a species of plover; (2) a dotard.

   1178. *coat*] i.e. the fool's motley.

   dicer] gambler.

   1179.] 'Yes, but you can play the fool without a costume' (*visor* = 'mask or
disguise'; *O.E.D.* sb. 3).

   1180.] Fancy, taking *visor* in the sense 'helmet', uses a metaphor from
jousting for this battle of wits: 'How did he rate in that bit of horse-play? Did he
thrust home?' (*O.E.D.* put v.¹ 3a, b). A line is wanting to rhyme with this, and it
should perhaps be divided into two two-stress lines, but several other unrhymed
lines occur in the play, see note on 552.

   1181. *blur*] smear. (To continue your metaphor, it wasn't a home thrust, but
he did draw blood.')

But where gat thou that mangy cur?

Fancy. Marry, it was his, and now it is mine.

Conveyance. And was it his and now it is thine?

Thou must have thy fancy and thy will,   1185

But yet thou shalt hold me a fool still.

Folly. [*To* CONVEYANCE] Why, weenest thou that *I*

cannot make thee play the fon?

Fancy. Yea, by my faith, good Sir John.

Conveyance. For you both it were enough.

Folly. [*To* CONVEYANCE] Why, weenest thou that *I*

were as much a fool as thou?   1190

Fancy. [*To* CONVEYANCE] Nay, nay, thou shalt

find him another manner of man.

Folly. In faith, I can do mast'ries, so I can.

Conveyance. What canst thou do but play Cock Wat?

Fancy. Yet, yes, he will make thee eat a gnat.

Folly. Yes, yes, by my troth, I hold thee a groat   1195

That I shall laugh thee out of thy coat.

Conveyance. Then will I say that thou hast no peer.

Fancy. Now, by the rood, and he will go near.

1189. enough] Inough *F*.   1194. Yet, yes] Yet yes *F*; Yes, yes *Dyce*; Yes, yet *Ramsay*.

1182. *mangy cur*] See 1122.

1188.] Fancy is supporting Folly here; 'Yes, what about *that*?'

Sir John] contemptuous appellation (often used for a priest; *O.E.D.* John 3). Cf. *Sir John Double-Cloak*, 605.

1189. *enough*] difficult enough (*O.E.D.* enough 3b). For the rhyme (F *Inough*) with *thou*, 1190, see note on 605.

1191. *him*] Folly.

1192. *do mast'ries*] perform feats (*O.E.D.* 5a).

1193. *Cock Wat*] 'the walking Spirit of Newgate . . . as I am priuatly knowne, & commonly cald by knaues, theeues and conicatchers, but more properly named *Cock Wary*, who giues warning to Court, citie and country' (Thomas Dekker, *Iests to Make you Merrie* (1607), in A. Grosart, ed., *The Non-Dramatic Works of Thomas Dekker*, Vol. II (New York, 1963), p. 299). Also mentioned in *Bowge*, 173–4; *Tongues*, 15.

1194. *eat a gnat*] Cf. *eat a fly*, 503, and the proverb cited there.

1195. *hold*] wager.

1198. *go near*] come close (i.e. to having 'no peer').

Folly. Hem, Fancy! *Regardes-voyes.*

> *Here* FOLLY *maketh semblant to take a louse from*
> CRAFTY CONVEYANCE *shoulder.*

Fancy. What hast thou found there?
Folly.   By God, a louse.   1200
Conveyance. By cock's heart, I trow thou liest.
Folly. By the mass, a Spanish moth with a grey list!
Fancy. Ha, ha, ha, ha, ha, ha!
Conveyance. Cock's arms! It is not so, I trow.

> *Here* CRAFTY CONVEYANCE *putteth off his gown.*

Folly. Put on thy gown again, for thou hast lost now.   1205
Fancy. Lo, John a Bonam, where is thy brain?
      Now put on, fool, thy coat again.
Folly. Give me my groat, for now thou hast lost.

> *Here* FOLLY *maketh semblant to take money of* CRAFTY
> CONVEYANCE, *saying to him:*

Shut thy purse, daw, and do no cost.

1199. *Regardes-voyes*] regardes voyes *F; regardes, voyes Dyce; regardes, voyes vous Ramsay.*   1201. liest] lyste *F.*   1202. moth] moght *F.*   1204.1. CONVEYANCE] *Dyce;* conuaunce *F.*   1205. for . . . now] *conj. Dyce;* for nowe thou has lost *F.*   1208. for . . . lost] *this ed.;* for thou has lost *F.*

1199. Regardes-voyes] regardez-vous. (There is no need to regularise or emend as does Ramsay (see Collation): Folly's French would inevitably be inaccurate.)

1199.1. Conveyance shoulder] Conveyance's shoulder (see note on 86).

1202.] This sounds like a reference to a particular sort of Spanish garment (*list* = 'stripe'), but I have not found any information to clarify it.

1203.] Another unrhymed line, but this is really an interjection, not part of the text.

1206. *John a Bonam*] Another contemptuous epithet, cf. *Sir John*, 1188. For the formation, see note on 579. A constable named *Jac a Bonam* appears among other foolish characters in the romance 'The Hunting of the Hare' (see Dyce, II, p. 256).

1209. *do no cost*] incur no expense.

Fancy. Now hast thou not a proud mock and a stark?   1210
Conveyance. With yes, by the rood of Woodstock park.
Fancy. Nay, I tell thee, he maketh no doubts
    To turn a fool out of his clouts.
Conveyance. [*Ironically*] And for a fool a man would
    him take.
Folly. Nay, it is I that fools can make: 1215
    For be he caiser, or be he king,
    To fellowship with folly I can him bring.
Fancy. Nay, wilt thou hear now of his schools,
    And what manner of people he maketh fools?
Conveyance. Yea, let us hear a word or twain.   1220
Folly. Sir, of my manner I shall tell you the plain:
    First I lay before them my bible,
    And teach them how they should sit idle,
    To pick their fingers all the day long;
    So in their ear I sing them a song,   1225
    And make them so long to muse,
    That some of them runneth straight to the stews;

1224. pick] pyke *F*.   1227. stews] stuse *F*.

1210. *proud mock*] splendid mocking.

stark] vigorous, thorough. With the word-order *a proud mock and a stark*, cf. *a goodly interlude and a merry* (title).

1211. *Woodstock*] In Oxfordshire, where Henry VIII had one of his palaces.

1212. *maketh no doubts*] does not scruple (*O.E.D.* sb.[1] 4a).

1213.] In *Wit and Science* (558–593) the fool Ignorance is turned out of his coat in order that it may be put on Wit.

clouts] clothing.

1216.] 'For whether a man be emperor or king'.

1218. *schools*] doctrine or lore (*O.E.D.* sb.[1] 11; usually used in the singular, but cf. *Wisdom*, 86: 'Teche me the scolys of yowr dyvynyte').

1221. *of my manner*] about my behaviour.

plain] plain fact (*O.E.D.* a.[1] 12b).

1222. *bible*] textbook (containing his 'doctrine', see note on 1218) (*O.E.D.* 2). Cf. *Jack a Thrum's bible*, 1428. The sense 'Bible' is probably also intended, for fools frequently preached 'mock-sermons' and were associated with clerical figures such as Friar Tuck. (See Enid Welsford, *op. cit.* (p. 64, note 150), pp 130, 147, 222, 232.) Folly probably carries his 'bible' with him, see 1295–7 (where he makes a reference to Genesis), and note on *tabulas* (1041.1).

1227. *stews*] brothels.

To theft and bribery I make some fall,
And pick a lock and climb a wall;
And where I spy a nysot gay,   1230
That will sit idle all the day
And cannot set herself to work,
I kindle in her such a lither spark
That rubbed she must be on the gall
Between the tappet and the wall.   1235
Conveyance. What, whoreson, art thou such a one?
Fancy. Nay, beyond all other set him alone.
Conveyance. Hast thou any more? Let see, proceed.
Folly. Yea, by God, sir; for a need,
I have another manner of sort   1240
That I laugh at for my disport,
And those be they that come up of nought,
(As some be not far and if it were well sought);
Such daws, whatsoever they be
That be set in authority,   1245
Anon he waxeth so high and proud,
He frowneth fiercely, brimly browed;
The knave would make it coy and he could;
All that he doth must be allowed;
And: 'This is not well done; sir, take heed';   1250

1229. pick] pyke *F*.   1232. work] warke *F*.   1235. tappet] *Dyce;* tap *F*.
1243. far] ferre *Dyce;* ferce *F*.   1245. authority] auctorite *F*.   1248. could]
cowde *F*.   1249. allowed] alowde *F*.   1250. done; sir, take] *this ed.;*
done, syr, take *Dyce;* done, Syr; take *Ramsay*.

1228. *bribery*] larceny (*O.E.D.* sb. 1).
1230. *nysot*] wanton.
1234. *rubbed . . . on the gall*] touched on a tender point (*O.E.D.* sb.² 1c).
1235. *tappet*] wall-hanging, tapestry. Cf. 'Ye bere out brothells lyke a bawde;
/ Ye get therby a slendyr laude / Betweyn the tappett and the walle' (*Garnesche*,
IV, 73–5).
1239. *for a need*] inevitably.
1240. *manner of sort*] kind [of people] (see note on 51).
1243.] Probably another dig at Wolsey. See Intro., p. 39.
1246. *he*] For the change from plural to singular, see note on 422.
1247. *brimly*] angrily.
1248. *make it coy*] behave disdainfully (*O.E.D.* a. 4).
and he could] if he knew how.

And maketh him busy where is no need;
He dances so long *Hey trolly lolly*,
That every man laugheth at his folly.

Conveyance. By the good Lord, truth he sayth.

Fancy. Thinkest thou not so, by thy faith?   1255

Conveyance. 'Think I not so', quod he! Else have I shame,
For I know divers that useth the same.

Folly. But now forsooth man, it maketh no matter;
For they that will so busily smatter,
So help me God, man, ever at the length   1260
I make hem lese much of their strength;
For with folly so do I them lead,
That wit he wanteth when he hath most need.

Fancy. Forsooth, tell on; hast thou any more?

Folly. Yes, I shall tell you or I go   1265
Of divers mo that haunteth my schools.

Conveyance. All men beware of such fools!

1261. hem] *this ed.*; hym *F*.   1264. more] *F*; mo *Dyce*.

1252. Hey trolly lolly] Another popular contemporary dance-song, which
appears in Henry VIII's manuscript (Stevens, Index no. 111). Cf. 'Wyth, Hey,
troly, loly, lo, whip here, Jak' (*Coystrowne*, 15); 'Sing, frisky jolly, with hey troly
lolly' (*The Four Elements*, Dodsley, I, p. 20), '*Hey, troly, loly*, / Let us see who
can descant on this same;' (*Hickscorner*, Dodsley, I, p. 179). (See *O.E.D.*
Trolly-lolly for further occurrences.) It had been in existence at least since the
latter part of the fourteenth century: 'And thanne seten somme and songen atte
nale, / And hulpen erie his half acre with "how! trolli-lolli!"' (*Piers Plowman*,
VI, 118–19).

1259. *smatter*] Here this seems to mean 'dabble superficially' (*O.E.D.* v. 3),
though elsewhere (*Why come*, 711; *Garlande*, 1194) Skelton uses it in the sense
'prate, chatter'; cf. *smattering*, 2096.

1260. *at the length*] finally.

1261. *hem*] F *hym* must be a misprint, the plural *their* being used in the same
context; see note on 1366.

1263.] Cf. '"I see wel," quod this wise man, "that the commune proverbe is
sooth, that 'good conseil wanteth whan it is moost nede'."' (*Canterbury Tales*,
VII.1047). Not cited by Tilley or Whiting.

he] Used impersonally = 'a man'; cf. 1216.

1264. *more*] Dyce emends to *mo*, for the rhyme, but cf. 604–5.

1266. *haunteth*] frequents.

schools] used here in the sense of 'educational establishments', but see 1218.

Folly. There be two lither, rude and rank,
    Simkin Titivel and Piers Pickthank;
    These lithers I learn them for to lere   1270
    What he sayth and she sayth, to lay good ear,
    And tell to his sovereign every whit,
    And then he is much made of for his wit;
    And be the matter ill more or less,
    He will make it mickle worse than it is;   1275
    But all that he doth and if he reckon well,
    It is but folly every deal.

Fancy. Are not his words cursedly couched?

Conveyance. By God, there be some that be shrewdly
    touched.

1272. sovereign] sufferayne *F*.   1273. wit] wyt *Dyce;* whyt *F*.   1276. deal]
dell *F*.   1279. shrewdly] shroudly *F*.

1268 ff.] This speech, like that of Countenance, 480 ff., sounds to be aimed at
particular individuals, see esp. 1279. No doubt Skelton's audience would
understand to whom he was referring.

1268. *two lither*] two evil men (the adjective is used substantively, as in 1270,
cf. *poor*, 868; for the singular noun used after a number, cf. *twenty mark*, 1108,
thousand pound, 1571. It would not be correct to consider *lither* an adjective like
rude and rank; this would necessitate a strong pause after *two*, and the caesura
should fall after the second stress.

rude and rank] probably 'coarse and loathsome' (*rude* means anything from
'ignorant' to 'barbarous', *rank*, 'grossly offensive').

1269.] For the formation of these names, see note on 917.; *Titivel* = 'Tell-
tale', cf. 'Thus the people telles / . . . And talkys lyke tytyuelles' (*Cloute*, 414,
418); 'Theis titiuyllis with taumpinnis wer towchid and tappid' (*Garlande*, 642);
'Sometime Tom Titivile maketh us a feast' (*Ralph Royster Doyster*, Dodsley, III,
p. 58).

Pickthank] 'Sycophant' or 'Tale-bearer'; cf. Dunbar's 'To the King', 43: 'To
be ane pykthank i wald prief'; 'many tales devised / Which oft the ear of
greatness needs must hear / By smiling pickthanks and base newsmongers'
(*1H4*, III.ii.23–5). A character Piers Pick*purse* is mentioned in *Respublica*, p.
282.

1270. *lithers*] See note on 1268.

lere] learn.

1271. *lay good ear*] listen well.

1274. *ill more or less*] evil to a greater or lesser extent.

1276. *and if he reckon*] if he considers.

1278. *couched*] contrived, so as to express their meaning allusively (*O.E.D.* v.
15b).

1279. *shrewdly*] 'sharply, pointedly', and punning on 'cursedly' (*O.E.D.* a.
1c).

But I say, let see and if thou have any more.   1280
Folly. I have an whole armoury of such haberdash
    in store:
    For there be other that folly doth use,
    That follow fond fantasies and virtue refuse—
Fancy. Nay, that is my part that thou speakest of now.
Folly. So is all the remenant, I make God avow;   1285
    For thou formest such fantasies in their mind,
    That every man almost groweth out of kind.
Conveyance. By the mass, I am glad that I came hither
    To hear you two rutters dispute together.
Fancy. Nay, but Fancy must be either first or last.   1290
Folly. But when Folly cometh, all is past.
Fancy. I wot not whether it cometh of thee or of me,
    But all is folly that I can see.
Conveyance. Marry, sir, ye may swear it on a book.
Folly. Yea, turn over the leaf, read there, and look   1295
    How frantic fancy first of all
    Maketh man and woman in folly to fall.
Conveyance. [*To* FANCY] Ah, sir, ah, ah! How by that?
Fancy. A perilous thing, to cast a cat
    Upon a naked man and if she scrat!   1300
Folly. So ho! I say, the hare is squat!

1281. *haberdash*] petty merchandise.

1282. *other*] another kind of person.

1284.] Fancy objects to Folly's reference to *fantasies*, as being *his* province.

1287. *out of kind*] unnatural.

1295.] Folly probably opens his 'bible' here.

look] see.

1296–7.] A reference to the Genesis account of the Fall; *fancy* probably being used here in the sense 'amorous inclination, love' (see note on 970–1), as well as 'caprice' or 'whim'.

1298. *How by that*?] 'What do you say to that?' Conveyance is getting his own back for Fancy's remarks in 1180.

1299. *cat*] Perhaps Fancy is using this epithet for Eve, in view of *naked man* in the next line. Otherwise the remark does not seem to have much point; it may be proverbial, but I have not found any other occurrences.

1300. *and if she scrat*] if she scratches.

1301. *the hare is squat*] i.e. 'I've got you in a corner' (metaphor from hare-coursing).

squat] couching, cowering to avoid observation.

For frantic Fancy, thou makest men mad,
And I Folly bringeth them to *qui fuit* gad;
With *qui fuit*, brainsick, I have them brought
From *qui fuit aliquid* to sheer shaking nought.   1305
Conveyance. Well argued and surely on both sides.
But for thee, Fancy, Magnificence abides.
Fancy. Why, shall I not have Folly with me also?
Conveyance. Yes, pardy, man, whether that ye ride or go;
Yet for his name we must find a shift.   1310
Fancy. By the mass, he shall hight Conceit.
Conveyance. Not a better name under the sun.
With Magnificence thou shalt wone.
Folly. God have mercy, good godfather.
Conveyance. Yet I would that ye had gone rather;   1315
For as soon as you come in Magnificence sight
All measure and good rule is gone quite.
Fancy. And shall we have liberty to do what we will?
Conveyance. Riot at liberty russheth it out still.

1310. shift] shyfte *F*; slyght *Dyce*.   1311. Conceit] consayte *F*.

1303. qui fuit *gad*] lit. 'the goad of "who was"'. Probably a proverbial
expression like 'Beware of "had I wist"' (see 211). *Qui fuit* must be part of a
Latin sentence which, when complete, would express 'He, who was something
(*qui fuit aliquid*, 1305) is now come to nothing (*sheer shaking nought*, 1305)'.
Possibly the beginning of a legal document?

1305. *sheer shaking nought*] absolute nothingness. Cf. 'Elynour began to
chyde, / They be wretchockes thou hast brought, / They are shyre shakyng
nought!' (*Rummyng*, 464–6).

1309. *pardy*] by God.
go] walk.

1310. *shift*] device. Dyce and Ramsay print *slyght*, for the rhyme, but *F*
shyft/*consayte* produces near-rhyme on its consonants, cf. 774/5.

1311. *Conceit*] (1) 'apprehension, understanding' (an ironic name for Folly);
(2) fancy or whim (confirming the connection between Fancy and Folly which
has been illustrated in their previous argument).

1314.] An ironic expresson of thanks. Cf. 'God-a-mercy, horse'; Tilley, G276
(1546).

1315. *rather*] sooner.

1316. *Magnificence sight*] Magnificence's sight (see note on 86).

1319.] 'Wanton living always dashes about freely' (for *russheth it out* see note
on 846) Cf. 'Wyth that came Ryotte, russhynge all at ones,/ A rusty gallande,
to-ragged and to-rente' (*Bowge*, 344–5). The gallant Riot in *Youth*, with a 'heart

Folly. Yea, but tell me one thing.
Conveyance.   What is that?   1320
Folly. Who is master of the mash-vat?
Fancy. Yea, for he hath a full dry soul.
Conveyance. Cock's arm's, thou shalt keep the
        brewhouse bowl.
Folly. But may I drink thereof whilst that I stare?
Conveyance. When Measure is gone what needest thou
        spare?   1325
    When Measure is gone we may slay care.
Folly. Now then go we hence. Away the mare!

                              [*Exit* FANCY *and* FOLLY.]

    CRAFTY CONVEYANCE *alone in the place*.

Conveyance. It is wonder to see, the world about,
        To see what folly is used in every place.
        Folly hath a room, I say, in every rout;   1330
        To put where he list Folly hath free chase;
        Folly and Fancy all where every man doth face and
            brace;

1321. mash-vat] masshe fat *F*.   1326. slay] slee *F*.   1327.1.] *Ramsay*.

---

as light as the wind', announces, 'I come lately from Newgate' (Dodsley, II, p. 14).

    1321. *mash-vat*] tub in which malt is brewed.
    1322.] Cf. 'Send ye any souls to heaven by water? /. . . By God, I have a dry soul should thither' (*The Four PP*, Farmer, *Heywood*, p.33).
    1324–6.] Cf. 'all good ale drynkers, / That wyll nothynge spare, / But drynke tyll they stare / And brynge themselfe bare, / With, Now away the mare, / And let vs sley care' (*Rummyng*, 106–11).
    1324. *whilst that I stare*] until my eyes are glazed (*O.E.D.* v. 3).
    1327. *Away the mare*] away with melancholy (*O.E.D.* mare sb.² 2). Proverbial; Tilley M646.
    1328. *the world about*] all over the world (cf. *the world environ*, 2).
    1330. *room*] place, position.
    1331. *put*] make his way (*O.E.D.* v.¹ 8b).
    free chase] free scope, 'full fling' (*O.E.D.* sb.¹ 1e).
    1332. *all where*] everywhere.
    face and brace] confront and embrace (as in a dance, see next line). To *face and brace* generally occurs as a doublet 'to swagger and bluster', used intransitively (*O.E.D.* brace v.²); cf. 'To prate and crake, / To face, to brace, / All voyde of grace' (*Scottes*, 32–4). But here used transitively, cf. 2221–2.

Folly footeth it properly, Fancy leadeth the dance,
And next come I after, Crafty Conveyance.

Who so to me giveth good advertence,   1335
Shall see many things done craftily:
By me conveyed is wanton insolence;
Privy pointments conveyed so properly;
For many times much kindess is denied
For dread that 'we dare not oft, lest we be spied'.   1340

By me is conveyed mickle pretty ware,
Sometime, I say, behind the door for need;
I have an hobby can make larks to dare;
I knit together many a broken thread.
It is great almesse the hunger to feed,   1345
To clothe the naked where is lacking a smock,
Trim at her tail or a man can turn a sock.

'What ho! Be ye merry, was it not well conveyed?'
'As oft as ye list, so honesty be saved;
Alas, dear heart, look that we be not perceived'.   1350
(Without craft nothing is well behaved).

1345. hunger] *F;* hungre *Dyce.*   1348. conveyed] conueyed *F.*   1350.
perceived] perseyuyd *F.*   1351. behaved] behauyd *F.*

1337.] There is a line wanting here, to complete the stanza. See note on 552.

1338. *Privy pointments*] private contracts (the pun on *privy* indicates that these
are sometimes of a sexual nature).

properly] (1) privately; (2) excellently (*O.E.D.* adv. 1, 4).

1343.] See Intro., pp. 34–5.

1345–6.] Ironically, to 'feed the hungry' and 'clothe the naked' are two of the
Seven Acts of Mercy (Matthew, xxv.35–6).

almesse] charity.

hunger] hungry (*O.E.D.* sb. 3; see note on 868).

1347.] [To make her] neat or pretty (behind) before anyone can turn a sock,
i.e. in a trice (with obvious sexual innuendo).

1349. *honesty*] reputation (*O.E.D.* sb. 1c).

1350. *perceived*] For the rhyme with *conveyed*,1348 (F *conueyed* /*perseyuyd*), cf.
534–5.

1351. *behaved*] managed (*O.E.D.* v. 2).

'Though I show you courtesy, say not that I crave;
Yet convey it craftily and hardily, spare not for me,'
So that there know no man but I and she.

Theft also, and petty bribery,   1355
Without me be full oft aspied;
My inwit dealing there can no man descry;
Convey it be craft, lift and lay aside;
Full much flattery and falsehood I hide;
And by crafty conveyance I will, and I can,   1360
Save a strong thief and hang a true man.

But some man would convey and can not skill,
As malapert taverners that check with their betters:
Their conveyance welteth the work all by will;
And some will take upon them to counterfeit letters,   1365
And therewithal convey hemself into a pair of
    fetters;
And some will convey by the pretence of sadness,
Till all their conveyance is turned into madness.

1352. courtesy] curtesy F.   crave] craue F; craued conj. Dyce.   1366.
hemself] this ed.; hymselfe F.

1352. *courtesy*] Although *curteys* was retained for reasons of metre in 1006, the
spelling is modernised here in order to be consistent with 1515.1, where the
spelling *courtesy* occurs in F.
   crave] 'I'm dying for it.' For the rhyme (F *craue* /*behauyd*), cf. 604–5.
   1357. *My inwit dealing*] the conduct of my conscience.
   1358. *be*] by.
   1360. *and*] if.
   1361. *strong*] 'flagrantly guilty' (*O.E.D.* adj. 11e).
   1362. *can not skill*] has no discrimination (see note on 1174).
   1363. *malapert*] impudent.
   check] quarrel.
   1364. *welteth*] overturns.
   will] wifulness.
   1365.] As Countenance had done for Fancy, though it was Liberty's undis-
closed activities that had put him in danger of fettering; see 30–1.
   1366. *hemself*] themselves. (F's *hymself* must be a misprint, in view of *them* in
the previous line; see note on 1261.)
   1367. *by the pretence of sadness*] by a false profession of seriousness (e.g.
Fancy's counterfeit letter said to be from Sad Circumspection; Collusion professing to be 'Sober Sadness').

Crafty conveyance is no child's game;
By crafty conveyance many one is brought up of
    nought;   1370
Crafty Conveyance can cloak himself from shame,
For by crafty conveyance wonderful things are
    wrought;
By conveyance crafty I have brought
Unto Magnificence a full ungracious sort,
For all hooks unhappy to me have resort.   1375

Here cometh in MAGNIFICENCE *with* LIBERTY *and* FELICITY.

Magnificence. Trust me, Liberty, it grieveth me right sore,
    To see you thus ruled and stand in such awe.
Liberty. Sir, as by my will it shall be so no more.
Felicity. Yet Liberty without rule is not worth a straw.
Magnificence. Tush, hold your peace, ye speak like
    an daw;   1380
    Ye shall be occupied, Wealth, at my will.
Conveyance. All that ye say, sir, is reason and skill.

Magnificence. Master Surveyor, where have ye been so
    long?
    Remember ye not how my Liberty by Measure ruled
    was?
Conveyance. In good faith sir, meseemeth he had the
    more wrong.   1385
Liberty. Marry, sir, so did he exceed and pass,
    They drove me to learning like a dull ass.

1374. Magnificence] Magnyfycence *Dyce;* magnyfyce *F*.

1374. *ungracious*] wicked (*O.E.D.* a.1).
1375. *hooks unhappy*] evil characters (*O.E.D.* hook sb. 12: 'Applied with certain qualifications to a person'—this is the earliest citation).
1376. *sore*] grievously.
1379. *not worth a straw*] Proverbial; Tilley S918.
1383. *Surveyor*] 'Sure Surveyance' is the assumed name of Conveyance.
1386. *he*] Measure.
1387. *They*] Measure and his associates.
drove me to learning] See 231.

Felicity. It is good yet that Liberty be ruled by reason.
Magnificence. Tush, hold your peace! Ye speak out of
    season.

    Yourself shall be ruled by Liberty and Largesse.   1390
Felicity. I am content, so it in measure be.
Liberty. Must measure, in the mare's name, you
        furnish and dress?
Magnificence. Nay, nay; not so, my friend Felicity.
Conveyance. Not and your grace would be ruled by me.
Liberty. Nay, he shall be ruled even as I list.   1395
Felicity. Yet it is good to beware of 'had I wist'.

Magnificence. Sir, by Liberty and Largesse I will that
    ye shall
    Be governed and guided; wot ye what I say?
    Master Surveyor, Largesse to me call.
Conveyance. It shall be done.
Magnificence.   Yea, but bid him come away   1400
    At once, and let him not tarry all day.

                  Here goeth out CRAFTY CONVEYANCE.

Felicity. Yet it is good wisdom to work wisely by wealth.
Liberty. Hold thy tongue and thou love thy health.
Magnificence. What will ye wast wind and prate thus in
    vain?

1395. ruled even] ruled euen *Dyce;* rulede uen *F.*

    1390. *Largesse*] i.e. Fancy.

    1391.] Cf. Magnificence's comment at 278. *He* has now changed his mind.

    1392. *in the mare's name*] an expletive: 'in the name of misery' (see note on
1327).

    furnish and dress] provide for you and put you in order.

    1396.] Cf. 211. Proverbial, but it is interesting that the warning here given to
Magnificence was also given to Wolsey in an anonymous ballad. See *Ballads*, p.
353, l. 36.

    1402.] Felicity repeats here the point made in his opening speech. Cf. the
proverb 'It is wisdom to suffer to win wealth', Whiting, W382; also 'it is wisdom
that thou look to thine own wealth' (*Utopia*, p. 86).

Ye have eaten sauce, I trow, at the Taylor's Hall.   1405
Liberty. [*To* FELICITY] Be not too bold, my friend, I
    counsel you; bear a brain.
Magnificence. And what so we say hold you content
    withal.
Felicity. Sir, yet without sapience your substance may
    be small;
    For where is no measure, how may worship endure?

          Here cometh in FANCY.

Fancy. Sir, I am here at your pleasure.   1410

    Your grace sent for me, I ween; what is your will?
Magnificence. Come hither, Largesse; take here Felicity.
Fancy. Why, ween you that I can keep him long still?
Magnificence. To rule as ye list, lo, here is Liberty.
Liberty. I am here ready.   1415
Fancy. What, shall we have Wealth at our guiding to
    rule as we list?
    Then farewell thrift, by him that cross kissed!

1406. friend, . . . you;] *this ed.;* frend; I counsell you, *Dyce.*   1415. ready.]
redy *F;* redy. *Fan.* What! shall we *Ramsay.*   1416. What, . . . have] what
shall we haue *F;* Haue *Ramsay.*   1417. kissed] kyst *F.*

1405. *Ye have eaten sauce*] 'To eat sauce' (to behave in a saucy fashion) is
proverbial; Tilley S100. Cf. 'To be so perte to prese so proudly vppe: / She sayde
she trowed that I had eten sause' (*Bowge*, 71–2).

    the Taylor's Hall] the hall of the guild of the Merchant Taylors, in Thread-
needle Street. For the possible significance of this remark, see Intro. p. 43.

1406. *bear a brain*] be cautious. The stresses in this line are on the syllables
bold, coun-, bear and *brain,* hence I place the semicolon after *you* (where the
caesura falls).

1407. *what so*] whatsoever.

1410. *pleasure*] The stress is, unusually, on the second syllable; cf. 1529.

1413. *still*] quiet (*O.E.D.* a. 2).

1415.] It is rare to find a two-stress line in the rhyme-royal stanza, and perhaps
part of this line is missing. Ramsay uses Fancy's *What shall we* (1416) to
complete this line, but 1416 is a typical line from a Vice, with extra (unstressed)
exclamatory syllables at its beginning (see Intro. p. 55), the stresses in 1416
being on *Wealth, guid-, rule,* and *list.*

1417. *that cross kissed*] who kissed the cross. Obscure.

Felicity. I trust your grace will be agreeable
    That I shall suffer none impeachment
    By their demeanance, nor loss reprivable. 1420
Magnificence. Sir, ye shall follow mine appetite and intent.
Felicity. So it be by measure I am right well content.
Fancy. What, all by measure, good sir, and none excess?
Liberty. Why, wealth hath made many a man brainless.

Felicity. That was by the means of too much liberty. 1425
Magnificence. What, can ye agree thus, and appose?
Felicity. Sir, as I say, there was no fault in me.
Liberty. Yea, of Jack a Thrum's bible can ye make a
    glose.
Fancy. Sore said, I tell you, and well to the purpose.
    [*To* FELICITY] What should a man do with you, lock
    you under key? 1430
Felicity. I say it is folly to give all wealth away.

Liberty. Whether should wealth be ruled by liberty,
    Or liberty by wealth; let see tell me that.
Felicity. Sir, as me seemeth, ye should be ruled by me.
Magnificence. What need you with him thus prate and
    chat? 1435

1430. man] *Dyce;* mau *F.*   key] kay *Dyce;* bay *F.*

1420. *demeanance*] 'behaviour', perhaps also 'belittling' though 'rare before 1700' (*O.E.D.* v.2).
  reprivable] reprehensible.
  1421. *appetite*] inclination.
  1424.] Cf. the proverb 'Wealth makes wits waver'; Tilley W201 (1598).
  1426. *appose*] raise objections.
  1428. *Jack a Thrum's bible*] 'And therto acordes too worthi preachers, Jacke a Throme and Jone Brest-Bale; these men seyd in the bibull that an ill drynker is unpossibull hevone for to wynne' (T. Wright and O. Halliwell, *Reliquiae Antiquae* (1841–43), I, 84. Cf. also 'he is a very fole; / Twyshe, set hym a chare, or reche hym a stole, / To syt hym vpon, and rede Iacke a thrummis bybille' (*Garlande*, 207–9). Kinsman, 'Olde Sayde Sawe', p. 108, suggests that this expression is proverbial, and it is cited by Whiting (J1), but with no other examples. Cf. also 'As wyse as Tom a thrum' (*Cloute*, 284).
  glose] (1) gloss; (2) flattering speech.
  1429. *Sore*] severely.
  1435. *chat*] talk idly.

Fancy. Show us your mind then, how to do, and what.
Magnificence. I say that I will ye have him in guiding.
Liberty. Master Felicity, let be your chiding;

And so as ye see it will be no better.
Take it in worth such as ye find.   1440
Fancy. What the devil, man, your name shall be the
        greater,
For wealth without largesse is all out of kind.
Liberty. And wealth is nought worth if liberty be behind.
Magnificence. Now hold ye content, for there is none
        other shift.
Felicity. Then waste must be welcome, and farewell thrift! 1445

Magnificence. [*To* FANCY] Take of his substance a sure
        inventory,
And get thou home together, for Liberty shall bide
And wait upon me.
Liberty. [*To* FANCY] And yet for a memory,
Make indentures how ye and I shall guide.
Fancy. I can do nothing but he stand beside.   1450
Liberty. Sir, we can do nothing the one without the other.
Magnificence. Well, get you hence then, and send me
        some other.

Fancy. Whom, lusty Pleasure, or merry Conceit?

1436. *mind*] intention or wish (*O.E.D.* sb.[1] 10).

1437. *him*] Felicity.

1440.] Cf. the proverbs 'To take one as we find him', and 'Take all things as
they come and be content'; Tilley T29 (1559), T196.

1443.] Felicity would agree with this if measure were included; see 219 ff.

1444. *shift*] means (open to you).

1446. *substance*] possessions (*O.E.D.* 16).

1448. *memory*] record (*O.E.D.* sb. 9).

1449. *indentures*] deeds of agreement.

guide] conduct ourselves.

1450. *he*] Liberty.

1453. *Pleasure*] the assumed name of Courtly Abusion.

Conceit] the assumed name of Folly.

Magnificence. Nay, first lusty Pleasure is my desire to have,
    And let the other another while await,   1455
    Howbeit that fond fellow is a merry knave.
    But look that ye occupy the authority that I you gave.

        Here goeth out FELICITY, LIBERTY, *and* FANCY.

        MAGNIFICENCE *alone in the place.*

Magnificence. For now, sirs, I am like as a prince should be:
    I have wealth at will, largesse and liberty.

    Fortune to her laws cannot abandon me,   1460
    But I shall of Fortune rule the rein;
    I fear nothing Fortune's perplexity.
    All honour to me must needs stoop and lean;
    I sing of two parts without a mean;
    I have wind and weather over all to sail,   1465
    No stormy rage against me can prevail.

    Alexander, of Macedony king,

1455. another while await] *this ed.;* another awayte *F;* another time awayte *conj.*
Dyce 1457. authority] auctoryte *F.* 1458. *Magnificence.*] *Ramsay;* fansy *F.*

1456.] Magnificence, then, has met Folly, although we have not yet seen them together.

1458 ff.] As Heiserman points out (pp. 84–8), the following speech resembles the ranting of tyrants like Herod, in the miracle plays, and World, in the moralities. Defiance of Fortune, however, is untypical of such figures, and closer to later heroes like Tamburlaine. See Intro., p. 29.

1462. *perplexity*] distress (*O.E.D.* 1b).

1464.] Contrast Measure's statement in 137.

1465–6.] But: *after a drought there falleth a shower of rain*, 12, and *Of terrestre treachery we fall in the flood,* / *Beaten with storms*, 2555–6. Poverty later tells Magnificence *Now must ye be stormy beaten with showers and rains*, 2018. See Kinsman, 'Olde Sayde Sawe', p. 100.

1467 ff.] A number of the heroes given in Magnificence's list are also cited in the catalogue of romance heroes of whom Jane Scrope has read (*Sparowe*, 612 ff.). There is something in common between Jane's naive admiration of these figures and Magnificence's admiration at himself for surpassing them. Alexander, Hannibal and Scipio are given as examples of men who lacked 'mesure' in Lydgate's 'Mesure', 33 ff., 44 ff., although Hercules is there cited as a moderate man, 137 ff.

Alexander] Alexander the Great, Alexander III of Macedon, 356–323 B.C.

That all the orient had in subjection,
Though all his conquests were brought to reckoning,
Might seem right well under my protection   1470
To reign, for all his martial affection;
For I am prince peerless proved of port,
Bathed with bliss, embraced with comfort.

Cyrus, that solemn sire of Babylon
That Israel released of their captivity,   1475
For all his pomp, for all his royal throne,
He may not be compared unto me;
I am the diamond, doubtless, of dignity;
Surely it is I that all may save and spill;
No man so hardy to work against my will.   1480

Porsenya, the proud provost of Turkey land,

1474. sire] syar *F*.   1476. royal throne] ryall trone *F*.

1468–70.] Cf. 'For all the whole Orent ys under myn obbeydeance, / . . . the most reydownid kyng Eyrodde, / Wyche thatt all pryncis hath under subjeccion / And all there whole powar vnder my proteccion' (*Pageant of the Shearmen and Taylors*, 502, 518–20, in *Two Coventry Corpus Christi Plays*, ed. Hardin Craig (E.E.T.S., 1957), p. 18).

1469.] 'Even if all his conquests were added up'.

1470. *protection*] patronage.

1471. *for*] in spite of.

affection] disposition (*O.E.D.* sb. 4).

1472.] Cf. Lucifer's 'I am pereles and prynce of pryde' (*The Fall of Lucifer*, 163, in *The Chester Plays*, I, ed. H. Deimling (E.E.T.S., 1892), p. 16; Pilate's 'I am a perelous prince' (*York Plays*, ed. L. T. Smith (1885), p. 220), World's 'Precyous prinse, prekyd in pride' (*The Castle of Perseverance*, 159)) and Mundus 'I am a prince perilous y-proved, / I-proved full perilous and pithily y-pight' (*Mundus and Infans*, Dodsley, I, p. 250).

peerless proved of port] found to be without equal in my state.

1473. *Bathed*] enveloped (*O.E.D.* v. 4b).

embraced with comfort] surrounded by pleasure.

1474. *Cyrus*] Cyrus the Great, the founder of the Persian empire.

solemn sire] grand lord. F *syar* was disyllabic.

1475. *captivity*] The Babylonian Captivity (*c*. 603–535 B.C.).

1479. *spill*] destroy, put to death.

1481. *Porsenya*] Lars Porsenna, prince of Clusium at the end of the sixth century B.C., who, according to tradition, marched against Rome in order to restore the Tarquins to the Roman throne.

Turkey] perhaps a mishearing of Tarquin?

That rated the Romans and made them ill rest,
Nor Caesar July, that no man might withstand,
Were never half so richly as I am dressed.
No, that I assure you, look who was the best.   1485
I reign in my robes, I rule as me list,
I drive down these dastards with a dint of my fist.

Of Cato the count, accounted the cane,
Darius, the doughty chieftain of Perse,
I set not by the proudest of them a prane,   1490
Ne by none other that any man can rehearse,
I follow in felicity without reverse;
I dread no danger, I dance all in delight;
My name is Magnificence, man most of might.

Hercules the hardy, with his stubborn clubbed mace, 1495
That made Cerberus to catch, the cur dog of Hell,

1487. these] *Dyce;* thse *F.*   1492. reverse] reuersse *Dyce;* reuesse *F.*

1482. *rated*] reproved.

1483. *Caesar July*] Julius Caesar. The inversion seems peculiar to Skelton.

1484.] Cf. the claim of Mundus: 'For I am richest in mine array' (Dodsley, I, p. 250).

1485. *look who was the best*] whoever was the best (*O.E.D.* look v. 4b).

1488. *Cato*] Marcius Porcius Cato, 'the Censor', 234–149 B.C.

count] Possibly puns on 'counter', i.e. Censor.

accounted the cane] who counted the tax (for the omission of the subject, see note on 504; for *cane* = 'the imposition of a tax' (deriving from O.F.), see Pollet p. 248).

1489. *Darius*] Darius I, who obtained the Persian throne in 521 B.C.

1490. *set not . . . a prane*] Cf. 'We set nat a prane / By suche a dronken drane' (*Albany*, 163–4). A variant of the proverb 'Not set (or 'Not worth') a preen' (= pin); Whiting, P364–5. But here *prane* = 'prawn', cf. 'Ye pycke no shrympes nor pranes' (*Cloute*, 209).

1491. *rehearse*] enumerate.

1492. *follow*] continue (*O.E.D.* v. 18).

1493.] Cf. the words of Mundus: 'I dawnse doun as a doo' (*The Castle of Perseverence*, 188).

1494. *most*] greatest.

1495. *stubborn*] rigid (*O.E.D.* a. 3 (1577)).

1496.] The twelfth labour of Hercules was to capture Cerberus, the triple-headed watchdog of Hades.

made Cerberus to catch] set out to catch Cerberus (*O.E.D.* make v. 34a, b).

And Theseus the proud, was Pluto to face,
It would not become them with me for to mell;
For of all barons bold I bear the bell;
Of all doughty I am doughtiest duke, as I deem;   1500
To me all princes to lowt man be seen.

Charlemagne, that maintained the nobles of France,
Arthur of Albion, for all his brim beard,
Nor Basian the bold, for all his bribance,
Nor Alericus, that ruled the Gothiance by sword,   1505
Nor no man on mould, can make me afeard;
What man is so mazed with me that dare meet,
I shall flap him as a fool to fall at my feet.

1497. the proud] the prowde *F;* that prowde *Dyce.*   1501. be seen] besene *F;*
beseme *conj. Dyce.*   1505. sword] swerd *F.*

1497.] Theseus descended with Pirithous to Hades to rescue Proserpina,
whom Pluto had carried off from the upper world. He was imprisoned in Hades
and rescued by Hercules.

was Pluto to face] who was to confront Pluto. (*O.E.D.* face v. 2; for the
omission of the pronoun see note on 504 and cf. 1488; for the construction with
was see Visser, II, p. 494, who remarks, however, that it is rare in More and
earlier English).

1498. *mell*] mingle, i.e. compete.

1499–1500.] Cf. Herod's boast: 'Of bewte and of boldness I bere ever-more the
belle / . . . I dynge with my dowtynes the devyl down to helle' (*Ludus Coventriae*, p. 151).

1500. *doughty*] men of valour (adjective used substantively, see *O.E.D.* a. 2).

1501. *to lowt*] to bow down, obey.

man] must (*man* is a variant of *O.E.D.* maun v.[1], a scots variant of 'must').
Manhood, when in the service of Mundus, also claims 'To me men lewt full low'
(Dodsley, I, p. 255).

1503. *Albion*] Britain.

brim] rugged.

1504. *Basian*] Antoninus Bassianus Caracalla, A.D. 186–217, Roman emperor
211–217. Originally named Bassianus, his nickname Caracalla was derived from
the long Gallic tunic he wore.

bribance] plundering. Not in *O.E.D.*

1505. *Alericus*] Alaric, *c.* 370–410, Gothic conqueror.

Gothiance] Goths.

1506. *mould*] earth.

1507. *mazed*] foolish.

1508. *flap*] strike with a sudden blow (*O.E.D.* v. 1).

Galba, whom his gallants garred for a gasp,
Nor Nero, that nother set by God nor man,   1510
Nor Vaspasian, that bare in his nose a wasp,
Nor Hannibal, again Rome gates that ran,
Nor yet Cipio, that noble Carthage won,
Nor none so hardy of them, with me that durst
    crake,
But I shall frounce them on the foretop and gar
    them to quake.   1515

Here cometh in COURTLY ABUSION *doing reverence and courtesy.*

Abusion. At your commandment, sir, with all due
    reverence.
Magnificence. Welcome, Pleasure, to our magnificence.
Abusion. Pleaseth it your grace to show what I do shall.

1513. Cipio] Cypyo *Dyce;* typyo *F.*

1509. *Galba*] Servius Sulpicius Galba, 3 B.C.–A.D. 69, Roman emperor in succession to Nero.

garred for a gasp] made to gasp (for his life—Galba was assassinated). This is an unusual construction, and the text may be corrupt. After *gar* one would expect either the simple infinitive (*agasp* or *gasp*, cf. 2068) or the construction 'for to gasp', cf. *gar them to quake*, 1515, and see Visser, II, p. 764.

1510. *set by*] cared for.

1511. *Vaspasian*] Vespasian, Roman emperor A.D. 70–79. The spelling Vaspasian is retained here for the pun: see next note.

that bare in his nose a wasp] According to the *Legenda Aurea*, Vespasian had suffered in youth from a plague of wasps which grew in his head and flew in and out of his nose. He was healed of this plague when converted to Christianity. (See W. Metcalfe, *Legends of the Saints* (1846), III, p. 120.)

1512. *Hannibal*] Hannibal, 247–182 B.C., was the great leader of the Carthaginians against Rome in the Second Punic War.

again Rome gates that ran] who charged the gates of Rome (*O.E.D* run v. 6b).

1513. *Cipio*] Scipio Africanus Major (Publius Cornelius Scipio) 236–*c.* 183 B.C., consul in the second year of the First Punic War. *Cipio* should probably be pronounced with a hard *c*, to alliterate with *Carthage*; I have not printed 'Scipio' for this reason. Alliteration in this passage is not consistent, however. See Intro., pp. 53–4.

1514. *that durst crake*] who dares brag.

1515. *frounce them on the foretop*] curl their hair (with fright, presumably).

gar] make (see note on 1509).

1515.1. doing reverence and courtesy] bowing and scraping.

1518. *what I do shall*] what I must do.

Magnificence. Let us hear of your pleasure, to pass the
    time withal.
Abusion. Sir, then, with the favour of your benign
    sufferance,   1520
    To show you my mind myself I will advance—
    If it like your grace to take it in degree.
Magnificence. Yes, sir; so good man in you I see
    And in your dealing so good assurance
    That we delight greatly in your dalliance.   1525
Abusion. Ah, sir, your grace me doth extol and raise,
    And far beyond my merits ye me commend and
        praise;
    Howbeit I would be right glad, I you assure,
    Anything to do that might be to your pleasure,
Magnificence. As I be saved, with pleasure I am surprised 1530
    Of your language, it is so well devised;
    Polished and fresh is your ornacy.
Abusion. Ah, I would to God that I were half so crafty,
    Or in elect utterance half so eloquent
    As that I might your noble grace content.   1535
Magnificence. Trust me, with you I am highly pleased,
    For in my favour I have you feoffed and seised;

1537. seised] seasyd *F*.

   1520. *sufferance*] permission.

   1522. *like*] please.

   in degree] apparently for 'in gree' = 'kindly, in good part'.

   1523. *so good man in you I see*] I see you to be such a good man.

   1524. *assurance*] confidence, trust.

   1525. *dalliance*] chat.

   1529. *pleasure*] Stress on second syllable; cf. 1410.

   1530–1.] Here *surprised*, 'overcome, affected', has two objects: 'I am overcome with pleasure; I am affected by your language'. 'Pleasure' being Abusion's
name, Magnificence means also that he is surprised by him.

   1532.] This is great praise; cf. Caxton's view of Skelton, quoted in Intro.,
p. 2.

   ornacy] ornateness (of style).

   1533. *crafty*] Abusion means 'skilful', but the sense 'cunning' is more appropriate to him.

   1534. *elect utterance*] carefully chosen words.

   1537.] 'For I have invested you legally with my favour' (*enfeoff*, 'put in legal
possession', and *seise*, 'invest with', are legal terms).

He is not living your manners can amend;

Marry, your speech is as pleasant as though it were
    penned.

To hear your common it is my high comfort;   1540

Point-device, all pleasure is your port.

Abusion. Sir, I am the better of your noble report.

But of your patience under the support,

If it would like you to hear my poor mind—

Magnificence. Speak, I beseech thee; leave nothing
    behind.   1545

Abusion. So as ye be a prince of great might,

It is seeming your pleasure ye delight,

And to acquaint you with carnal delectation,

And to fall in acquaintance with every new fashion;

And, quickly your appetites to sharp and address,   1550

To fasten your fancy upon a fair mistress

That quickly is envived with ruddies of the rose,

Inpurtured with features after your purpose,

The strains of her veins as azure indy blue,

1554. indy] Inde *F*.

1538. *can*] who can (see note on 504).

1540. *common*] discourse.

1541. *Point-device*] to perfection. Cf. 842.

1542. *of*] for.

1543. *under the support*] See note on 61.

1544. *mind*] opinion.

1546. *So as*] since.

1547. *seeming*] fitting.

1548. *And to acquaint you*] and that you should acquaint yourself.

carnal] A pun on 'cardinal'. See Intro., note 98.

1550. *sharp and address*] whet and direct.

1552 ff.] Cf. *Knolege*, esp: 'Your ruddys wyth ruddy rubys may compare; / Saphyre of sadnes, enuayned wyth indy blew' (16–17); 'Relucent smaragd' (21); 'Illumynyd wyth feturys far passyng my reporte;' (23); see Intro., p. 52.

quickly] vigorously.

envived] enlivened.

ruddies] reds.

1553. *Inpurtured*] adorned. Not in *O.E.D.*

after] befitting (*O.E.D.* adv. 15).

1554. *strains*] = contents? *O.E.D.* does not record this meaning, but Skelton's use here seems related to 3: 'The germinal vesicle in the yolk of an egg'.

indy blue] indigo.

Enbudded with beauty and colour fresh of hue,　　1555
As lily white to look upon her lere,
Her eyen relucent as carbuncle so clear,
Her mouth enbalmed, delectable and merry,
Her lusty lips ruddy as the cherry—
How like you? Ye lack, sir, such a lusty lass.　　1560
Magnificence. Ah, that were a baby to brace and to buss!
I would I had, by Him that Hell did harrow,
With me in keeping such a Philip Sparrow.
I would hawk whilst my head did wark,
So I might hobby for such a lusty lark.　　1565
These words in mine ear they be so lustily spoken,
That on such a female my flesh would be wroken;
They touch me so thoroughly, and tickle my conceit,
That weryed I would be on such a bait.
Ah, cock's arms, where might such one be found?　　1570
Abusion. Will ye spend any money?
Magnificence.　　　　　　　　　　Yea, a thousand pound.

1556. lere] leyre *Dyce;* heyre *F.*　　1561. buss] basse *F.*

1556. *lere*] countenance. Dyce's emendation is clearly correct; it was conventional to compare a lady's *lere* with lilies; cf. 'With lilye-white leres lossum he [i.e. she] is' (*The Harley Lyrics,* ed. G. L. Brook (1956), p. 31).

1557. *relucent*] shining.

1558. *enbalmed*] made sweet and fragrant.

1560. *How like you?*] How does that please you?

1561. *baby*] doll, puppet (*O.E.D.* sb. 2 (1552)).

to brace and to buss] to embrace and kiss.

1563. *Philip Sparrow*] i.e. a sweet little bird: sparrows were reported to be lecherous. '*Philip*, or *Phip* was a familiar name given to a sparrow from its note being supposed to resemble that sound' (Dyce, II, p. 121). Skelton's *Sparowe,* an epitaph for a departed favourite killed by a cat, would be recalled here: Magnificence wants to pursue the lady as Gib the cat did Philip (see 1569).

1564–5.] See Intro., pp. 34–5.

wark] ache.

1565. *hobby*] hawk with a hobby (small falcon).

1567. *wroken*] gratified.

1568. *conceit*] fancy.

1569. *weryed*] See *O.E.D.* worry v. 3c: 'To bite at or upon (an object); to kiss or hug vehemently'; cf. 'Gib, I saye, our cat / Worrowyd her on that / Which I loued best' (*Sparowe,* 28–30). F spelling is retained because the modern 'worried' would not give the right sense, and is considerably different in sound.

Abusion. Nay, nay, for less I warrant you to be sped;
    And brought home and laid in your bed.
Magnificence. Would money, trowest thou, make such
    one to the call?
Abusion. Money maketh merchants, I tell you, over all. 1575
Magnificence. Why, will a mistress be won for money
    and for gold?
Abusion. Why, was not for money Troy both bought and
    sold?
    Full many a strong city and town hath been won
    By the means of money, without any gun.
    A mistress, I tell you, is but a small thing;   1580
    A goodly ribbon, or a gold ring,
    May win with a sault the fortress or the hold;
    But one thing I warn you, press forth and be bold.
Magnificence. Yea, but some be full coy and passing hard-
    hearted.
Abusion. But, blessed be our Lord, they will be soon
    converted.   1585
Magnificence. Why, will they then be entreated, the most
    and the least?
Abusion. Yea, for *omnis mulier meritrix si celari potest*.
Magnificence. Ah, I have spied ye can much broken
    sorrow.

1582. or] *this ed.; of F.*   1587. *meritrix*] *F;* meretrix *Dyce.*

1572. *sped*] successful.

1574. *to the call*] immediately available. The hawking and luring metaphor is continued in *call*: 'A particular sound or cry used to attract or decoy birds' (*O.E.D.* sb. 3).

1575.] Proverbial; Tilley M1078. For its possible implications here, see Intro., p. 43, note 140.

1577.] 'The first destruction of Lamedon's Troy (which preceded Priam's) was due in classical myth to his failure to pay Poseidon (the earth-shaker) his wages for building it' (D. Pearsall, *John Lydgate* (1970), p. 124).

1582. *sault*] assault.

hold] stronghold.

1584. *coy*] unresponsive (*O.E.D.* 2a).

1587.] 'Yes, for "every woman is a whore if it can be hidden".' Cf. the proverb 'All women would be whores if men besought them'; Whiting W484.

1588. *can much broken sorrow*] know much petty misery (?); the meaning of

Abusion. I could hold you with such talk hence till to-
     morrow;
     But if it like your grace more at large   1590
     Me to permit my mind to discharge,
     I would yet show you further of my conceit.
Magnificence. Let see what ye say; show it straight.
Abusion. Wisely let these words in your mind be weighed:
     By wayward wilfulness let each thing be conveyed; 1595
     Whatsoever ye do, follow your own will,
     Be it reason or none it shall not greatly skill;
     Be it right or wrong, by the advice of me
     Take your pleasure and use free liberty;
     And if you see anything against your mind,   1600
     Then some occasion or quarrell ye must find,
     And frown it and face it as though ye would fight,
     Fret yourself for anger and for despite;
     Hear no man whatsoever they say,
     But do as ye list and take your own way.   1605
Magnificence. Thy words and my mind oddly well accord.
Abusion. What should ye do else? Are not you a lord?
     Let your lust and liking stand for a law;
     Be wresting and writhing, and away draw;

1601. occasion or] occacyon or *Ramsay;* accacyon or *F;* occacyon of *Dyce.*

---

broken sorrow is uncertain. Cf. 'They konne so muchel craft on Wades boot, / So
muchel broken harm' (*Canterbury Tales*, IV.1424–5, and Robinson's note, p.
714, where *broken harm* is glossed as 'petty annoyances'). In *Mankind* Mercy says
of the Vices that 'þei kan moche sorow' (*Macro*, p. 162, l. 256).

   1589. *hence*] from now.
   1592. *conceit*] opinion.
   1597. *skill*] matter.
   1599.] Although the concepts 'pleasure' and 'liberty' in general are mainly
meant here, this reminds us that 'Pleasure' (Abusion) and Liberty are played by
the same actor. See Intro., p. 48.
    1600. *against your mind*] in opposition to your wish (*O.E.D.* mind sb.[1] 9e).
    1601. *occasion*] opportunity of fault-finding (*O.E.D.* sb.[1] 1).
    1602. *frown it and face it*] look stern and bullying.
    1608. *lust and liking*] (1) pleasure; (2) sexual appetite.
    1609. *wresting and writhing*] turning and twisting.
    draw] move.

And ye see a man that with him ye be not pleased, 1610
And that your mind cannot well be eased,
(As if a man fortune to touch you on the quick),
Then feign yourself diseased, and make yourself sick;
To stir up your stomach you must you forge;
Call for a caudle and cast up your gorge, 1615
With: 'Cock's arms, rest shall I none have
Till I be revenged on that whoreson knave!
Ah, how my stomach wambleth! I am all in a sweat.
Is there no whoreson that knave that will beat?'

Magnificence. By cock's wounds, a wonder fellow thou
art, 1620
For ofttimes such a wambling goth over my heart;
Yet I am not heart-sick but that me list;
For mirth I have him curried, beaten, and blissed,
Him that I loved not, and made him to lowt;
I am forthwith as whole as a trout; 1625
For such abusion I use now and then.

Abusion. It is none abusion, sir, in a noble man,
It is a princely pleasure, and a lordly mind;
Such lusts at large may not be left behind.

Here cometh in CLOAKED COLLUSION *with* MEASURE.

Collusion. [*Aside to* MEASURE] Stand still here, and ye
shall see 1630

1615. caudle] caudell *conj. Dyce;* candell *F.*   1623. curried] coryed
F.   1626. then] than *F.*

1614. *forge*] pretend.
1615. *caudle*] 'A warm drink . . . given chiefly to sick people' (*O.E.D.* sb. 1).
Dyce's conjecture that F *candell* was a misprint, though he later retracted it (see
Dyce, II, p. 487), seems right in view of *cast up your gorge* (= 'vomit'), and *you
were wont to have caudles for your head*, 2009.
1618. *wambleth*] heaves with nausea.
1621. *wambling*] feeling of nausea.
1622. *but that me list*] except as it pleases me.
1623. *curried*] thrashed.
blissed] beaten.
1625. *as whole as a trout*] Proverbial; Tilley T536.
1630. *here*] i.e. at some distance from Magnificence, and not visible to him or
Abusion (see 1686).

That for your sake I will fall on my knee.

Abusion. Sir Sober Sadness cometh; wherefore it be?

[COLLUSION *kneels.*]

Magnificence. Stand up, sir; ye are welcome to me.

Collusion. Please it your grace, at the contemplation

    Of my poor instance and supplication,   1635

    Tenderly to consider in your advertence—

    Of our blessed Lord, sir, at the reverence—

    Remember the good service that Measure hath you

       done,

    And that ye will not cast him away so soon.

Magnificence. My friend, as touching to this your mo-

    tion,   1640

    I may say to you I have but small devotion;

    Howbeit at your instance I will the rather

    Do as much as for mine own father.

Collusion. Nay sir, that affection ought to be reserved,

    For of your grace I have it nought deserved;   1645

    But if it like you that I might roun in your ear,

    To show you my mind I would have the less fear.

Magnificence. [*To* ABUSION] Stand a little aback, sir,

    and let him come hither.

Abusion. With a good will, sir. God speed you both

    together.

Collusion. [*Aside of* MAGNIFICENCE] Sir, so it is: this

    man is here by   1650

1632. *wherefore it be?*] why is it?

1634 ff.] This speech is made in a very formal manner, quite unlike Collusion's usual style. See Intro., p. 52.

contemplation] petition (*O.E.D.* 5b).

1635. *instance*] urgent entreaty (*O.E.D.* sb. 1).

1637. *at the reverence*] in honour.

1639.] This line completes the request begun in *Please it your grace,* 1634.

1640. *as touching to*] with regard to.

1641. *devotion*] enthusiasm (*O.E.D.* sb. 5).

1642. *rather*] more quickly.

1644. *affection*] feeling, disposition.

reserved] kept back, restrained.

1646. *roun*] whisper.

1650. *this man*] i.e. Measure.

That for him to labour he hath prayed me heartily;
Notwithstanding to you be it said
To trust in me he is but deceived;
For so help me God, for you he is not meet.
(I speak the softlier because he should not weet).   1655
Magnificence. [*To* ABUSION] Come hither, Pleasure;
      you shall hear mine intent.
   Measure, ye know well, with him I cannot be
      content;
   And surely as I am now advised,
   I will have him rehaited and despised.
   How say ye, sirs? Herein what is best?   1660
Abusion. By mine advice, with you, in faith, he shall not
      rest.
Collusion. Yet sir, reserved your better advisement,
   . It were better he spake with you or he went,
   That he know not but that I have supplied
   All that I can his matter for to speed.   1665
Magnificence. Now by your troth, gave he you not a
      bribe?
Collusion. Yes, with his hand I made him to subscribe
   A bill of record for an annual rent.

1652. Notwithstanding] Notwithstandynge *Dyce;* Notwithstanyynge
F. said] sayde *F.*   1653. deceived] dyssayued *F.*   1659. rehaited]
rehayted *F.*

1652–3.] For the rhyme (F *sayde/dyssayued*), cf. 604–5.

1655. *weet*] know.

1659. *rehaited*] Obscure. *O.E.D.* considers it a variant of rehete v.[2], one
meaning of which is 'rebuke, scold'. Dyce, comparing *inhateth*, 2431 (the
meaning of which is also uncertain), suggested the meaning 're-hated'. Com-
parison with 'rehatour', in Dunbar's *Flyting of Dunbar and Kennedie* (244, 401),
is unhelpful, since this is also 'A term of abuse of obscure origin and meaning'
(*O.E.D.*).

1662. *reserved your better advisement*] with due respect for your superior
opinion.

1664. *supplied*] supplicated.

1665. *speed*] cause to succeed.

1666.] This shows how far Magnificence errs in his judgement of Measure.

1667. *subscribe*] sign his name to.

1668. *bill of record*] legal document, deed.

Abusion. But for all that he is like to have a glent.

Collusion. Yea by my troth, I shall warrant you for me,   1670
    And he go to the devil, so that I may have my fee
    What care I?

Magnificence.   By the mass, well said.

Abusion. What force ye, so that ye be paid?

Collusion. [*To* ABUSION] But yet, lo, I would or that he
    went,
    Lest that he thought that his money were evil spent,   1675
    That he would look on him, though it were not long.

Magnificence. Well canst thou help a priest to sing a
    song.

Collusion. So it is all the manner nowadays,
    For to use such hafting, and crafty ways.

Abusion. He telleth you truth, sir, as I you ensure.   1680

Magnificence. Well, for thy sake the better I may endure
    That he come hither, and to give him a look
    That he shall like the worse all this week.

Collusion. I care not how soon he be refused,
    So that I may craftily be excused.   1685

Abusion. Where is he?

1671. devil] deuyll *Dyce;* deull *F.*   1673. ye be] *Dyce;* he be *F.*   1676.
That he] *F;* That ye *Dyce.*   1682. That he] *Dyce;* Tha the *F.*   *look*]
loke *F.*   1683. week] woke *F.*

1669.] This probably means: 'But even so, he will probably glimpse (that you have deceived him)'. Dyce, comparing 'glint' = 'slippery' in *Garlande* 572, suggested that *glent* = 'slip, fall'. However, the usual meaning of *glent* is 'glance, gleam', and *O.E.D.* cites no other examples with Dyce's suggested meaning.

1670. *for me*] for my part.

1673. *What force ye*] what do you care. This echoes Collusion's *What care I* (1672); the line is clearly addressed to Collusion and I therefore follow Dyce in emending *he* to *ye*, though Ramsay retains *he*, commenting that Abusion addresses this line to Magnificence.

1674. *he*] i.e. Measure.

1676. *he*] Magnificence. Here F seems correct, although both Dyce and Ramsay emend to *ye*. Collusion is replying to Abusion's question in the previous line.

1677.] i.e. 'You're a fine hypocrite'.

1684. *refused*] rejected.

Collusion.   Marry, I made him abide,
    Whilst I came to you, a little here beside.
Magnificence. Well, call him, and let us hear him reason;
                          [COLLUSION *goes to* MEASURE.]
    And we will be commoning in the mean season.
Abusion. This is a wise man, sir, wheresoever ye him had.   1690
Magnificence. An honest person, I tell you, and a sad.
Abusion. He can full craftily this matter bring about.
Magnificence. Whilst I have him I need nothing doubt.

    Here let COLLUSION *bring* MEASURE *forward,*
    MAGNIFICENCE *looking on with a very haughty expression.*

Collusion. [*To* MEASURE] By the mass, I have done that
        I can,
    And more than ever I did for any man;   1695
    I trow ye heard yourself what I said.
Measure. Nay indeed, but I saw how ye prayed,
    And made instance for me be likelihood.
Collusion. Nay, I tell you, I am not wont to fode
    Them that dare put their trust in me;   1700
    And thereof ye shall a larger proof see.
Measure. Sir, God reward you as ye have deserved.
    But think you with Magnificence I shall be reserved?
Collusion. By my troth, I cannot tell you that;
    But and I were as ye, I would not set a gnat   1705

1693.1–2.] Hic introducat colusion mesure magnyfycence aspectante vultu
elatissimo. *F.*

1689. *commoning*] talking together.
mean season] meantime.
1690. *This*] i.e. Collusion.
1691. *a sad*] A reference to Collusion's assumed name, 'Sober Sadness'.
1692. *craftily*] See note on 1533.
1693. *doubt*] fear.
1693.2. with a very haughty expression] Cf. 572.2.
.1697. *prayed*] entreated.
1698. *be likelihood*] as it seemed.
1699. *fode*] beguile.
1702.] A touch of irony here, whether intended by Measure or not.
1703. *reserved*] retained.
1705. *not set a gnat*] Cf. the proverb 'To set not a fly'; cited in note on 412.

By Magnificence, nor yet none of his;

For go when ye shall, of you shall he miss.

Measure. Sir, as ye say.

Collusion. Nay, come on with me; [*They approach*
     MAGNIFICENCE]

Yet once again I shall fall on my knee

For your sake, whatsoever befall;   1710

[*Aside*]. I set not a fly and all go to all.

Measure. [*To* MAGNIFICENCE] The Holy Ghost be with
     your grace.

Collusion. [*Kneels*] Sir, I beseech you let pity have some
     place

In your breast towards this gentleman.

Magnificence. [*To* MEASURE] I was your good lord till
     that ye began   1715

So masterfully upon you for to take

With my servants, and such mast'ries gan make

That wholly my mind with you is miscontent;

Wherefore I will that ye be resident

With me no longer.

Collusion.   Say somewhat now, let see,   1720

For yourself.

Measure.   Sir, if I might permitted be,

I would to you say a word or twain—

Magnificence. What, wouldst thou, lurden, with me brawl
     again!

1718. miscontent] myscontente *Dyce;* myscon tente *F.*   1720–1.] *line
arrangement conj. Dyce;* with me no longer | Clokyd colusyon ❡ Say some-
what nowe let se/for your selfe *F.*

1707. *of you shall he miss*] he will feel the want of you (*O.E.D.* miss v.[1] 23f).

1711. *set not a fly*] See note on 412.

and all go to all] finally ('when everything is summed up' *O.E.D.* all 8e).

1716–17.] The verb has two objects: 'take upon yourself', and take (i.e. 'deal',
O.E.D. v. 26) with my servants': 'To take upon yourself to deal so overbearingly
with my servants'. (Cf. 1530–1.)

such mast'ries gan make] dominated so (*O.E.D.* mastery 1).

1718. *miscontent*] dissatisfied.

1721. *For yourself*] These words are printed with the previous line in F.

Have him hence I say, out of my sight!
That day I see him I shall be worse all night.   1725

Here MEASURE *goeth out of the place [forcibly removed by*
ABUSION].

Abusion. Hence, thou hainiard! Out of the doors, fast!
Magnificence. Alas, my stomach fareth as it would cast!
Collusion. Abide, sir, abide; let me hold your head.
Magnificence. A bowl or a basin I say, for God's bread!
     [*He is given a bowl.*]
     Ah, my head! But is the whoreson gone?   1730
     God give him a mischief! Nay, now let me alone.
Collusion. A good drift, sir; a pretty feat.
     By the good lord, yet your temples beat.
Magnificence. Nay, so God me help, it was no great vexa-
          tion,
     For I am panged ofttimes of this same fashion.   1735
Collusion. Cock's arms, how Pleasure plucked him
          forth!
Magnificence. Yea, walk he must; it was no better worth.
Collusion. Sir, now methink your heart is well eased.
Magnificence. Now Measure is gone I am the better
          pleased.
Collusion. So to be ruled by Measure it is a pain.   1740
Magnificence. Marry, I ween he would not be glad to
          come again.
Collusion. So I wot not what he should do here,

1725.1. forcibly removed] See 1736.
1726. *hainiard*] Another obscure term of abuse, probably meaning 'wretch'.
Not in *O.E.D.*, but cf. 'hayne': 'A term of reproach: A mean wretch, a niggard'.
   Out of the doors] See Intro., p. 44, and cf. 568.
1727 ff.] Magnificence proceeds to follow Abusion's advice in 1613 ff.
1727. *cast*] vomit.
1728. *Abide*] hold on.
1729.1. given a bowl] Perhaps by a member of the audience. See Intro., p.
45.
1732. *drift*] device.
1736. *plucked*] dragged.
1737. *it was no better worth*] there was no alternative.

Where men's bellies is measured there is no cheer;
For I hear but few men that give any praise
Unto measure, I say, nowadays.   1745
Magnificence. Measure? Tut, what the devil of Hell,
Scantly one with measure that will dwell.
Collusion. Not among noble men, as the world goth.
It is no wonder, therefore, though ye be wroth
With Measure. Whereas all nobleness is, there I
    have passed,   1750
They catch that catch may, keep and hold fast,
Out of all measure themself to enrich,
No force what though his neighbour die in a ditch.
With polling and plucking out of all measure,
Thus must ye stuff and store your treasure.   1755
Magnificence. Yet sometime, pardy, I must use largesse.
Collusion. Yea marry, sometime—in a mess of vergesse,
As in a trifle or in a thing of nought:
As giving a thing that ye never bought.
It is the guise now, I say, over all,   1760
Largesse in words—for rewards are but small.
To make fair promise what are ye the worse?
Let me have the rule of your purse.
Magnificence. I have taken it to Largesse and Liberty.
Collusion. Then is it done as it should be.   1765
But use your largesse by the advice of me,

1743.] Cf. the proverb 'A fasting belly may never be merry'; Tilley B292
(1536).

1747. *Scantly*] hardly.

1750. *Whereas*] where.

there I have passed] where I have been.

1751. *catch that catch may*] Proverbial; Tilley C189.

1753. *force*] matter.

1754. *polling and plucking*] plundering and stripping.

1757. *mess of vergesse*] dish of verjuice ('The acid juice of green or unripe
grapes, crab-apples, or other sour fruit, expressed and formed into a liquor'
(*O.E.D.*)).

1758. *trifle*] (1) trivial thing; (2) probably, in view of *mess of vergesse*, 'A dish
composed of cream boiled with various ingredients' (*O.E.D.* sb. 6 (1598)).

1764. *taken*] entrusted (*O.E.D.* v. 60).

    And I shall warrant you wealth and liberty.

Magnificence. Say on; methink your reasons be
      profound.

Collusion. Sir, of my counsel this shall be the ground:

    To chose out two, three of such as you love best,   1770
    And let all your fancies upon them rest.

    Spare for no cost to give them pound and penny;
    Better to make three rich than for to make many.
    Give them more than enough, and let them not
      lack,

    And as for all other, let them truss and pack.   1775
    Pluck from an hundred and give it to three;
    Let neither patent scape them, nor fee;
    And wheresoever you will fall to a reckoning,
    Those three will be ready even at your beckoning,
    For them shall you have at liberty to lowt.   1780
    Let them have all, and the other go without.
    Thus joy without measure you shall have.

Magnificence. Thou sayst truth, by the heart that God
      me gave!

    For as thou sayst, right so shall it be.
    And here I make thee upon Liberty   1785
    To be supervisor, and on Largesse also,
    For as thou wilt so shall the game go.
    For in Pleasure and Surveyance and also in thee

1780. them] *conj. Dyce;* then *F.*

1768. *reasons*] observations (*O.E.D.*sb.[1] 3).
1769. *ground*] basis.
1770. *To chose*] that you should chose.
1771. *fancies*] inclinations or whims.
1772. *Spare for no cost*] Cf. 890.
1775. *all other*] all the rest.
truss and pack] take themselves off (*O.E.D.*truss v. 4).
1777. *patent*] licence of privilege.
scape] elude.
1778. *fall to a reckoning*] take account.
1781. *the other*] the rest.
1785. *upon*] over.
1788. *Pleasure and Surveyance*] i.e. Abusion and Conveyance.

    I have set my whole felicity,
    And such as you will shall lack no promotion.   1790
Collusion. Sir, sith that in me ye have such devotion,
    Committing to me and to my fellows twain
    Your wealth and felicity, I trust we shall obtain
    To do you service after your appetite.
Magnificence. In faith, and your service right well shall
    I acquite.   1795
    And therefore hie you hence, and take this oversight.
Collusion. Now Jesu preserve you, sir, prince most of might.

> *Here goeth* CLOAKED COLLUSION *away and leaveth*
> MAGNIFICENCE *alone in the place.*

Magnificence. Thus, I say, I am environed with solace;
    I dread no dints of fatal destiny.
    Well were that lady might stand in my grace,   1800
    Me to enbrace and love most specially;
    Ah lord, so I would halse her heartily!
    So I would clip her, so I would kiss her sweet!

> *Here cometh in* FOLLY [*with his hawk, injured*].

Folly. Marry, Christ grant ye catch no cold on your feet!

Magnificence. Who is this?

1803. clip] clepe *F*.

    1791. *devotion*] loyalty.
    1793–4. *obtain / To do*] succeed in doing.
    1795. *acquite*] requite.
    1796. *oversight*] superintendence.
    1798. *environed with solace*] surrounded by comfort.
    1799.] But cf. 1879.
    1800. *might*] who might (see note on 504).
    1802. *halse*] embrace.
    1803. *clip*] hug.
    1803.1. with his hawk, injured] The hawk which he acquired from Fancy, in exchange for his dog; for its 'injury' see 1811.
    1804 ff.] Folly proceeds to entertain Magnificence with what Dodsley (I, p. 50) calls 'a string of nonsensical incongruities', a device frequently used for comic effect in the interludes. Cf. the speeches of Ignorance in *The Four*

Folly.   Conceit, sir, your own man.   1805

Magnificence. What tidings with you, sir? I befool thy
      brain-pan.

Folly. By our lakin sir, I have been a-hawking for the
      wild swan;

    My hawk is rammish, and it happed that she ran—

    Flew I should say—into an old barn

    To reach at a rat. I could not her warn;   1810

    She pinched her pinion, by God, and catched harm.
      [*Shows off injured hawk.*]

    It was a runner. Nay, fool, I warrant her blood-warm.

Magnificence. Ah sir, thy gerfalcon and thou be
      hanged together!

Folly. And sir, as I was coming to you hither,

    I saw a fox suck on a cow's udder;   1815

1813. gerfalcon] Iarfawcon *F*.   1814. hither] hyder *F*.   1815. udder]
ydder *F*.

Elements (Dodsley, I, pp. 49–50); of Covetous in *Enough* (306–53); of Inclination
in *The Trial of Treasure* (Dodsley, III, pp. 267–8), and of Courage in *Tide
Tarrieth* (251–75).) Typical in this nonsense is the inclusion of a string of
marvellous or unlikely events: 'The Moon lying in childbed of her last son'
(*Enough*, 307), 'I can remember since Noe's ship / Was made, and builded on
Salisbury Plain' (*The Trial of Treasure*, p. 267). They often involved the natural
world, as in 1815 here. These speeches have the riddling quality of some
medieval lyrics: cf. 'heringes in parkes hornes boldly blowe, . . . And mice
mowe corn with waveying of ther tailes' (*Medieval English Lyrics*, ed. R. T.
Davies (1963), pp. 223–4). The use of this device for Folly, in his rôle as court
fool to Magnificence, is particularly appropriate.

1804.] This line may be addressed to the audience, rather than to
Magnificence.

  1806. *I befool thy brain-pan*] See note on 875.

  1808. *rammish*] wild.

  1810. *reach at*] get at.

  warn] prevent.

  1811. *pinion*] wing.

  1812. *It*] i.e. the rat.

  Nay, fool] This may be addressed to a member of the audience, who is
lamenting the hawk's 'death'. Folly always calls Magnificence 'sir', so he is not
speaking to him. Alternatively, he may be talking to himself.

  I warrant her blood-warm] I guarantee she is alive (*O.E.D.* blood-warm a.
(1577)).

  1813. *gerfalcon*] large falcon.

And with a lime-rod I took them both together.

I trow it be a frost, for the way is slidder;

See, for God avow, for cold as I chidder.

Magnificence. Thy words hang together as feathers in the
        wind.

Folly. Ah sir, told I not you how I did find   1820

A knave and a carl, and all of one kind?

I saw a weathercock wag with the wind,

Great marvel I had, and mused in my mind;

The hounds ran before, and the hare behind;

I saw a losel lead a lurden, and they were both blind;   1825

I saw a souter go to supper or ever he had dined.

Magnificence. By cock's heart, thou art a fine merry
        knave.

Folly. [*Aside*] I make God avow ye will none other men
        have.

Magnificence. What sayst thou?

Folly.   Marry, I pray God your
        mastership to save.

1816. together] togyder *F*.   1817. slidder] slydder *F*.   1818. chidder]
chydder *F*.

1816. *lime rod*] rod smeared with bird-lime (for catching birds, normally).
took] captured.

1817. *slidder*] slippery.

1818. *chidder*] shiver (Not in O.E.D., but cf. chitter v. 3).

1819.] Cf. the proverbs 'Words and feathers the wind carries away'; Tilley
W831 (1591), and 'As wavering as feathers in the wind'; Tilley F162. Especially
comparable are 'But my words as feathers in the wind you have weighed'
(*Enough*, 158), and 'A song much like thauthour of the same, / It hangeth
together like fethers in the winde' (*The Longer*, Diir — not cited in Tilley). See
note on 984–5.

1822.] Cf. Inclination's 'the weathercock of Paul's caught the pip' (*The Trial
of Treasure*, Dodsley, III, p. 267); Covetous's 'he carried away the weathercock
in spite of the people' (*Enough*, 333).

wag] sway.

1823. *marvel*] astonishment.

1824.] Contrast the proverb 'To chase (or follow) as hound does the hare';
Whiting H577, H582.

1825.] Cf. the proverb 'If the blind lead the blind they both fall into the ditch';
Tilley, B452.

1826. *souter*] cobbler.

I shall give you a gaud of a gosling that I gave   1830
The gander and the goose both grazing on one
    grave;
Then Rowland the reeve ran, and I began to rave,
And with a bristle of a boar his beard did I shave.

Magnificence. If ever I heard sic another God give me
    shame.

Folly. Sim Saddle-goose was my sire, and Dawcock my
    dame;   1835
I could, and I list, gar you laugh at a game
How a woodcock wrestled with a lark that was lame;
The bitter said boldly that they were to blame;
The fieldfare would have fiddled, and it would not
    frame;
The crane and the curlew thereat gan to grame;   1840
The snite snivelled in the snout and smiled at the game.

Magnificence. Cock's bones! Heard you ever such
    another?

Folly. See, sir, I beseech you, Largesse my brother.

Here FANCY *cometh in.*

1835. sire] syer *F*.

1830–1.] A combination of two proverbs: 'Goose and gander and gosling are
three sounds but one thing'; Tilley, G351 (1659), and 'He hopes to eat of the
goose that shall graze on your grave'; Tilley, G353.

    1830. *gaud*] jest.

    1832. *reeve*] bailiff (christened 'Rowland' to alliterate, probably).

    1835. *Saddle-goose*] 'a nickname for a fool' (*O.E.D.*).

    sire] F *syer*, disyllabic.

    Dawcock] another name for a fool; a favourite of Skelton's. Cf. 'This doctour
Dawcocke, Drede, I wene, he hyghte' (*Bowge*, 303); '*Domine* Dawcocke! / Ware
the hawke' (*Hauke*, 244–5 and *passim*); 'This is the tenor of my byl, / A daucock
ye be, and so shalbe styll' (*Why come*, 1247–8).

    1838. *bitter*] bittern.

    1839. *fiddled*] played the fiddle.

    frame] succeed.

    1840. *grame*] fret.

    1841. *snite*] snipe.

    1843.] Fancy enters appropriately after Magnificence's question.

Magnificence. What tidings with you sir, that you look
    so sad?
Fancy. When ye know that I know, ye will not be glad. 1845
Folly. What, brother Brainsick! How farest thou?
Magnificence. Yea, let be thy japes, and tell me how
    The case requireth.
Fancy.   Alas, alas, an heavy meeting!
    I would tell you and if I might for weeping.
Folly. What, is all your mirth now turned to sorrow?   1850
    Farewell till soon; adieu till tomorrow.

> *Here goeth* FOLLY *away*.

Magnificence. I pray thee, Largesse, let be thy sobbing.
Fancy. Alas sir, ye are undone with stealing and robbing.
    Ye sent us a supervisor for to take heed;
    Take heed of yourself, for now ye have need.   1855
Magnificence. What, hath Sadness beguiled me so?
Fancy. Nay, madness hath beguiled you, and many mo;
    For Liberty is gone, and also Felicity.
Magnificence. Gone! Alas, ye have undone me!
Fancy. Nay, he that ye sent us, Cloaked Collusion,   1860
    And your painted 'Pleasure', Courtly Abusion,
    And your 'demeanour' with Counterfeit
        Countenance,
    And your 'Surveyor', Crafty Conveyance,

1848. meeting] metynge *F*.   1849. weeping] wepynge *F*.   1863. 'Surveyor'] suruayour *Dyce;* superuysour *F*.

1847–8. *how / The case requireth*] what the situation calls for (*O.E.D.* require v. 6b).

1848–9.] For the rhyme (F *metynge / wepynge*), cf. 534–5.

1854. *a supervisor*] i.e. 'Sober Sadness' or Collusion; see 1785–6.

1858.] Although Fancy is speaking primarily of the characters Liberty and Felicity (hence they are capitalised), the meaning is also that Magnificence has lost his power of choice and happiness in general.

1861. *painted*] feigned (*O.E.D.* ppl. a. 2b).

1862. *demeanour*] 'behaviour'; 'Good Demeanance' was the assumed name of Countenance.

1863. '*Surveyor*'] 'Sure Surveyance' was the assumed name of Conveyance. (Dyce's emendation is sound, for the 'supervisor' was Collusion; see note on 1854.)

Or ever we were ware, brought us in adversity,
And had robbed you quite from all felicity.   1865
Magnificence. Why, is this the largesse that I have used?
Fancy. Nay, it was your fondness that ye have used.
Magnificence. And is this the credence that I gave to the
    letter?
Fancy. Why, could not your wit serve you no better?
Magnificence. Why, who would have thought in you
    such guile?   1870
Fancy. What, yes, by the rood, sir, it was I all this while
That you trusted, and Fancy is my name;
And Folly my brother, that made you much game.

Here cometh in ADVERSITY.

Magnificence. Alas, who is yonder that grimly looks?
Fancy. Adieu, for I will not come in his clokes.   1875
                    [*Exit* FANCY.]
Magnificence. Lord, so my flesh trembleth now for dread!

Here MAGNIFICENCE *is beaten down and spoiled
    from all his goods and raiment.*

Adversity. I am Adversity, that for thy misdeed

1874. who] *F(CUL);* why *F(BL).*   looks] lokys *F.*   1875. clokes] clokys
F.   1875.1.] *Ramsay.*

1867. *fondness*] foolishness. Fancy here reveals *his* true character.

1868. *the letter*] See 311 ff.

1875. *clokes*] clutches, perhaps literally claws; see Intro., p. 46.

1876.1. beaten down] by a *dint* of Adversity's (?clawed) hand, see 1880; 1885
suggests how this is done.

spoiled from] deprived of (*O.E.D.* v.[1] 8). Cf. the scene in *The Longer*, where
God's Judgement orders Confusion to 'spoyle' the fool Moros 'of his aray' and
'geue him his fooles coate' (Giir).

1877 ff.] Adversity's tone and terminology is similar to that of Death in some
medieval plays. With his description of himself as *The stroke of God* and the
reference to *the dint of my hand*, cf. 'I am deth goddys masangere / . . . Ayens my
dredful dentys it vayleth nevyr to plete / . . . Ffor now I go to sle hym with
strokys sad and sore' (*Ludus Coventriae*, pp. 174, 175). There, Mors is punishing
Herod, whom Magnificence resembles; see note on 1458 ff. The impartiality of
Death (or perhaps his *penchant* for the great), expressed, for example, in 'I set
not . . . by pope, emperour, kynge, duke, ne prynces' (*Everyman*, 125–6, ed.
A. C. Cawley (1961), p. 4) is recalled here too in 1884.

From God am sent to quite thee thy meed.
Vile veliard, thou must not now my dint withstand;
Thou mayst not abide the dint of my hand.   1880
Lie there, losel; for all thy pomp and pride,
Thy pleasure now with pain and trouble shall be
　　tried.

[*To audience*] The stroke of God, Adversity, I hight;
I pluck down king, prince, lord, and knight;
I rush at them roughly and make them lie full low;   1885
And in their most trust I make them overthrow.
This losel was a lord and lived at his lust;
And now like a lurden he lieth in the dust.
He knew not himself, his heart was so high;
Now is there no man that will set by him a fly.   1890
He was wont to boast, brag, and to brace;
Now dare he not for shame look one in the face.
All worldly wealth for him too little was;
Now hath he right nought, naked as an ass.
Sometime without measure he trusted in gold;   1895
And now without measure he shall have hunger and
　　cold.
Lo, sirs, thus I handle them all
That follow their fancies in folly to fall;
Man or woman, of what estate they be,

1880. mayst] *F(CUL)*; must *F(BL)*.　　1881. losel; . . . pride,] *this ed.*; losell,
for all thy pomp and pride; *Dyce*.　　1884. pluck] plucke *F(CUL)*; pluke
F(BL).

1878. *quite*] pay.

1879. *veliard*] a nonce-word = old man (?) (*O.E.D.* suggests derivation from
Fr. *vieillard*.)

1880. *abide*] withstand (*O.E.D.* v. 14).

1881. *for*] in spite of (though here also 'because of').

1882. *tried*] purified; a metaphor from alchemy. ('To remove (the dross or
impurity) from metal by fire', *O.E.D.* v. 3.)

1886. *most trust*] [moment of] greatest confidence.

overthrow] fall down (*O.E.D.* v. 5).

1890. *set . . . a fly*] See note on 412.

1891. *brace*] bluster.

1894. *naked as an ass*] Cf. the proverb 'As lewd as an ass'; Whiting, A220.
(Whiting also lists 'As naked as an ass'; A221, but gives only this example.)

I counsel them beware of adversity.   1900
Of sorrowful servants I have many scores:
I visit them sometime with blains and with sores;
With botches and carbuncles in care I them knit;
With the gout I make them to groan where they sit;
Some I make lepers and lazars full hoarse;   1905
And from that they love best some I divorce;
Some with the marmol to halt I them make;
And some to cry out of the bone-ache;
And some I visit with burning of fire;
And some I wring of the neck like a wire;   1910
And some I make in a rope to totter and walter;
And some for to hang themself in an halter;
And some I visit with battle, war, and murder,
And make each man to slay other,
To drown or to slay themself with a knife,   1915
And all is for their ungracious life.
Yet sometime I strike where is none offence,
Because I would prove men of their patience.

1903. carbuncles] carbuckyls *F*.   1909. burning] brennynge *F*.   1910.
And some] *this ed.;* Of some *F*.   1913. visit with] vysyte with *conj. Dyce;*
vysyte to *F*.   murder] murther *F*.

1902. *visit*] (1) inflict; (2) punish (*O.E.D.* v. 3, 5).
blains] blisters.
1903. *botches*] boils.
carbuncles] tumours, boils.
in care I them knit] I entangle them in suffering.
1905. *lazars*] lepers.
1906. *divorce*] separate.
1907. *marmol*] mormal; 'An inflamed sore, esp. on the leg' (*O.E.D.*).
halt] limp.
1908. *of*] from.
1911. *totter*] swing to and fro (*O.E.D.* v. 1; 1b 'to swing from the gallows'
(1530) is also suggested here).
walter] roll.
1917–18.] On the testing of patience in adversity, cf. *The Clerk's Tale*, esp.
'For greet skile is, he preeve that he wroghte / . . . He preeveth folk al day, it is
no drede, / And suffreth us, as for oure excercise, / With sharpe scourges of
adversitee /Ful ofte to be bete in sondry wise' (*Canterbury Tales*, IV.1152,
1155–8).
1918. *prove*] test.

But nowadays to strike I have great cause,
Lidderins so little set by God's laws.   1920
Fathers and mothers that be negligent,
And suffer their children to have their intent,
To guide them virtuously that will not remember,
Them or their children ofttimes I dismember;
Their children because that they have no meekness, 1925
I visit their fathers and mothers with sickness;
And if I see thereby they will not amend,
Then mischief suddenly I them send;
For there is nothing that more displeaseth God,
Than from their children to spare the rod   1930
Of correction, but let them have their will.
Some I make lame, and some I do kill,
And some I strike with a franesy;
Of some of their children I strike out the eye;
And where the father by wisdom worship hath won 1935
I send ofttimes a fool to his son.
Wherefore of adversity look ye beware,
For when I come, cometh sorrow and care;
For I strike lords of realms and lands
That rule not by measure that they have in their
    hands,   1940
That sadly rule not their household men.

1926. sickness] sekenesse *F*.   1933. some] *Dyce*; syme *F*.

1920. *Lidderins*] rascals.
1921 ff.] This digression would have been of great interest to Tudor audiences. Cf. the speech in *Calisto and Melibaea*, Dodsley, I. p. 90–1, esp. 'The
bringers-up of youth in this region / Have done great harm because of their
negligence'; the section 'Of the erudicion of neglygent faders anenst theyr
chyldren' in *Ship*, I, pp. 45–52; the remarks on the 'euill bringing vp of youth'
in *The Longer*, Aiir, Diiiv, and Liberty's comments 2134 ff. The whole of *Nice
Wanton* develops the proverb 'Spare the rod and spoil the child' (Tilley R155),
cf. 1930.
1922. *suffer*] allow.
1925.] 'Because their children show no obedience'.
1930.] See note on 1921 ff.
1933. *franesy*] delirium.
1936. *to*] as.
1941. *sadly*] firmly.

I am God's prepositor; I print them with a pen;
Because of their negligence and of their wanton
    vages,
I visit them and strike them with many sore plagues.
To take, sirs, example of that I you tell,   1945
And beware of adversity, by my counsel.
Take heed of this caitiff that lieth here on ground;
Behold how Fortune of him hath frowned.
For though we show you this in game and play,
Yet it proveth earnest, ye may see, every day.   1950
For now will I from this caitiff go,
And take mischief and vengeance of other mo
That hath deserved it as well as he.
How, where art thou? Come hither, Poverty;
Take this caitiff to thy lore. [*Exit* ADVERSITY.]   1955

Here cometh in POVERTY.

Poverty. Ah, my bones ache, my limbs be sore;
    Alas, I have the sciatica full evil in my hip!
    Alas, where is youth that was wont for to skip?
    I am lousy and unliking and full of scurf;
    My colour is tawny, coloured as a turf.   1960
    I am Poverty, that all men doth hate.
    I am baited with dogs at every man's gate;
    I am ragged and rent, as ye may see;
    Full few but they have envy at me.

1948. of him] *F;* on hym *conj. Dyce.*   1955. S.D.] *Ramsay.*

1942. *prepositor*] prefect.
print them with a pen] write down their names (*O.E.D.* print v. 4).
1943. *vages*] tricks.
1945. *To take*] take.
1948. *of him*] because of him, at his behaviour (*O.E.D.* prep. 13).
1955. *lore*] tuition.
1957. *full evil*] very badly.
1959. *lousy*] ridden with lice.
unliking] unpleasant.
1960. *turf*] clod of earth.
1964.] 'Few do not feel enmity for me'; a litotes for 'Everyone hates me' (*O.E.D.* envy sb. 1).

Now must I this carcase lift up;   1965
He dined with delight, with poverty he must sup.
Rise up sir, and welcome unto me.

Here let him set about lifting MAGNIFICENCE
and he will place him on a bed.

Magnificence. Alas, where is now my gold and fee?
    Alas, I say, whereto am I brought?
    Alas, alas, alas, I die for thought.   1970
Poverty. Sir, all this would have been thought on before;
    He wotteth not what wealth is that never was sore.
Magnificence. Fie, fie, that ever I should be brought in
        this snare!
    I weened once never to have known of care.
Poverty. Lo, such is this world! I find it writ: 1975
    'In wealth to beware', and that is wit.

1967.1–2.] *this ed.;* Hic accedat ad leuandum magnyfycence et locabit eum
super locum stratum. *F.*

1967.2. on a bed] Based on emendation of F to *super stratum*; I believe *locum*
(see Collation) to have been printed in error after *locabit*. The 'bed' derives from
Adversity's associations with death (see note on 1877 ff.): in *The Castle of
Perseverance* mankind lies on a bed to die, and his 'soul' crawls out from under it
(*Macro*, p. 1); in the Cornish miracle play *The Creacion of the World* (2000 s.d.)
Death strikes Adam with his spear and he falls on a bed (ed. Paula Neuss,
forthcoming (Garland)). Here, as in *The Massacre at Paris*, where the Admiral
'enters' in his bed (226 s.d.), the bed represents sickness and poverty rather than
death, for although Magnificence says *I die* (1970), he does not. (The bed is
placed at some distance from the main action, see 2107.)

Ramsay glosses *super locum stratum* 'upon a couch', although in his introduction (p. xlvii) he apparently thinks that *stratum* means street. (In medieval Latin
the word for 'street' is *strata*, not *stratus* (see Du Cange).) For the view that *super
locum stratum* means 'upon a "spread place"', acting as 'a symbol of poverty' and
being 'very comparable to the allusive skeleton properties used on the Japanese
Noh stage', see Southern, pp. 198–200.

1968. *fee*] possessions. Magnificence refers to the 'goods' which were taken
from him by Adversity (1876.1–2).

1970. *thought*] sorrow, distress (*O.E.D.* sb.[1] 5).

1971. *would*] ought to.

1972.] Proverbial; Whiting, W137, (Although this instance is cited sepa-
rately, W144).

sore] distressed (*O.E.D.* a.[1] 11).

1976. *'In wealth to beware'*] Proverbial; Tilley, W196. Cf. 2160.

Magnificence. In wealth to beware if I had had grace,
    Never had I been brought in this case.
Poverty. Now, sith it will no nother be,
    All that God sendeth take it in gree;   1980
    For though you were sometime a noble estate
    Now must you learn to beg at every man's gate.
Magnificence. Alas, that ever I should be so shamed!
    Alas that ever I Magnificence was named!
    Alas that ever I was so hard happed   1985
    In misery and wretchedness thus to be lapped!
    Alas that I could not myself no better guide!
    Alas in my cradle that I had not died.
Poverty. Yea sir, yea, leave all this rage,
    And pray to God your sorrows to assuage.   1990
    It is folly to grudge against his visitation.
    With heart contrite make your supplication
    Unto your maker that made both you and me;
    And when it pleaseth God, better may be.
Magnificence. Alas, I wot not what I should pray.   1995
Poverty. Remember you better, sir; beware what ye say.
    For dread ye displease the high deity.
    Put your will to his will, for surely it is he
    That may restore you again to felicity,
    And bring you again out of adversity.   2000
    Therefore poverty look patiently ye take,
    And remember he suffered much more for your
        sake;

1996. Remember] Remembre *Dyce;* Remmbre *F.*

1979. *no nother*] no different.

1980. *in gree*] See note on 1522.

1985. *happed*] (1) fortuned; (2) wrapped up (*O.E.D.* v.² 2; cf. 2019), i.e. in the bedding Poverty has provided, see 2038.

1986. *lapped*] wrapped.

1989. *rage*] passion.

1994. *better*] something better, better times (*O.E.D.* a. 6).

1996. *Remember you*] recollect yourself.

1997. *For dread*] for fear that.

1998.] Cf. *Enough,* 1363, where worldly man is told 'you must put your will to God's will'.

    Put] apply.

Howbeit of all sin he was innocent
And ye have deserved this punishment.
Magnificence. Alas, with cold my limbs shall be marred.   2005
Poverty. Yea sir, now must ye learn to lie hard,
That was wont to lie on featherbeds of down;
Now must your feet lie higher than your crown.
Where you were wont to have caudles for your head,
Now must you munch mammocks and lumps of
    bread;   2010
And where you had changes of rich array,
Now lap you in a coverlet, full fain that you may;
And where that ye were pomped with what that ye
    would,
Now must ye suffer both hunger and cold;
With courtly silks ye were wont to be draw,   2015
Now must ye learn to lie on the straw;
Your skin that was wrapped in shirts of Raynes,
Now must ye be stormy beaten with showers and rains;
Your head that was wont to be happed, most
    droopy and drowsy;
Now shall ye be scabbed, scurvy and lousy.   2020

2015. with courtly silks] with courtely sylkes *F(BL)*; with curteyns of sylke
F(CUL).   2018. stormy beaten] stormy beten *F*; storm ybeten *conj.*
Dyce.   2019. happed, . . . drowsy;] *this ed.*; happed moost drowpy and
drowsy, *Dyce*; happed moost drowpy and drowsy—*Ramsay*.

2008.] I am unable to explain this, unless perhaps Magnificence is lying with
his head hanging over the edge of the bed, cf. *droopy and drowsy*, 2019.

2010. *mammocks*] scraps.

2012. *lap you*] wrap yourself.

full fain that you may] very glad that you are able to.

2013. *pomped*] pampered.

2015. *courtly silks*] *CUL*, which has the 'corrected' forme, prints *curteyns of
sylke*. This reading may have arisen from a misunderstanding of the meaning of
draw ('covered'), and I believe the 'uncorrected' version to be the true one.

2017. *shirts of Raynes*] 'shirts made of the delicate species of linen manufac-
tured at Rennes in Brittany' (Dyce, II, p. 268).

2018. *ye*] for you (ethic dative).

stormy] stormily; adjective used adverbially, as often in this text, see note on
1010. Dyce conjectures *storm ybeten*, however.

2019. *droopy and drowsy*] dejected and sluggish. Cf. 'vgly of chere, / Droupy
and drowsy, / Scuruy and lowsy' (*Rummynge*, 14–16), which confirms that this

Magnificence. Fie on this world full of treachery!
    That ever nobleness should live thus wretchedly!
Poverty. Sir, remember the turn of Fortune's wheel,
    That wantonly can wink, and winch with her heel.
    Now she will laugh, forthwith she will frown;   2025
    Suddenly set up and suddenly plucked down;
    She danceth variance with mutability,
    Now all in wealth, forthwith in poverty;
    In her promise there is no sickerness;
    All her delight is set in doubleness.   2030
Magnificence. Alas, of Fortune I may well complain.
Poverty. Yea sir, yesterday will not be called again.
    But yet, sir, now in this case,
    Take it meekly, and thank God of his grace;
    For now go I will beg for you some meat.   2035
    It is folly against God for to plete.
    I will walk now with my beggar's bags,
    And hap you the whiles with these homely rags.

Despairingly let him say these words:

2021. treachery] trechery *F.*   2022. wretchedly] wretchydly *F.*   2038.1.]
this ed.; Difidendo dicat ista verba *F; Discedendo dicat ista verba. Dyce.*

---

phrase is meant to refer to the *present* state of Magnificence's head. (Dyce,
however, sees it as qualifying *happed*: 'wrapped most heavily and drowsily' i.e.
'in a sleep-inducing fashion'.)

2021–2.] For the near-rhyme (F *trechery* / *wretchydly*), cf. 604–5.
2024. *wink*] 'give a significant glance' (*O.E.D.* v.¹ 7).
winch] kick.
2025–6.] Cf. 2525–6, 2532–3.
2027. *She danceth variance*] she moves in a changeable fashion; a phrase
analogous to 'to dance attendance' (*O.E.D.* dance v. 5); see note on 840.
2028.] Cf. 2523.
2029. *sickerness*] certainty, security.
2030. *doubleness*] deceitfulness.
2032.] Proverbial; Tilley, Y31.
2035.] Perhaps from the audience?
2036. *plete*] contend.
2038. *hap*] See note on 1985.
2038.1. Despairingly] Based on emendation of F *Difidendo* to *Diffidendo*.
Dyce conjectured *Discedendo*: 'departing'; this was followed by Ramsay. Southern suggests *diffindendo*: 'breaking off' (p. 185).

Ah, how my limbs be lither and lame.
Better it is to beg than to be hanged with shame,   2040
Yet many had lever hanged to be,
Than for to beg their meat for charity.
They think it no shame to rob and steal,
Yet were they better to beg, a great deal;
For by robbing they run to *in manus tuas* queck,   2045
But begging is better medicine for the neck.
Yea, marry, is it, yea, so mote I go;
Ah lord God, how the gout wringeth me by the toe!

                                    [*Exit* POVERTY.]

Here MAGNIFICENCE *dolorously maketh his moan.*

Magnificence. O feeble fortune, O doleful destiny,
    O hateful hap, O careful cruelty,   2050
    O sighing sorrow, O thoughtful misery,
    O redeless ruth, O painful poverty,
    O dolorous heart, O hard adversity,
    O odious distress, O deadly pain and woe,
    For worldly shame I wax both wan and blo.   2055

2048.1.] *Ramsay.*   2052. redeless] rydlesse *F.*

2039. *lither*] withered.

2041. *had lever*] would prefer.

2045. in manus tuas *queck*] i.e. hanging. *In manus tuas* is the beginning of the prayer said by the dying: 'Into thy hands I commend my spirit' (Ps. xxx.6; Luke xxiii.46); *queck* is an onomatopoeic word representing the sound of choking (see note in *Macro*, p. 223). Cf. 'For drede of in manus tuas qweke' (*Mankind*, 516); 'the wrest is twist so sore, / For as soon as they have said *In manus tuas* once, / By God, their breath is stopped at once' (*Hickscorner*, Dodsley, I, p. 158); 'And if I fall, I catch a queck; / I may fortune to break my neck' (*Youth*, Dodsley, II, p. 8).

2047. *so mote I go*] as I hope to live.

2048.] Cf. 'A pox of this gout! or, a gout of this pox! for the one or the other plays the rogue with my great toe' (*2H4*, I.ii.232–5).

2048.1.] Perhaps Poverty does not actually go out (of the hall). See Intro., p. 44.

2050. *careful*] full of care.

2051. *thoughtful*] anxious (*O.E.D.* 2).

2052. *redeless*] unavailing.

2055. *blo*] livid.

Where is now my wealth and my noble estate?
Where is now my treasure, my lands, and my rent?
Where is now all my servants that I had here a late?
Where is now my gold upon them that I spent?
Where is now all my rich habiliment?   2060
Where is now my kin, my friends, and my noble blood?
Where is now all my pleasure and my worldly good?

Alas my folly, alas my wanton will!
I may no more speak till I have wept my fill.

[*Enter* LIBERTY.]

Liberty. [*Sings*] With yea marry, sirs, thus should
    it be: 2065
I kissed her sweet, and she kissed me;
I danced the darling on my knee;
I garred her gasp, I garred her glee,
With dance on the lea, the lea!
I bussed that baby with heart so free;   2070
She is the bote of all my bale.

Ah! so that sigh was far-fet!
To love that lovesome I will not let,

2064.1.] *Ramsay.*

2057. *rent*] source of revenue.

2058. *a late*] of late.

2060. *habiliment*] apparel.

2064.1.] Liberty enters appropriately upon Magnificence's reference to his *wanton will*, singing of delights the prince had relished before his fall. He does not notice Magnificence until 2106.

2065 ff.] Liberty's song is no doubt a garbled version of some popular contemporary lyric.

2066. *sweet*] sweetly.

2068. *gasp*] pant (for air).

   glee] squint (presumably, here, with ecstasy).

2071. *bote of all my bale*] remedy for all my sorrows. Normally used in religious contexts, but see A. C. Cawley, *The Wakefield Pageants in the Towneley Cycle* (1958), pp. xxviii–ix, who comments on a similar parody ('This is boyte of our bayll, / Good holsom ayll') in the *Prima Pastorum*.

2073. *lovesome*] lovable one.

   let] desist (*O.E.D.* v.² 2).

My heart is wholly on her set.
I plucked her by the patlet;   2075
At my device I with her met,
My fancy fairly on her I set;
So merrily singeth the nightingale!

In lust and liking, my name is Liberty:
I am desired with highest and lowest degree.   2080
I live as me list, I leap out at large,
Of earthly thing I have no care nor charge.
I am president of princes; I prick them with
    pride;
What is he living that liberty would lack?
A thousand pound with liberty may hold no tack;   2085
At liberty a man may be bold for to brake;
Wealth without liberty goth all to wrake.
But yet sirs, hardily, one thing learn of me:
I warn you beware of too much liberty,
For *totum in toto* is not worth an haw.   2090
Too hardy, or too much, too free of the daw,
Too sober, too sad, too subtle, too wise,
Too merry, too mad, too giggling, too nice,
Too full of fancies, too lordly, too proud,

2075. *patlet*] 'An article of apparel worn about the neck and upper part of the chest . . . a collar or ruff' (*O.E.D.*).

2076. *device*] pleasure (*O.E.D.* sb. 3).

2079. *In*] belonging to, inherent in (*O.E.D.* prep. 25).

2080. *with*] among.

2083.] A line is needed to rhyme with this. But see note on 552.

prick] spur.

2085. *hold no tack*] not match (*O.E.D.* sb.[1] 11a).

2086. *brake*] Either 'torture on the rack' (*O.E.D.* v.[2]), or 'vomit' (as Magnificence did, 1727), or 'break wind' (*O.E.D.* v.[6]).

2087. *wrake*] ruin.

2089. *warn*] advise.

2090. totum in toto] all in all.

not worth an haw] i.e. worthless. Proverbial; Tilley, H221.

2091. *much*] great.

free of the daw] unrestrictedly foolish.

Too homely, too holy, too lewd and too loud,   2095
Too flattering, too smattering, too too out of har,
Too clattering, too chattering, too short and too far,
Too jetting, too jagging, and too full of japes,
Too mocking, too mowing, too like a jackanapes:
Thus *totum in toto* groweth up, as ye may see,   2100
By means of madness and too much liberty.
For I am a virtue if I be well used,
And I am a vice where I am abused.

Magnificence. Ah, woe worth thee Liberty, now thou
    sayst full true!
That I used thee too much sore may I rue.   2105

Liberty. [*To audience*] What, a very vengeance, I say!
    Who is that?
What brothel, I say, is yonder, bound in a mat?

Magnificence. I am Magnificence that sometime thy
    master was.

Liberty. What, is the world thus come to pass?
[*To audience*] Cock's arms, sirs, will ye not see   2110
How he is undone by the means of me?
For if measure had ruled liberty as he began,
This lurden that here lieth had been a noble man.
But he abused so his free liberty,
That now he hath lost all his felicity;   2115

2095. *lewd*] common, vulgar.

2096. *smattering*] given to superficial talk.

2097. *clattering*] tattling.

too short and too far] too limited and too far-reaching (*O.E.D.* short a. 3h; far a. 2).

2098. *jetting*] strutting (in the 'new jet'); see note on 465.

jagging] Either 'thrusting' (*O.E.D.* v.¹ 1c), or 'wearing fashionably slashed garments' (*O.E.D.* jag sb.¹ 1, 'a slash or cut made in the surface of a garment').

2099. *mowing*] grimacing.

jackanapes] monkey.

2104. *woe worth thee*] curse you.

2106. *a very vengeance*] Imprecation, 'used to strengthen interrogations' (*O.E.D.* 3).

2107. *brothel*] wretch.

mat] See note on 1027. Here a reference to the *homely rags* in which Magnificence was wrapped by Poverty.

Not thorough largesse of liberal expense,
But by the way of fancy insolence;
For liberality is most convenient
A prince to use with all his whole intent,
Largely rewarding them that have deserved;   2120
And so shall a noble man nobly be served;
But nowadays as hucksters they huck and they stick,
And pinch at the payment of a pudding-prick;
A laudable largesse, I tell you, for a lord
To prate for the patching of a potsherd,   2125
Spare for the spense of a noble that his honour
    might save,
And spend an hundred shillings for the pleasure of
    a knave;
But so long they reckon with their reasons amiss,
That they lose their liberty and all that there is.

Magnificence. Alas that ever I occupied such abusion!   2130
Liberty. Yea, for now it hath brought thee to confusion;
    For where I am occupied and used wilfully,
    It cannot continue long prosperously;
    As evidently in reckless youth ye may see
    How many come to mischief for too much liberty,   2135

2125. potsherd] pot sharde *F*.   2128. they reckon] they rekyn *Dyce;* theyr
rekyn *F*.   2134. reckless] retchlesse *F*.

2116–17.] Liberty here contrasts the true largesse or liberality appropriate to
a prince, with the false largesse resulting from fancy. See Intro., p. 26.
  2116. *thorough*] through.
expense] expenditure.
  2117. *fancy insolence*] capricious arrogance.
  2119. *A prince*] for a prince.
  2120. *Largely*] generously.
  2122. *hucksters*] retailers of small goods.
huck] haggle.
stick] hesitate.
  2123. *pudding-prick*] skewer.
  2125. *for*] because of.
potsherd] piece of broken earthenware.
  2126. *Spare for the spense of*] refrain from spending.
  2128. *reckon*] calculate.
  2130. *occupied*] practised (*O.E.D.* v. 6).

And some in the world, their brain is so idle
That they set their children to run on the bridle,
In youth to be wanton, and let them have their will,
(And they never thrive in their age, it shall not
    greatly skill);
Some fall to folly themself for to spill,   2140
And some fall preaching at the Tower Hill;
Some hath so much liberty of one thing and other,
That nother they set by father and mother;
Some have so much liberty that they fear no sin,
Till, as ye see many times, they shame all their kin; 2145
I am so lusty to look on, so fresh and so free,
That nuns will leave their holiness and run after me;
Friars with folly I make them so fain
They cast up their obedience to catch me again,
At liberty to wander and walk over all,   2150
That lustily they leap sometime their cloister wall.

> *Here someone blows a horn from the back*
> *behind the audience.*

Yonder is a whoreson for me doth rechate;
Adieu, sirs, for I think lest that I come too late!

                                        [Exit LIBERTY.*]*

2151.1.] Hic aliquis buccat in cornu a retro post populum. *F.*   2153.1.]*Ramsay.*

2137. *to run on the bridle*] to run free (the parents abandon control of their children). Proverbial; Whiting, B539.

2138. *In youth to be wanton*] As shown in *Nice Wanton*, see note on 1921 ff.

2139.] 'It will not matter very much if they never prosper in their maturity.'

2141. *Tower Hill*] Where executions were held. (F *toure*: monosyllabic.) Dyce compares 'he did promote thee, / To make thee preach at the gallow-tree' (*Youth*, Dodsley, II, p. 15).

2143. *set by*] esteem (*O.E.D.* v. 91c).

2148. *Friars*] F *Freers*; monosyllabic.

2149. *again*] in return.

2150. *walk over all*] go everywhere.

2151. *lustily*] gaily.

2151.1. someone] If this was one of the five actors, it must have been the boy playing Fancy, since the other four are all occupied.

2152. *for me doth rechate*] who summons me with a horn.

2153. *think*] am concerned, take care (*O.E.D.* does not record quite this sense, but cf. thought sb.[1] 5).

Magnificence. O good lord, how long shall I endure
          This misery, this careful wretchedness?   2155
          Of worldly wealth, alas, who can be sure?
          In Fortune's friendship there is no steadfastness.
          She hath deceived me with her doubleness.
          For to be wise all men may learn of me,
          In wealth to beware of hard adversity.   2160

          Here cometh in CRAFTY CONVEYANCE [*and*]
          CLOAKED COLLUSION, *with a lusty laughter.*

Conveyance. Ha, ha, ha! For laughter I am like to burst.
Collusion. Ha, ha, ha! For sport I am like to spew and
          cast.
Conveyance. What hast thou gotted, in faith, to thy
          share?
Collusion. In faith, of his coffers the bottoms are bare.
Conveyance. As for his plate, of silver and such trash,   2165
          I warrant you I have given it a lash.
Collusion. What, then he may drink out of a stone cruse.
Conveyance. With yea sir, by Jesu that slain was with
          Jews,
          He may rinse a pitcher, for his plate is to wed.
Collusion. In faith, and he may dream on a dagswain
          for any feather bed.   2170
Conveyance. By my troth, we have rifled him meetly
          well.

2161. burst] brast *F.*   2170.] *Dyce; two lines in* F.

2160. *In wealth to beware*] See note on 1976.
    2166. *a lash*] This probably means 'as payment for a debt'; cf. *his plate is to
wed*, 2169, *made chevisance*, 2237. See 'to run in or upon the lash': to incur more
debts than one can pay' (*O.E.D.* sb.[1] 4).
    2167. *cruse*] jar.
    2169. *rinse*] clean out. With *rinse a pitcher*, cf. *O.E.D.* rinse-pitcher: 'a toper'.
to wed] used as security.
    2170. *dagswain*] 'A coarse coverlet of rough shaggy material' (*O.E.D.*).
Magnificence *is bound in a mat* (2107), but the Vices have not yet noticed him.

Collusion. Yea, but thank me thereof every deal.

Conveyance. Thank thee thereof, in the devil's date!

Collusion. Leave thy prating, or else I shall lay thee on
    the pate.

Conveyance. Nay, to wrangle, I warrant thee, it is but a
    stone-cast.   2175

Collusion. By the mass, I shall cleave thy head to the
    waist.

Conveyance. Yea, wilt thou cleanly cleave me in the clift
    with thy nose?

Collusion. I shall thrust in thee my dagger—

Conveyance.   Thorough the leg into the hose.

Collusion. Nay, whoreson, here is my glove; [*throws down
    glove*] take it up and thou dare.

Conveyance. Turd, thou art good to be a man of war!   2180

Collusion. I shall skelp thee on the scalp; [*strikes him*] lo,
    seest thou that?

Conveyance. What, wilt thou skelp me? Thou dare not
    look on a gnat.

Collusion. By cock's bones, I shall bliss thee and thou be
    too bold.

Conveyance. Nay then, thou wilt ding the devil and thou
    be not hold.

2176. waist] waste *F*.   2177. cleave] cleue *Dyce;* clene *F*.

2174. *lay*] beat.

2175.] i.e. 'We're not far off quarrelling'. *Stone-cast* ('stone's throw') may be
used here literally as well as metaphorically.

2177. *cleanly*] completely.

clift] crutch.

nose] penis. (See Partridge, p. 154, 'nose').

2178.] Cf. 'I shal thrust hym thorowe the ars with my dagger' (*Impatient
Poverty*, Dir.).

Thorough the leg into the hose] i.e. 'Impossible'.

2179. [throws down glove]] As this is a clowning scene, perhaps some other
object may have been thrown.

2181. *lo, seest thou that?*] Probably addressed to a member of the audience.

2183. *bliss*] thrash.

2184. *ding*] thump.

and thou be not hold] if you are not prevented.

Collusion. But wottest thou, whoreson, I rede thee to be
　　　　wise?　　　　　　　　　　　　　　　　　　　　　2185
Conveyance. Now I rede thee beware, I have warned thee
　　　　twice.
Collusion. Why, weenest thou that I forbear thee for
　　　　thine own sake?
Conveyance. Peace, or I shall wring thy be in a brake!
　　　　[*Pulls out dagger.*]
Collusion. Hold thy hand, daw, of thy dagger, and stint
　　　　of thy din,
　　　　Or I shall falchion thy flesh, and scrape thee on
　　　　　　the skin.　[*Gestures with sword.*]　　　　　2190
Conveyance. Yea, wilt thou, hangman, I say, thou cavel!
Collusion. Nay, thou rude ravener, rain-beaten javel!
Conveyance. What, thou Colin Coward, known and
　　　　tried!
Collusion. Nay, thou false-hearted dastard, thou dare
　　　　not abide!
Conveyance. And if there were none to displease but
　　　　thou and I,　　　　　　　　　　　　　　　　　　2195
　　　　Thou should not scape, whoreson, but thou
　　　　　should die.

2185. whoreson, . . . wise?] *this ed.;* horson? I rede the to be wyse. *Dyce*.
2190. falchion] fawchyn *F*.　　　2191. hangman] *Dyce;* hagman *F*.

2188. *thy be*] No doubt 'thy behind'. Ramsay's suggestion that *be* is used as a
quibbling echo of that in the preceding dialogue, so that this line means 'I'll put
thy *be* (i.e. thy injunction) on the rack' (p. 88), is unconvincing.
　brake] rack.
　2189. *stint of*] stop.
　2190. *falchion*] cut with a falchion (a broad sword).
　2191. *cavel*] 'low fellow' (*O.E.D.* sb.[2] 2).
　2192. *ravener*] plunderer.
　rain-beaten] A term of abuse, similar to the modern 'wet'. Colin Clout calls his
verse 'rudely rayne beaten' (*Cloute*, 55).
　javel] rascal.
　2193. *Colin Coward*] See note on 917. This particular name is chosen partly
because it alliterates with 'Cloaked Collusion', probably.
　2194. *abide*] stand firm.

Collusion. Nay, ich shall wring thee, whoreson, on
    the wrist.
Conveyance. Marry, I defy thy best and thy worst.

           [*Enter* COUNTENANCE.]

Countenance. What, a very vengeance, need all these
    words?
    Go together by the heads, and give me your swords. 2200
               [*They hand him their weapons.*]
Collusion. So he is the worst brawler that ever was born.
Conveyance. In faith, so to suffer thee it is but a scorn.
Countenance. Now let us all be one, and let us live in rest;
    For we be, sirs, but a few of the best.
Collusion. By the mass, man, thou shall find me
    reasonable.   2205
Conveyance. In faith, and I will be to reason agreeable.
Countenance. Then trust I to God and the holy rood
    Here shall be not great shedding of blood.
Collusion. By our lakin sir, not by my will.
Conveyance. By the faith that I owe to God, and I will
    sit still.   2210
Countenance. Well said. But in faith, what was your
    quarrel?
Collusion. Marry sir, this gentleman called me javel.
Conveyance. Nay, by Saint Mary, it was ye called me
    knave.
Collusion. Marry, so ungoodly language you me gave.

2198.1.] *Dyce.*   2199. *Countenance.*] *Dyce; not in F.*

    2197. *ich*] I.
    2198.1.] Countenance must have been making his way forward during the
preceding dialogue; his opening line shows that he has heard at least part of it.
    2200. *Go together by the heads*] come to an agreement. See note on 566.
    2201. *So*] introductory particle (*O.E.D.* adv. 5c (1593)).
    2202. *suffer*] endure.
    2212.] See 2192.
    2213.] Conveyance's memory is not as good as Collusion's; the word *knave*
was not used.
    2214. *ungoodly*] bad.

Countenance. Ah, shall we have more of this matters yet? 2215
   Methink ye are not greatly accumbered with wit.
Conveyance. God's foot, I warrant you I am a gentleman
      born;
   And thus to be faced I think it great scorn.
Countenance. I cannot well tell of your dispositions.
   [*To* CONVEYANCE]. And ye be a gentleman, ye
     have knave's conditions.   2220
Collusion. By God, I tell you I will not be outfaced.
Conveyance. By the mass, I warrant thee I will not be
     braced.
Countenance. Tush, tush, it is a great default;
   The one of you is too proud, the other is too haut.
   Tell me briefly whereupon ye began.   2225
Collusion. Marry, sir, he said that he was the prettier man
   Than I was, in opening of locks.
   And I tell you I disdain much of his mocks.
Conveyance. Thou saw never yet but I did my part
   The lock of a casket to make to start.   2230
Countenance. Nay, I know well enough ye are both well
     handed
   To grope a gardeviance, though it be well banded.

2223. default] defaute *F*.

   2215. *this matters*] this business.
   2216. *accumbered*] overloaded.
   2218. *faced*] treated impudently.
   2219. *of your dispositions*] about your qualities (*O.E.D.* 6).
   2220.] Cf. 'no gentylmen but gentyl condycyons' (*Gentleness*, 502).
   conditions] behaviour (*O.E.D.* sb. 11b).
   2221. *outfaced*] impudently put down or contradicted.
   2222. *braced*] bullied, insulted.
   2223. *default*] defect.
   2226. *prettier*] more ingenious.
   2228. *disdain much of*] am very offended at.
   2230. *start*] break loose.
   2232. *grope a gardeviance*] rummage in a chest.
   banded] fastened with bands.

Collusion. I am the better yet in a budget.
Conveyance.   And I the better in a mail.
Countenance. Tush, these matters that ye move are
          but sops in ale;
     Your trimming and tramming by me must be tanged, 2235
     For had I not been ye both had been hanged
     When we with Magnificence goods made chevisance.
Magnificence. [*Addressing them from his bed.*] And
          therefore our Lord send you a very vengeance!
Countenance. What beggar art thou, that thus doth ban
          and wary?
Magnificence. Ye be the thieves, I say, away my goods
          did carry.   2240
Collusion. Cock's bones, thou beggar, what is thy name?
Magnificence. Magnificence I was, whom ye have
          brought to shame.
Countenance. Yea, but trow you, sirs, that this is he?
Conveyance. Go we near and let us see. [*They approach*
          MAGNIFICENCE.]
Collusion. By cock's bones, it is the same.   2245
Magnificence. Alas, alas, sirs, ye are to blame!
     I was your master, though ye think it scorn;
     And now on me ye gaure and spurn.

2233. budget] bowget *F*.

2233. *budget*] pouch or wallet.
   mail] wallet or travelling bag.
2234. *move*] mention (*O.E.D.* v. 14).
2235. *trimming and tramming*] trifling nonsense. (Not in *O.E.D.*, but cf. trim-tram sb. 2 'an absurdity; a piece of nonsense'.)
   tanged] given point.
2237. *Magnificence*] Magnificence's (see note on 86).
   made chevisance] contracted a loan (*O.E.D.* sb. 7; *to wed*, 2168, confirms that this is the meaning here, and that the citation under *O.E.D.* sb. 6, 'booty', is incorrect).
2239. *ban and wary*] curse.
2240. *did carry*] who did carry (see note on 504).
2247. *think it scorn*] disdain it (*O.E.D.* sb. 4).
2248. *gaure*] gape.
   spurn] treat with contempt.

Countenance. Lie still, lie still now, with ill hail.
Conveyance. Yea, for thy language cannot thee avail.   2250
Collusion. Abide sir, abide; [*Aside to* COUNTENANCE
    and CONVEYANCE.] I shall make him to piss.
Magnificence. Now give me somewhat, for God sake,
    I crave!
Conveyance. In faith, I give the four quarters of a knave.
Countenance. In faith, and I bequeath him the tooth-
    ache.
Collusion. And I bequeath him the bone-ache.   2255
Conveyance. And I bequeath him the gout and the gin.
Collusion. And I bequeath him sorrow for his sin.
Countenance. And I give him Christ's curse,
    With never a penny in his purse.
Conveyance. And I give him the cough, the murr, and
    the pose.   2260
Collusion. Yea, for *requiem eternam* groweth forth of
    his nose.
    But now let us make merry and good cheer.
Countenance. And to the tavern let us draw near.
Conveyance. And from thence to the Half Street,
    To get us there some fresh meat.   2265
Collusion. Why, is there any store of raw mutton?
Countenance. Yea, in faith; or else thou art too great
    a glutton.

2249. *ill hail*] misfortune.
2251.] A line is needed to rhyme with this. But see note on 552.
2253. *the four quarters of a knave*] See note on 1167.
2256. *gin*] rack; perhaps metaphorical here, as in being 'racked with pain'.
2260. *the murr, and the pose*] catarrh.
2261.] Cf. the proverb 'Hunger drops out of his nose'; Tilley, H813.
requiem eternam] eternal rest.
2264. *the Half Street*] On the Bankside, Southwark, where the brothels were.
2265. *meat*] 'The flesh of a whore or a wanton' (Partridge, p. 147: 'meat').
2266-7] Cf. the proverb 'Mutton is good meat for a glutton'; Whiting, M813.
mutton] slang for 'prostitute' (*O.E.D.* 4). With *raw mutton*, cf. 'one that is the chefe / Whiche is not fedd / so ofte with rost befe / As with rawe motten' (*Rede me*, p. 39, referring to Wolsey).

Conveyance. But they say it is a queasy meat;
    It will strike a man mischievously in a heat.
Collusion. In fay, man, some ribs of the mutton be so
        rank   2270
    That they will fire one ungraciously in the flank.
Countenance. Yea, and when ye come out of the shop,
    Ye shall be clapped with a collop
    That will make you to halt and to hop.
Conveyance. Some be wrested there that they think on it
        forty days,   2275
    For there be whores there at all assays.
Collusion. For the passion of God, let us go thither.

            And let them leave the place hurriedly.

Magnificence. Alas, mine own servants to show me such
        reproach,
    Thus to rebuke me and have me in despite;
    So shamefully to me their master to approach,   2280
    That sometime was a noble prince of might!
    Alas, to live longer I have no delight;
    For to live in misery it is harder than death;
    I am weary of the world, for unkindness me slay'th.

2277.1.] Et cum festinacione discedant a loco. *F.*   2284. slay'th] sleeth *F.*

2268. *queasy*] unsettling to the stomach.
2269. *mischievously*] in such a way as to cause damage.
heat] fever.
2270. *fay*] faith.
2271.] A reference to the probability of catching venereal disease (see 2273).
fire] inflame.
ungraciously] severely.
2272. *the shop*] i.e. the brothel.
2273. *clapped with a collop*] (1) beaten with a piece of meat; (2) given the clap by a prostitute.
2275. *wrested*] (1) racked with pain (*O.E.D.* v. 7b); (2) (with sexual innuendo) twisted, screwed (*O.E.D.* v. 1b).
2277.] A line is needed to rhyme with this. But see note on 552.
2278. *mine own servants to show*] that my own servants should show.
2279. *despite*] contempt.
2284. *unkindness*] ingratitude.

Here enters DESPAIR.

Despair. [*To audience*] Despair is my name, that
      Adversity doth follow,   2285
    In time of distress I am ready at hand.
    I make heavy hearts with eyen full hollow,
    Of fervent charity I quench out the brand;
    Faith and good hope I make aside to stand;
    In God's mercy, I tell them, is but folly to trust;   2290
    All grace and pity I lay in the dust.

    [*To* MAGNIFICENCE] What liest thou there
      ling'ring, lewdly and loathsome?
    It is too late now thy sins to repent.
    Thou hast been so wayward, so wrangling, and
      so wrothsome,
    And so far thou art behind of thy rent,   2295
    And so ungraciously thy days thou hast spent,
    That thou art not worthy to look God in the face.
Magnificence. Nay, nay, man, I look never to have part of
    his grace,

    For I have so ungraciously my life misused,
    Though I ask mercy, I must needs be refused.   2300

Despair. No, no; for thy sins be so exceeding far,
    So innumerable, and so full of despite,
    And again thy maker thou hast made such war,
2284.1.] Hic intrat dyspare. *F.*   2285. follow] folowe *Dyce;* felowe *F.*

2285. *Despair*] The ultimate 'sin against the Holy Ghost' where a man believed
himself too evil to obtain God's mercy; see 2290, 2336 ff.

2292. *lewdly and loathsome*] vilely and hatefully.

2294. *wrothsome*] angry.

2295. *thy rent*] what you owe (to God).

2296. *ungraciously*] wickedly.

2298. *part of*] a share in (*O.E.D.* sb. 7).

2301. *No, no;*] Despair means: 'No, do not even think of asking for mercy'.
far] great (*O.E.D.* a. 2c).

2302. *despite*] defiance.

2303. *again*] against.

That thou canst not have never mercy in his sight.

Magnificence. Alas, my wickedness! That may I wite!   2305
  But now I see well there is no better rede,
  But sigh and sorrow, and wish myself dead.

Despair. Yea, rid thyself rather than this life for to lead;
  The world waxeth weary of thee; thou livest too long.

  Here enters MISCHIEF [*with a halter and a knife*].

Mischief. And I Mischief am, comen at need,   2310
  Out of thy life thee for to lead;
  And look that it be not long
  Or that thyself thou go hang
  With this halter good and strong;
  Or else with this knife cut out a tongue   2315
  Of thy throat-boll, and rid thee out of pain;
  Thou art not the first himself hath slain.
  Lo, here is thy knife and a halter; and or we go further
  Spare not thyself, but boldly thee murder.

Despair. Yea, have done at once without delay.   2320

2309.1.] Hic intrat myschefe. *F.*   2310. I Mischief am,] *this ed.;* I, Myschefe,
am *Dyce.*   2313. hang] honge *F.*   2318. further] ferther *F.*   2319.
murder] *F.*

2304. *not . . . never*] i.e. never (the use of a double negative for emphasis was
common).

2305. *wite*] blame.

2306. *rede*] plan.

2308. *rid*] destroy.

2309.1.] Mischief, 'harm or evil', is the personification of suicide here, as in
Mankind. See Sister M. P. Coogan, *An Interpretation of the Moral Play, Mankind*
(1947), pp. 58–61.

a halter and a knife] See 2314–15.

2310. *I Mischief am*] This parallels *Despair is my name* (2285), and the caesura
falls after *am.*

at need] in the emergency.

2316. *Of thy throat-boll*] from thy throat (*throat-boll*: 'adam's apple' used
metonymically for the throat).

rid thee] deliver yourself.

2317. *himself hath slain*] who has killed himself.

Magnificence. Shall I myself hang with an halter? Nay;
Nay, rather will I choose to rid me of this life
In sticking myself with this fair knife.

Here MAGNIFICENCE *would slay himself with a knife.*

Mischief. Alarum, alarum, too long we abide!
Despair. Out, harrow, hell burneth! Where shall I me
hide?   2325

Here enters GOOD HOPE *while* DESPAIR *and* MISCHIEF
are running away. Let GOOD HOPE *suddenly snatch
the sword from him and say:*

Good Hope. Alas, dear son, sore cumbered is thy mind,
Thyself that thou would slo against nature and kind.
Magnificence. Ah, blessed may ye be sir. What shall I
you call?
Good Hope. Good Hope, sir, my name is; remedy
principal
Against all faults of your ghostly foe.   2330
Who knoweth me himself may never slo.
Magnificence. Alas, sir, so I am lapped in adversity,
That Despair well nigh had mischieved me;

2324. *Mischief.*] Dyce; Magnyfycence F. 2325.1–3. *follows Dyce;* Hic intrat
Goodhope fugientibus dyspayre et myschefe repente good hope surripiat illi
gladio et dicat. *F;* . . . gladium . . . *Dyce.*   2330. faults] fautes *F:* sautes *Dyce.*

2321–3.] Cf. 'I may / Finish my life with cord or with knife, / The dispatch
whereof I will not delay' (*Tide Tarrieth*, 1591–3).
2323.1.] Cf. *She would stick herself with a knife* (s.d. in *Nice Wanton*, Dodsley,
II, p. 181).
2324–5.] Mischief sees Good Hope approaching, and warns Despair that they
should run away.
2324. abide] stay.
2325. *Out, harrow, hell burneth*] Exclamations of distress. Craik, taking *hell*
literally, suggests that Despair and Mischief are devils (p. 52); but Magnificence
calls Despair *man* in 2298.
2326. *cumbered*] troubled.
2327. *slo*] kill.
against nature and kind] unnaturally (a doublet).
2330. *faults*] failings.
ghostly] spiritual.
2333. *mischieved*] ruined.

For had ye not the sooner been my refuge,
Of damnation I had been drawn in the luge. 2335
Good Hope. Undoubted ye had lost yourself eternally;
There is no man may sin more mortally
Than of wanhope through the unhappy ways
By mischief to breviate and shorten his days.
But, my good son, learn from despair to flee; 2340
Wind you from wanhope and acquaint you with me.
A great misadventure, thy maker to displease,
Thyself mischieving to thine endless disease.
There was never so hard a storm of misery,
But through good hope there may come remedy. 2345
Magnificence. Your words be more sweeter than any
precious nard,
They mollify so easily my heart that was so hard;
There is no balm ne gum of Araby
More delectable than your language to me.
Good Hope. Sir, your physician is the grace of God. 2350
That you hath punished with his sharp rod.
Good Hope your potecary assigned am I.

2334. *the sooner*] speedily (*O.E.D.* adv. 12).

2335. *luge*] Scottish form of 'lodge'.

2336. *ye had*] you would have.

2337. *more mortally*] Because in the state of despair, a man thinks himself incapable of God's mercy, and therefore cannot be forgiven. 'Wanhope, that makyth a man nogt to trusten in goddys mercy; for hym thynketh his synne is so myche, that he may neuere haue forgiuenesse, and so peradventure, he may sle hym-self thrug the feendys combryng' (*Jacob's Well*, ed. A. Brandeis (*E.E.T.S.*, 1890), p. 112).

2338. *wanhope*] despair.
unhappy] disastrous.

2339. *breviate*] abbreviate.

2341. *Wind you*] take yourself (*O.E.D.* v.[1] 26).

2342–3.] [It would be] a great misfortune to offend your maker by injuring yourself to your eternal misery.

2346. *nard*] ointment.

2347. *mollify*] make tender.

2348. *gum of Araby*] gum arabic.

2351. *That you hath punished*] who has punished you.

2352. *potecary*] apothecary. See Intro., note 87.

That God's grace hath vexed you sharply
And pained you with a purgation of odious
    poverty,
Mixed with bitter aloes of hard adversity,   2355
Now must I make you a lectuary soft:
I to minister it, you to receive it oft;
With rhubarb of repentance in you for to rest;
With drams of devotion your diet must be dressed;
With gums ghostly of glad heart and mind   2360
To thank God of his sond, and comfort ye shall find.
Put fro you presumption and admit humility,
And heartily thank God of your adversity;
And love that lord that for your love was dead,
Wounded from the foot to the crown of the head;   2365
For who loveth God can ail nothing but good.
He may help you, he may mend your mood;
Prosperity by him is given solaciously to man,
Adversity to him therewith now and then,
Health of body his busyness to achieve,   2370
Disease and sickness his conscience to descrive,

2368. by him] by hym *conj. Dyce;* to hym *F.*   2369. then] than *F.*

2353. *That*] now that, since.
vexed] afflicted.
2355. *aloes*] 'A drug of nauseous odour, bitter taste, and purgative qualities, procured from the inspissated juice of plants of the genus *Aloe*' (*O.E.D.* 3).
2356. *lectuary*] electuary: 'A medicinal conserve or paste, consisting of a powder or other ingredient mixed with honey, preserve, or syrup of some kind' (*O.E.D.*).
2358. *rhubarb*] This was used for medicinal purposes, as a purgative.
in you for to rest] to remain in you (qualifying *repentance*).
2359. *drams*] small draughts of cordial.
2360. *gums*] Certain gums were used as drugs, or for other medicinal purposes.
of] for.
2361. *sond*] 'sending'; grace, dispensation.
2366. *ail*] be affected by (*O.E.D.* v. 4b).
2367. *mend your mood*] improve your disposition.
2368. *solaciously*] comfortingly.
2370. *busyness*] labour. (The spelling with y is retained here so that a syllable is not lost, and because 'business' has a different sense.)
2371. *his conscience to descrive*] to reveal his inmost heart (*O.E.D.* descrive 4 '= descry v.¹ 2').

Affliction and trouble to prove his patience,
Contradiction to prove his sapience,
Grace of assistance, his measure to declare,
Sometime to fall, another time to beware;   2375
And now ye have had, sir, a wonderous fall,
To learn you hereafter for to beware withal.
How say you, sir, can ye these words grope?
Magnificence. Yea, sir, now am I armed with good hope,
And sore I repent me of my wilfulness;   2380
I ask God mercy of my negligence,
Under Good Hope enduring ever still,
Me humbly committing unto God's will.
Good Hope. Then shall you be soon delivered from
      distress,
For now I see coming to youward Redress.   2385

Here enters REDRESS.

Redress. Christ be among you, and the Holy Ghost.
Good Hope. He be your conduct, the Lord of mights
      most.
Redress. [*To* GOOD HOPE] Sir, is your patient anything
      amended?
Good Hope. Yea sir, he is sorry for that he hath offended.
Redress. [*To* MAGNIFICENCE] How feel you yourself,

2380. wilfulness] wylfulnesse *F*.   2381. negligence] neglygence *F;* neglygesse *conj. Dyce.*   2385.1.] Hic intrat Redresse. *F.*

2374.] 'The grace of his presence, to display his [i.e. God's] measure' (*O.E.D.*
assistance 1).
2376. *wonderous*] astonishing.
2378. *grope*] apprehend.
2381. *negligence*] Dyce conjectured *neglygesse*, for the rhyme, but this near-
rhyme (F. *wylfulnesse /neglygence*) is acceptable; cf. 604–5.
2385. *to youward*] towards you.
Redress] Reparation.
2387. *conduct*] guide (*O.E.D.* sb.¹ 3).
of mights most] of greatest power.
2388. *anything*] at all.
2389. *for that he hath offended*] that he has sinned.

my friend? How is your mind?   2390

Magnificence. A wretched man, sir, to my maker unkind.

Redress. Yea, but have ye repented you with heart
        contrite?

Magnificence. Sir, the repentance I have no man can
        write.

Redress. And have ye banished from you all despair?

Magnificence. Yea, wholly to Good Hope I have made my
        repair.   2395

Good Hope. Questionless he doth me assure
        In good hope alway for to endure.

Redress. Then stand up sir, in God's name,
        [MAGNIFICENCE *rises*]
        And I trust to ratify and amend your fame.
        Good Hope, I pray you with hearty affection   2400
        To send over to me Sad Circumspection.

Good Hope. Sir, your request shall not be delayed.

                                And let him go out.

Redress. Now surely, Magnificence, I am right well
        apayed
        Of that I see you now in the state of grace.
        Now shall ye be renewed with solace: 2405
        Take now upon you this habiliment,

2402.1.] Et exiat. *F.*

2390. *mind*] state of mind, inclination (*O.E.D.* b.[1] 15).

2391. *unkind*] unnatural, or ungrateful.

2393. *write*] describe (in writing?). The meaning seems to be simply 'describe'; *O.E.D.* does not record this sense.

2395. *made my repair*] returned (*O.E.D.* repair sb.[1] 4b).

2399. *ratify*] sanction.

amend your fame] repair your reputation.

2401. *send over*] When we last heard of Circumspection, he was abroad, his letter having supposedly come from Pontoise. (See 343.)

2403. *apayed*] contented.

2404. *Of that*] in that.

2405. *renewed with solace*] restored by comfort.

2406. *this habiliment*] The garment symbolises Magnificence's regeneration. The presentation of new clothing is a common device in the interludes: Everyman, for example, puts on a garment of 'Contrycyon', and Youth is given 'a newe araye' by Charity; see Craik, pp. 78–82.

[*Hands him a garment*]
And to that I say give good advisement.

Let MAGNIFICENCE *receive the garment.*

Magnificence. To your request I shall be confirmable.
Redress. First, I say, with mind firm and stable
 Determine to amend all your wanton excess,   2410
 And be ruled by me, which am called Redress.
 Redress my name is, that little am I used
 As the world requireth, but rather I am refused.
 Redress should be at the reckoning in every account,
 And specially to redress that were out of joint;   2415
 Full many things there be that lacketh redress,
 The which were too long now to express;
 But Redress is redeless and may do no correction.
 Now welcome, forsooth, Sad Circumspection.

Here cometh in SAD CIRCUMSPECTION *saying:*

Circumspection. Sir, after your message I hied me hither
 straight,   2420
 For to understand your pleasure and also your
 mind.
Redress. Sir, to account you, the continue of my conceit
 Is from adversity Magnificence to unbind.
Circumspection. How fortuned you, Magnificence, so far
 to fall behind?

2407.1.] Magnyfycence accipiat indumentum. *F.*   2409. *Redress.*] *Dyce;* ¶
F.   2414. account] accompte *F.*   2422.] *this ed.;* Syr, to accompte you
the contynewe of my consayte, *Dyce.*

2407. *advisement*] attention.
2408. *be confirmable*] conform.
2412. *that little am I used*] who am little used.
2415. *that*] anything that.
2418. *redeless*] powerless to advise.
2422. *account*] recount, tell (*O.E.D.* v. 8b).
 continue of my conceit] substance of my personal opinion (*O.E.D.* contenu;
conceit sb. 4).

Magnificence. Sir, the long absence of you, Sad
    Circumspection,   2425
    Caused me of adversity to fall in subjection.

Redress. All that he sayth of truth doth proceed:
    For where sad circumspection is long out of the
      way,
    Of adversity it is to stand in dread.
Circumspection. Without fail, sir, that is no nay;   2430
    Circumspection inhateth all running astray.
    But, sir, by me to rule first ye began.
Magnificence. My wilfulness, sir, excuse I ne can.

Circumspection. Then ye repent you of folly in times past?
Magnificence. Soothly, to repent me I have great cause;   2435
    Howbeit from you I received a letter,
    Which contained in it a special clause
    That I should use largesse.
Circumspection.   Nay sir, there a pause.
Redress. Yet let us see this matter thoroughly engrossed.
Magnificence. Sir, this letter ye sent to me at Pontesse
    was enclosed.   2440

2434.] *Word order as in F;* Then ye of Foly in tymes past you repent *Ramsay.*   2436. a letter] *F;* a letter sent *Ramsay.*

2426.] 'Caused me to fall subject to adversity'.

2428. *out of the way*] absent. (See note on 213.)

2429.] 'Adversity is to be feared.'

2430. *no nay*] not to be denied.

2431. *inhateth*] a nonce-word; (?) hates intensely. (See note on 1659.)

2436.] The text may be corrupt here, since this does not rhyme with 2434. The changes suggested by Dyce's reviewer in the *Gentleman's Magazine*, adopted by Ramsay (see Collation), seem too great a departure from the text, however. This last part of the play is corrupt or incomplete in other places (see notes on 2462 ff., 2496), and perhaps the incompleteness is Skelton's own, rather than that of his printer.

2438. *there a pause*] [there is] matter for doubt there.

2439. *engrossed*] sorted out (*O.E.D.* v. 1b).

2440. *Pontesse*] See note on 343.

Circumspection. Who brought you that letter? Wot ye
   what he hight?
Magnificence. Largesse, sir, by his credence, was his
   name.
Circumspection. This letter ye speak of never did I write.
Redress. To give so hasty credence ye were much to
   blame.
Magnificence. Truth it is, sir; for after he wrought me
   much shame,   2445
   And caused me also to use too much liberty,
   And made also Measure to be put fro me.

Redress. Then Wealth with you might in no wise abide.
Circumspection. Aha! Fancy and Folly met with you,
   I trow.
Redress. It would be found so if it were well tried.   2450
Magnificence. Surely my wealth with them was
   overthrow.
Circumspection. Remember you, therefore, how late ye
   were low.
Redress. Yea, and beware of unhappy Abusion.
Circumspection. And keep you from counterfeiting
   of Cloaked Collusion.

Magnificence. Sir, in good hope I am to amend.   2455
Redress. Use not then your countenance for to
   counterfeit.
Circumspection. And from crafters and hafters I you
   forfend.

2442. *by his credence*] according to his credentials (*O.E.D.* sb. 4).
2445. *after*] afterwards.
2450. *tried*] put to the test.
2451. *overthrow*] ruined.
2456. *Use not . . . to counterfeit*] do not be in the habit of counterfeiting
(*O.E.D.* use v. 20).
2457. *crafters and hafters*] tricksters and deceivers.
forfend] prohibit.

Here enters PERSEVERANCE.

Magnificence. Well, sir, after your counsel my mind I
will set.
Redress. What, brother Perseverance! Surely well met.
Circumspection. Ye come hither as well as can be thought. 2460
Perseverance. I heard say that Adversity with
Magnificence had fought.

Magnificence. Yea, sir, with Adversity I have been vexed,
But Good Hope and Redress hath mended
mine estate,
And Sad Circumspection to me they have annexed.
Redress. What this man hath said, perceive ye his
sentence? 2465
Magnificence. Yea, sir; from him my corage shall never
flit.
Circumspection. According to truth they be well devised.
Magnificence. Sirs, I am agreed to abide your ordinance;
Faithfully assuring with good peradvertance.

2457.1.] Hic intrat perseueraunce. *F.*   2464. annexed] annexyd *Dyce;*
amexyd *F.*   2469. Faithfully assuring] *this ed.;* Faythfully assuraunce *F;*
faythful assuraunce *Dyce.*

2460.] i.e. 'Your arrival is very fortunate'. (Perseverance, unlike Circumspection, had not been sent for.)

2462 ff.] This stanza has imperfect rhyme, and contains eight lines. Ramsay
prints with hiatus after 2464 and 2467, suggesting that a speech by Perseverance
has been omitted. But the verse is not deficient in *sense*, only in form. See note on
2436.

2462. *vexed*] troubled.

2463. *mended mine estate*] improved my condition.

2465. *this man*] Circumspection, in 2452 ff., where Redress was supporting
him.

sentence] sentiments, opinion.

2466. *corage*] mind, spirit.

2467. *they*] Circumspection's words.

devised] ordered (*O.E.D.* v. 5).

2468. *abide*] submit to (*O.E.D.* v. 15).

2469. *assuring*] promising (F *assurance* was misprinted, being contaminated
by *peraduertaunce*).

peradvertance] thorough attention.

Perseverance. If you be so minded we be right glad.   2470
Redress. And ye shall have more worship than ever ye
    had.
Magnificence. Well I perceive in you there is much
    sadness,
    Gravity of counsel, providence and wit;
    Your comfortable advice exceedeth all gladness.
    But friendly I will refrayne you further, or we flit: 2475
    Whereto were most meetly my corage to knit?
    Your minds I beseech you herein to express,
    Commencing this process at master Redress.

Redress. Sith unto me formest this process is erected,
    Herein I will afforce me to show you my mind: 2480
    First, from your magnificence sin must be abjected
    In all your works more grace shall ye find;
    Be gentle, then, of corage, and learn to be kind,
    For of nobleness the chief point is to be liberal,
    So that your largesse be not too prodigal.   2485

Circumspection. Liberty to a lord belongeth of right,
    But wilful waywardness must walk out of the way;
    Measure of your lusts must have the oversight;
    And, not all the niggard nor the chincherd to play,

2474. advice exceedeth] *this ed.*; aduyse and wyt excedyth *F*.   2489. And,
. . . play,] *this ed.*; And not all the nygarde nor the chyncherde to play; *Dyce*.

2474. *comfortable*] comforting.
2475.] 'But I will question you further, in a friendly fashion, before we go'
(*O.E.D.* refrayne v. 'To question or examine'; *friendly* adjective used adverbially).
2476.] 'On what it would be most suitable to fix my mind'.
2479. *process*] argument or discussion.
erected] (?) directed (*O.E.D.* records this with a query under erect v. 11; Dyce
compares *arect*; see note on 94).
2480. *afforce me*] do my best.
2481. *abjected*] rejected.
2486. *of right*] by right.
2489. *not . . . to play*] so that you do not play.
chincherd] miser.

Let never niggardship your nobleness affray;   2490
In your rewards use such moderation
That nothing be given without consideration.

Perseverance. To the increase of your honour then
        arm you with right,
   And fumously address you with magnanimity;
   And ever let the dread of God be in your sight;   2495
   And know yourself mortal, for all your dignity;
   Set not all your affiance in Fortune full of guile;
   Remember this life lasteth but a while.

Magnificence. Redress, in my remembrance your
        lesson shall rest;
   And Sad Circumspection I mark in my mind;   2500
   But Perseverance, meseemeth your problem was
        best:
   I shall it never forget nor leave it behind,
   But wholly to perseverance myself I will bind,
   Of that I have misdone to make a redress,
   And with sad circumspection correct my
        wantonness.   2505

Redress. Unto this process briefly compiled,

2490. niggardship] negarshyp *F.*

2490. *niggardship*] niggardliness.
affray] attack.
2494. *fumously*] passionately.
address you] equip yourself.
2496.] A line is needed to rhyme with this. See note on 2436.
2497. *affiance*] faith.
2500. *mark*] attend to (*O.E.D.* v. 14).
2501. *problem*] 'A question proposed for academic discussion or scholastic disputation' (*O.E.D.* 2).
2506. *process*] (1) argument or discussion; (2) series of actions or events (*O.E.D.* sb. 4, 5). Magnificence refers to the immediately preceding discussion between the Virtues, and also to the play as a whole.
compiled] constructed.

Comprehending the world casual and transitory,
Who list to consider shall never be beguiled,
If it be regist'red well in memory;
A plain example of worldly vainglory: 2510
How in this world there is no sickerness,
But fallible flattery enmixed with bitterness.

Now well, now woe, now high, now low degree;
Now rich, now poor, now whole, now in disease;
Now pleasure at large, now in captivity;   2515
Now lief, now loath, now please, now displease;
Now ebb, now flow, now increase, now discrease:
So in this world there is no sickerness,
But fallible flattery enmixed with bitterness.

Circumspection. A mirror encleared is this interlude,   2520
This life inconstant for to behold and see:
Suddenly advanced, and suddenly subdued;
Suddenly riches, and suddenly poverty;
Suddenly comfort, and suddenly adversity;
Suddenly thus Fortune can both smile and frown,   2525
Suddenly set up, and suddenly cast down.

Suddenly promoted, and suddenly put back;
Suddenly cherished, and suddenly cast aside;
Suddenly commended, and suddenly find a lack;

2511. sickerness] sekernesse *Dyce;* sekenesse *F.*   2516. lief] leue *F.*

2507. *Comprehending*] summing up, describing.
casual] precarious.
2508. *consider*] give consideration (with *unto*, 2506).
2509. *regist'red*] recorded.
2513.] Cf. 'But nowe hye nowe lowe, vnstable as a flode' (*Ship*, I, p. 190).
2516. *lief*] beloved.
2517.] Cf. 'Nowe flode of ryches nowe ebbe of pouerte' (*Impatient Poverty*, Eiir).
discrease] decrease.
2520. *mirror*] i.e. a faithful reflection.
encleared] made bright.

Suddenly granted, and suddenly denied;   2530
Suddenly hid, and suddenly spied;
Suddenly thus Fortune can both smile and frown,
Suddenly set up, and suddenly cast down.

Perseverance. This treatise, devised to make you disport,
  Showeth nowadays how the world cumbered is.   2535
  To the pith of the matter who list to resort:
  Today it is well, tomorrow it is all amiss;
  Today in delight, tomorrow bare of bliss;
  Today a lord, tomorrow lie in the dust;
  Thus in this world there is no earthly trust.   2540

  Today fair weather, tomorrow a stormy rage;
  Today hot, tomorrow outrageous cold;
  Today a yeoman, tomorrow made of page;
  Today in surety, tomorrow bought and sold;
  Today masterfast, tomorrow he hath no hold;   2545
  Today a man, tomorrow he lieth in the dust;
  Thus in this world there is no earthly trust.

Magnificence. This matter we have moved, you mirths
      to make,
  Pressly purposed under pretence of play,
  Showeth wisdom to them that wisdom can take: 2550
  How suddenly worldly wealth doth decay;
  How wisdom thorough wantonness vanisheth away;
  How none estate living of himself can be sure,
  For the wealth of this world cannot endure.

2549. Pressly] Precely *F*.

2534. *treatise*] either 'book' (*O.E.D.* sb. 1), or 'story' (1b).
2536.] 'If anyone wishes to go to the heart of the matter'.
2543. *made of*] treated as (*O.E.D.* v. 21a).
2544. *in surety*] guaranteed.
2545. *masterfast*] bound to a master.
2548. *moved*] treated of (*O.E.D.* v. 27).
2549.] 'Forcefully put forward for consideration in the guise of a play'.
(*O.E.D.* glosses *pressly* 'expressly', but see press v. 8 etc.; purpose v. 1; pretence sb. 3, 4.)

Of the terrestre treachery we fall in the flood,　　　2555
Beaten with storms of many a froward blast,
Ensorded with the waves savage and wood:
Without our ship be sure it is likely to burst.
Yet of magnificence oft made is the mast,
Thus none estate living of him can be sure,　　　2560
For the wealth of this world cannot endure.

Redress.　Now seemeth us sitting that ye then resort
　　Home to your palace with joy and royalty.
Circumspection.　Where everything is ordained after your
　　　　noble port.
Perseverance.　There to endure with all felicity.　　　2565
Magnificence.　I am content, my friends, that it so be.
Redress.　[*To audience*]　And ye that have heard this
　　　　disport and game,
　　Jesus preserve you from endless woe and shame.

AMEN

Cum privilegio.

2555. treachery] trechery *conj. Dyce;* rechery *F*.　　2557. Ensorded] ensordyd
F; Ensorbyd *conj. Dyce.*　　2558. burst] brast *F*.　　2560. him] hym *F;*
hymselfe *conj. Dyce.*

2555. *terrestre treachery*] earthly deceit (F *rechery*; the emendation suggested by
alliteration, and also *Fie on this world full of treachery*, 2021).

2556. *froward*] adverse.

2557. *Ensorded*] Made grimy. Cf. Latin *sordeo*, 'to be dirty'; *O.E.D.* sordes,
'dirt' (1640). A nonce-word, which *O.E.D.* (ensorde) cites wrongly as from
Cloute. Ramsay adopts Dyce's conjecture *ensorbyd* 'sucked in' (Latin *sorbeo*).
Were this the correct reading, it would also be a nonce-word.

wood] violent.

2558. *Without*] unless.

2560. *him*] magnificence, the concept mentioned in the previous line. Dyce,
comparing 2553, emends to *hymself*, but cf. the variations *lie* (2539), and *he lieth*
(2546), in the previous refrain.

Cum privilegio] i.e. *Cum privilegio regali.*

Glossarial Index to the Commentary

The following list is not intended to be complete. Words and phrases are referred to their first annotated occurrence in a particular sense. Citation is normally in the forms given in the text, but where more than one form occurs, reference may be to the uninflected form. An asterisk indicates that the annotation supplements the *O.E.D.* or, for proverbial references, Tilley and Whiting.